THE DEFINITIVE GUIDE
TO **B2B DIGITAL**
TRANSFORMATION

THE DEFINITIVE GUIDE TO **B2B DIGITAL TRANSFORMATION**

How to Drive Uncommon Growth by Prioritizing Customers over Technology

BY **FRED GEYER**
AND **JOERG NIESSING**

B2BDigitalTransformation.com

First Printing, 2020

ISBN 978-1-7342969-0-7
ePub ISBN 978-1-7342969-1-4

B2BDigitalTransformation.com
P.O. Box 400841
1953 Massachusetts Ave
Cambridge, Ma 02140

Visit www.B2BDigitalTransformation.com for news, insights, cases, events, and forums tailored to the needs of B2B transformation leaders.

Cover design: Kelly Redling
Design and composition: Maureen Forys/Happenstance Type-O-Rama
Illustration: Harold Cheng
Editing: J. K. West and Susan Berge

CONTENTS

Part 1
TRANSFORMATION 1:
THE DIGITAL SELLING SHIFT

Part 2
TRANSFORMATION 2:
THE DIGITAL EXPERIENCE MAKEOVER

Part 3

TRANSFORMATION 3:
THE DIGITAL PROPOSITION PIVOT

Part 4
ENABLE DIGITAL TRANSFORMATION

LIST OF ILLUSTRATIONS

PREFACE

Why This Guide?

This book is for B2B leaders seeking pragmatic ways to profitably grow their business. From the B2B growth leader's perspective, the constant drumbeat of reporting about the coolest contraption, the newest start-up, and the hippest digital entrepreneur misses the point. To them, riding each and every trend is not only impossible but also imprudent. Just keeping up is daunting enough. B2B growth leaders want to know how to effectively apply the technologies that are most relevant to their customers, their industry, and the unique growth challenges they face.

Over the last two decades, we have helped B2B leaders from many of the world's largest companies use digital transformation to drive growth. We wrote this book to share what we've learned. Fred contributes the insights he's gained at Prophet consulting with major B2B financial services, healthcare, and technology clients, such as Zurich Financial, Johnson & Johnson, and Avery Dennison. Fred's own experience as president of Crayola Canada and chief marketing officer, North America, for Electrolux Floor Care enables him to bring a practitioner's perspective to making transformation work in the real world. Joerg brings his perspectives as a member of the faculty at INSEAD, where he has engaged with more than three thousand executives from the likes of KONE, Roche, Google, Maersk, Michelin, IBM, Thales, Sanofi, and KION just in the past five years. Joerg is also the program director of INSEAD's two flagship programs, "B2B Marketing Strategies" and "Leading Digital Marketing Strategy." His prior experience as a strategy consultant and head of Prophet's Insight and Analytics practice, along with his previous work as a marketing data scientist, ensures that our recommendations are sound and executable.

Our frameworks and methods have been successfully applied and refined through discussions with senior executives at INSEAD and in consulting work at Prophet with companies in a wide range of B2B industries around the world.

Today we are witnessing a profound shift in how B2B buyers use digital to consume information, make informed buying decisions, and engage with suppliers. Though the shift is easy to see, addressing it isn't easy to do. Over and over, the leaders we work with beg us for proven methods with which to chart a path forward. This guide will help them bypass the buzzwords and will arm them with the tools they need to take the best next steps for the challenges they face.

The danger growth leaders must avoid is becoming what MIT and Capgemini call "digital fashionistas" in their zeal to participate in important digital trends and their fear of being left behind if they don't act immediately.[1] The applications for digital customer interaction are so broad and so diverse that novices risk letting their enthusiasm for the latest data, the most talked-about digital trends, and the most heavily boosted new technologies drive their investment decisions.

We believe that leaders must take a step-by-step approach tailored to their organization and to their market to become more customer centric, agile, and digital. The most common question we hear from executives starting to feel the pressure of going digital is "Where do I start?" The answer is "Where it makes the most sense from a customer point of view." Companies that leverage digital technologies and data to create value for their customers will create value for themselves.

However, CEOs report that many of their digital transformation efforts fail. Of the 1,350 senior industrial executives Accenture interviewed for its 2019 digital transformation study, 78 percent failed to exceed their return on digital investment goals.[2] In the first wave of digital customer engagement in B2B, which is only now coming to an end, companies invested millions in websites, customer portals, social marketing, and other vehicles without clear customer objectives and, all too often, with little evidence to justify the investment. Many company leaders were seduced by suppliers' promises of easy benefits (including revenue and margin growth) that were simply not achievable with the customer-centric tools, methods, and metrics at hand. Few of these initiatives were integrated into core revenue- and margin-building parts of the business. Granted, a certain amount of digital foundation building was needed. However, CEOs consistently report their dissatisfaction with the returns from these investments.[3]

The first wave also generated a good deal of dissatisfaction among B2B customers. According to a 2017 study by the IBM Institute for Business Value, there is an alarming disconnect between executive investment in digital experiences and what customers actually care most about.[4] In this study of six hundred supplier executives and six thousand customers, two-thirds of customers claimed that exploring products using virtual reality, interactive digital displays, or voice commands was disappointing and did not live up to their expectations. As a result, they decided not to adopt these products for future use. This finding demonstrates how urgently companies need to transform their digital interactions with customers.

This book is also a rejection of the myopia that what works in B2C will work in B2B. This myopia afflicts those who don't appreciate the profound differences between growing a B2B company and growing a consumer business. B2B businesses cannot be Uber or Tesla because they cannot rely on bypassing existing sales and communication channels to reach a single key decision-making consumer. Success in B2B relies on navigating complex value chains and addressing the disparate needs of multiple commercial decision makers and decision influencers. Leaders who do not appreciate the differences between B2C and B2B have spearheaded B2C look-alike digital investments that have generated false starts and dissatisfaction.[5] Myopia has thus set back the development of digital marketing in B2B by making many B2B growth leaders skeptical of the whole concept of digital customer engagement. They realized that B2C copycats were unlikely to succeed, but they could not see other, more B2B-suitable, ways to engage their customers digitally.

This situation compelled us to develop this step-by-step guide to help B2B leaders build the momentum and capabilities needed to transform their companies into agile, customer-centric digital organizations. We offer advice on how to use digital technology to address customer needs and how to enable the organization to deliver the transformation this entails. We chose a guide format because it can outlast the rapid pace of digital advancements. Understanding individual technologies such as the latest social media tools, artificial intelligence (AI) developments, and

Internet of Things (IoT) applications is important. But these technologies evolve quickly, and their relevance varies from industry to industry. Our interest is in arming B2B leaders with the principles they need to take a technology-agnostic approach to tackling digital transformation. Emerging technologies and new applications are merely tools; although technical learning is needed to use new tools, successful outcomes result from leveraging the entire toolbox intelligently based on your customers' needs and your organization's digital capabilities. The ability to leverage more and more of the toolbox comes from building momentum: as the organization moves through phases of implementation, it progressively builds organizational capabilities, as employees learn more and more about what customers value most.

The evidence is already in: customers and employees are the key to successful digital transformation.[6] They deserve the attention that most managers instead devote to technology selection. This guide is fundamentally based on our discovery that digital transformations succeed by putting people first—and last. Every transformation project must begin by understanding customers' needs, and no transformation project can be completed until the challenges of employee learning, development, and motivation as well as talent management, governance, and measurement are addressed. This guide offers many ideas on collecting and deploying customer data effectively—another key to success in digital transformation. When seen through the lens of customers, employees, and data, digital transformation is clearly a continuous, multistep process. Success lies in achieving ever-increasing levels of customer centricity, in which employees learn from customers every step of the way, and customers recognize that the company is increasingly attentive to their needs.

HOW TO USE THIS GUIDE

This book is designed as a practical, in-depth guide to three types of digital transformation. Parts 1, 2, and 3 of the book are organized by transformation type: first, the Digital Selling Shift, then the Digital Experience Makeover, and finally, the Digital Proposition Pivot. The concluding section, part 4, delves into what companies need to do to enable these transformations.

The Digital Selling Shift and the Digital Experience Makeover can be undertaken independently or in combination. The Digital Proposition Pivot almost always first demands the transformation of selling and experience. Because businesses are at different starting points in their digital maturity and face different challenges and opportunities, they may benefit from one transformation more than another. The reader should feel free therefore to use this guide in whole or in part depending on their needs. Delve into just one of the transformations, and put aside the book until the opportunity arises to undertake one of the others.

Each part begins with a discussion of the challenges particular to a transformation type, followed by a case study of a B2B company that has undertaken the transformation. We then tackle the four essential questions growth leaders must address to undertake the transformation: Where to Play, How to Win, What to Do, and Who Is Needed.

► **Where to Play.** This chapter describes a key area of focus or tool for gaining customer insights, identifying growth opportunities, and prioritizing those opportunities. The Digital Selling Shift relies on building customer use cases; the Digital Experience Makeover, on mapping the customer experience; and the Proposition Pivot, on building a demand landscape.

- ▶ **How to Win.** Here, we provide a strategic framework that answers the question "How can the company succeed at winning and keeping customers in the face of existing and new competitors?" The Digital Selling Shift depends on the 4C approach to digital customer strategy: clarify, capture, cultivate, and convert. The Digital Experience Makeover relies on a design approach for touchpoint, service, product, and end-to-end experience design. And the Proposition Pivot outlines a proposition-based approach to defining the growth strategy.

- ▶ **What to Do.** This chapter tackles one of the most important and chronically ignored topics in the discussion of digital transformation: what leaders can do to put in place an actionable and pragmatic plan to galvanize the organization into executing the strategy. The Digital Selling Shift deploys the "implementation sprint" to mobilize implementation, the Digital Experience Makeover relies on "experience pilots" to turn strategy into action, and the Proposition Pivot utilizes the "new solution launch" to trigger execution.

- ▶ **Who Is Needed.** Every part concludes with this chapter, which addresses the key question "Who does the organization need to make the transformation happen?" In the Digital Selling Shift section, we review the role of the analytics team. In the Digital Experience Makeover, we introduce the key elements of a digital experience development organization. In the Digital Proposition Pivot, we discuss the importance of a transformation management office.

A book that focuses on digital transformation as a path to uncommon growth would be woefully incomplete without addressing two critical enablers: data and people. Yet the failure to address the challenges inherent in managing data and people is cited by C-suite executives as the single biggest cause of digital transformation failure. The last part of the book deals with data management and organizational capability building within each of the three transformations. Customer data management, with its many dimensions and its complexity, is an area in which senior leaders often fumble, losing sight of what matters most: building a complete view of the customer and assembling a set of flexible digital platforms to turn data into action. In chapter 4.2, "Use Customer Data More Effectively," we delve into specific aspects of these two imperatives, including why the decisions about data platforms are too important to leave to the IT department and should be carefully considered at the highest levels of the company. Managing internal change—in organizational structure, leadership, processes, governance, talent and incentives, and culture—is the backbone of every successful digital initiative. In chapter 4.3, "Mobilize for Employee Enablement," we talk about the organization's Body/Mind/Soul, a metaphor that is a useful way to think about the people side of digital transformation.

We believe it's important to address every one of the transformations from a people-first-and-last point of view. People first, to keep the customer first and foremost. The customer viewpoint is valuable to customers and will therefore provide value to B2B organizations.[7] People last, because no transformation is sustainable unless the organization develops capabilities. Making people a priority ensures that talent, processes, teaming, measurement, and continuous improvement will go hand in hand with the introduction of new technologies, data sources, and platforms so the organization can deliver effectively.

In writing this book, we drew extensively from the collective lessons of Prophet clients, INSEAD executive learning program participants, and case study contributors. We have included examples from these companies that are in the public domain. This guide also relies extensively on proven frameworks, checklists, and road maps based on real-life examples and case studies. Wherever possible, we provide examples of companies we have worked with. But few companies are able to divulge the actual metrics, figures, and other confidential information that populated these tools. To offer the reader specificity while respecting confidentiality, we created three hypothetical, but typical, B2B companies—ACME Commercial Insurance, ACME Distribution Software, and ACME Medical Devices—to illustrate in detail how the real work of transformation gets done. Each ACME company is a composite drawn from between three and seven actual companies in that industry. No confidential company information was used. Finally, although our frameworks provide clear structure and guidance, they cannot be construed as cookie-cutter solutions. As with the lessons from any book, they must be adapted for each company's specific circumstances and needs.

INTRODUCTION

Digital Transformation and Uncommon Growth in B2B

D igital is profoundly changing our economy and the way we work.[1] Adapting to the ongoing digitization of the economy, and of society more broadly, is one of the biggest challenges B2B growth leaders face in the next decade. Traditional B2B industries, such as medical devices, commercial insurance, agricultural supply, component manufacturing, packaging, and business software, have deployed digital technologies to enhance internal operations but not the customer experience. To a large extent, B2B companies have been somewhat shielded from deep disruption in their customer interactions.[2] Not for much longer, though.

What's changed? The main drivers of disruption—access to customer data and business-accessible digital channels and touchpoints—have arrived in B2B.[3] The Internet of Things (IoT), AI, robotics, and digital automation have created an explosion of data throughout the value chain. Intermediaries such as hospitals, farm cooperatives, commercial brokers, distributors, systems integrators, and purchasing agents no longer have a monopoly on customer data. Common data-sharing standards, application programming interfaces (APIs), and the growing exchange of customer data are also reducing the balkanization of data in B2B, where customer data that historically resided in discrete databases or paper files under the control of individual participants in the supply chain is now widely available.

Broader access to data in B2B is accelerating quickly.[4] The ability to migrate customer data to the cloud is breaking down silos that arose from legacy systems within large enterprises, such as commercial insurance companies, which until now have found it extremely difficult to view the whole customer. In healthcare and financial services, data aggregators are emerging, bundling data within and across enterprises to provide a more complete view of the customer. As more elements of the B2B buying and ownership experience move online, end-to-end customer data is becoming available for the very first time.

The number of digital content delivery alternatives is also growing rapidly in B2B. Digital learning, technical support, e-commerce, and mobile-commerce are skyrocketing because of richer content vehicles such as video and chat, smart content (more personalized and tailored to the buying occasion), and the anytime-anyplace advantages of mobile devices. These channel and content alternatives are enabling established sellers to partner with—or bypass completely—intermediaries in ways that add value to the end customer. They are also helping insurgent players gain access to customers who were previously monopolized by well-established incumbents with scale advantages in sales and support.

The impact of these changes is fundamental within B2B value chains: companies are gaining access to data about their customers and their customers' customers, and buyers are more able to see and compare data about the offerings of their providers and their providers' providers. This increased access has produced three types of disruption:

- ▶ **Data-driven commoditization.** With more and greater information and data available to compare relevant alternatives, buyers can examine a broader set of viable competitors, including low-cost insurgents. This information access also enables buyers to disaggregate products from support services, such as training or maintenance. Low-cost competitors are able to cherry-pick the common and least differentiated items in the line, leaving full-range suppliers to support more complex offerings without the volume they need to sustain profitability. Cherry-picking is rampant in medical devices, where insurgent low-cost suppliers have gained a sufficient foothold in the market to pressure the margins of major players such as Johnson & Johnson, Medtronic, and Stryker.[5]

- ▶ **Data-driven disintermediation.** Greater access to data and information about companies' offers, along with the enhanced ability to use digital tools to request or exchange information directly from and with providers, means that buyers' need for intermediaries is reduced or even eliminated. The complete bypassing of intermediaries is not as common in B2B as it is in B2C commerce. Often in B2B, the mix of services, information, and touchpoints shifts to include greater supplier-to-end-customer interaction but doesn't eliminate hard-to-avoid intermediary functions such as local field service or complex advice giving. Engie, the French gas supplier, has pioneered a digital transformation that uses data and sophisticated analytics to monetize the reductions in energy consumption by large enterprises.[6] In doing so it is creating a direct relationship with public and private organizations such as Ohio State University's Columbus, Ohio, campus, where it both disintermediates and partners with the outsourced facility management company Axium Infrastructure.

▶ **Data-driven innovation.** With more data available, suppliers have more ammunition to combat commoditization, by moving from product-based to data-driven solutions. Data-driven solutions integrate data, product and services, and event software into bundles that price-oriented producers cannot compete with. The most innovative suppliers are going one step further by moving away from stand-alone solutions to data-driven solutions that integrate into the customer or industry ecosystem. For example, Decision Support Systems, a division of Change Healthcare, integrates patient medical record data with treatment scenarios based on the guidelines of the American Radiological Association to guide physicians who are ordering imaging tests.[7]

In examining successful digital transformation initiatives, we've discovered that the current technology-led digital transformation paradigm is flawed. In fact, it should be the converse. Prioritizing customers over technology is the key to driving uncommon growth through digital transformation. Our examination of digital transformation cases has revealed three customer-first transformational shifts that address the disruptive forces of data-driven commoditization, disintermediation, and innovation: the digital selling shift, the digital experience makeover, and the digital proposition pivot.

TRANSFORMATION 1:
THE DIGITAL SELLING SHIFT

Leverage digital technologies to engage and sell more effectively

The digital selling shift is about moving away from the classic but inefficient B2B sales and marketing model to a more integrated model that combines selling and digital marketing in powerful new ways. In the classic model, members of the sales force "own" the customer relationship, and marketing is a support function that assists them and builds market awareness. The emergence of new sources of customer data and digital technologies for interacting and engaging with customers makes the idea that sales owns the customer relationship obsolete. It also blurs the distinction between relationship-driven sales teams and communication-driven marketing teams; more than ever, the two functions need to be seamlessly integrated. Selling is becoming too big a job to leave to the sales force alone. B2B companies must reorient themselves to utilize the new digital tools and technologies, which can help them acquire new customers and forge new and stronger relationships, increase the share of wallet among established customers, and expand the number of buying centers within existing customer organizations. In this shift, digital marketers and data analysts play a greater role in lead generation, securing renewals, cross-selling, and upselling. Thanks to recent advances in digital targeting, personalization, outreach, content creation, account-based marketing (ABM), and always-on marketing, they are becoming the stewards of integrated personal outreach and one-on-one sales interaction.

In the initial stages of this transformation, digital technologies and data are a value-add to the sales force. They boost sellers' effectiveness, freeing up their time so they can focus on sending the right messages to the best prospects and paying more attention to underserved or overlooked customers.

Once salespeople gain competence in digital, digital-marketing lead generation and digital-marketing-enabled launch initiatives can now become the central focus. Digital marketing takes over the role of the sales force for certain activities such as prospecting and lead generation.

Digital marketing may replace the sales force completely for entire product categories or customer segments because of its capacity to lower costs while also precision targeting large numbers of customers. Such substitution is particularly valuable in a couple of cases—for example, when a large number of customers must be reached in a short period of time, such as during a new-product launch, or when the company is competing in price-sensitive categories or among price-sensitive segments, where lowering the total cost to serve (including the cost of the sales force) is paramount. Even partial substitution means that marketing has to transform fundamentally from being a handmaiden to sales to becoming the driving force in understanding, creating, communicating, and delivering value—to customers as well as to the company.

During the past few years, this integrated digital marketing and sales model has begun to take hold in traditional sales-force-intensive industries. Pharmaceutical companies selling to physicians is one example. The new integrated digital model has permeated three crucial phases of drug sales: premarket conditioning, launch sell-in, and post-launch market development. Up until recently, these activities took place within a classic selling model, in which marketing teams developed the messaging, the visual selling aids, and the content for events, and the sales and physician affairs teams conducted the preponderance of physician interactions, supported by targeted media and conference sponsorships.

But physicians' growing time constraints, regulatory limits on pharma-company-sponsored events, and the high cost of maintaining a large sales force have triggered a radical selling shift. Now, pharma marketing teams (aided by physicians' greater comfort with multichannel digital information gathering) are establishing a digital dialogue with physicians whom they target individually. Indegene, a provider of market research and management services in healthcare, conducted a global physician survey in 2019 that demonstrated how rapidly pharma marketing has changed.[8] Of the thirteen communication channels physicians most preferred for learning about pharmaceutical products, nine were digital: online journals, websites, marketing emails, webinars, self-directed web detailing, emails from representatives, live remote detailing, social apps, and text messaging. In fact, that same survey found that more physicians prefer communicating with pharma companies through digital channels than through sales reps. And the shift to digital is accelerating: at the 2019 Eyeforpharma conference in Philadelphia, five of the largest global pharmaceutical companies reported at least one brand launch that was fully digital and replaced their own sales force in whole or in part during the launch period.[9]

TRANSFORMATION 2:
THE DIGITAL EXPERIENCE MAKEOVER

Leverage digital technologies to innovate and enrich customer experiences

The customer journey from purchase to deployment to expanded use to maintenance to upgrade and finally to loyal customer involves a multitude of experiences delivered by B2B companies and their intermediaries. Digital technologies represent a powerful tool for redesigning B2B customer experiences by making them more tailored, configurable, dynamic, and easy to use and thus more relevant to customers.[10] Relevance at key points in the customer journey such as onboarding, reordering, and technical support ensures that the experiences conform to the individual customer's needs and are less generic. And when combined with a reduction in pain points, relevance accelerates the customer's path to realizing value and establishes the competitive differentiation that B2B companies need to win and grow.

B2B companies should begin the digital experience makeover by fixing broken steps in the customer journey—investing in listening to customers and addressing customers' pain points.[11] Sounds pretty straightforward, right? But in reality, many B2B suppliers are so focused on selling, product, and price that the customer experience is treated as just one of many operational processes—optimized from an internal perspective but not from the customer's. Creating a culture of listening to the customer and fixing pain points—such as complicated billing, sluggish or subpar technical support, and hard-to-reach claims adjusters—can have a significant impact on customer retention.[12] To address customer pain points, teams must be able to fully understand the journeys of all their different types of customers. They must also learn to distinguish the pain points that matter most.

Pain point resolution is a great way to begin to improve customer experiences, but meeting expectations is rarely sufficient to make a significant impact in customers' working lives or to generate competitive advantage. A higher level of innovation is required, one that relies on customer-inspired redesign to dramatically enhance experiences or add valuable new experiences to the customer journey. Take, for example, Schneider Electric's mobile app for electrical contractors that lets them specify their requirements for new building sites.[13] The app condensed a once time-consuming, multistep process—taking notes in the field, then inputting requirements at a desktop computer, and then interacting with Schneider's customer service center by phone and email—into a one-stop operation that handled the entire job from a mobile phone or tablet. It not only saved the customer time, but it also enabled Schneider to suggest add-on products. Most importantly, it gave Schneider real-time data with which to learn more about contractors' needs and to monitor the results of any pilots they ran to improve the experience.

A digital experience makeover doesn't necessarily call for adding new touchpoints, as Schneider did with the introduction of its mobile app. Often breakthrough improvement can come from enhancing the customer journey through the inspired, data-driven redesign of existing touchpoints. The key is to go beyond fixing pain points and eliminating hassles to understanding what will delight customers.

In 2018 Thyssenkrupp's Elevator unit completely overhauled its customer experience by partnering with Microsoft to redesign its elevator repair and maintenance offering.[14] Thyssenkrupp Elevator wanted to gain a competitive edge by focusing on what matters most to its customers: reliability. Drawing on the IoT and Microsoft's Azure technology, the company now connects its elevators to the cloud, gathering data from embedded sensors and systems and transforming it into valuable business intelligence. In this way, Thyssenkrupp has been able to offer customers what its competitors have not: predictive and preemptive maintenance. Based on the data, the system, known as MAX, calculates the remaining lifetime of key components, determining which parts will require maintenance, and when. The system also flags potential repair issues. Predictive modeling increases efficiency and reduces elevator downtime. Because they are based on machine learning, the predictive models have been continuously improving, as they rely on data the company has been collecting even in the years before adoption. As a result, Thyssenkrupp is confident that MAX can reduce elevator downtime by up to 50 percent, making its predictive models second to none in the global elevator industry.

MAX is a major milestone in Thyssenkrupp Elevator's business strategy. Within the eighteen-month launch period, the company aims to connect some 180,000 units in North America and Europe; the US, Germany, and Spain will be the pilot countries. The solution now features an enhanced customer service portal, which grants building managers access to important real-time information about their elevators' performance, thus helping them to facilitate timelier and more effective repair work with Thyssenkrupp's maintenance engineers. Thyssenkrupp is now also using Microsoft Willow Twin, a digital twin (digitalized virtual model) of the physical building to revolutionize the way buildings are maintained. The digital twin captures live data from IoT sensors that are embedded in all the building's systems—from lighting and elevators to heating, ventilation, and air conditioning—along with data about the way space is being used and occupied. It makes all the data available to building owners, managers, and maintenance staff in real time. They can then track usage patterns, identify problems, and gain insights about how they operate a building and the way people use it. The digital twin opens the door to creating new and better experiences for tenants and visitors.

TRANSFORMATION 3:
THE DIGITAL PROPOSITION PIVOT

Leverage digital technologies to pivot to data-powered solutions

The third transformation addresses the shift from providing products and services to providing data-powered solutions. Most successful B2B companies are adept at bundling offerings focused on the portfolio of products and services that they provide. But digital technologies such as RFID, IoT, AI, and blockchain are revolutionizing these offerings. Even product-engineering-oriented powerhouses such as Siemens, Johnson & Johnson, and BASF are incorporating one or more of these data-sharing technologies into their current or planned innovations for the next decade.[15] Many new offerings are focusing on sharing, integrating, and learning from data gathered through an industry ecosystem such as digital medical records. As a result, an enormous array of B2B product and service companies are turning into data-driven solution providers. These companies must pivot to offer data-driven solution propositions. A good example is Hilti, which pivoted from selling tools and machinery for the construction and mining industries to providing a fleet management solution that allows customers to pay for equipment on an as-used basis (pay per hour). Hilti is using the data to anticipate when new tools are needed, to replace worn parts and accessories, and to address surges in tool utilization.[16]

In this pivot to data-powered solutions, every aspect of the value proposition that companies have relied on, such as training, premium pricing, value-added services, feature upgrades, call center help, and distribution access, is a candidate for fundamental change. Companies can now unleash the power of digital technologies and data to connect customers and devices, to make data accessible, to configure solutions on demand, and to partner with other suppliers. Data-powered solutions also often require finding new ways to monetize the benefits that digitization delivers. The go-to-market proposition for companies competing in this new world must address these new dynamics. Because the list of potential changes is so vast, it's up to company leaders to take control and guide their organization to focus on those that matter most.

Consider how digitizing a value proposition could generate revenue as well as save costs.

- ► **Digital as a revenue generator.** Innovation needn't be limited to R&D for new products. Digital can unleash it across a wider range of functions and areas—for example, rethinking pricing by moving to a subscription-based model or introducing consulting services as part of the offer bundle.

- ► **Digital as a cost saver.** Companies can automate costly, in-person, on-site-delivered support services (such as technical support) or employee training, thus reducing the cost to serve and enabling them to compete more effectively. Data transparency and analytics can also give companies the ability to spot potential cost savings for customers (for example, identifying opportunities for volume discounting) or cost-saving efficiencies with suppliers. Digital thus allows companies to partner with customers as well as with other supply chain entities for mutual benefit.

Adobe's 2012 pivot from packaged-software maker to cloud-based subscription provider of solutions such as the Adobe Creative Suite is an example of a proposition pivot that increased Adobe's revenues and margins while allowing customers to pay only for what they use.[17] By 2011, Adobe had emerged as the clear leader in packaged design software that bundled products such as Photoshop, Illustrator, Acrobat, and InDesign to help a wide range of B2B customers create compelling visual output. But sales were flattening as the company reached the limits of market penetration for software that cost approximately $3,000 per user just to get started. The quickening pace of change on the intranet and other digital channels required frequent updates that were almost impossible to support in the annual to eighteen-month cycles for upgrading prepackaged software.

Adobe's customers weren't asking for subscriptions; a large proportion of its customer base was happy with the product as it was. Subscribing to, rather than buying, software was still a new idea that involved considerable change for Adobe's customers. Still, Adobe embarked on a proposition pivot to a software as a service (SaaS) solution. This changed how the company developed software, delivered it, engaged with customers (now directly, instead of through resellers), provided upgrades, billed customers, and recognized revenue. The central idea was to sell Adobe's products and services via download from a cloud environment that would monitor customer needs, update the software frequently, make upgrades easy to undertake, and provide inexpensive data storage to customers.

Selling software on a monthly basis meant forgoing a large up-front payment in favor of monthly ones that the subscriber could cancel with only two months' notice. The deferred payoff, potentially significant profitability gains, would come only if Adobe succeeded in sustaining customer satisfaction and loyalty over the long term. But among the many advantages of Adobe's SaaS, it opened the door for doing so by creating a direct relationship between Adobe and the professional designers who were its core customers. This direct relationship cut out software resellers and allowed Adobe to augment margins while helping the customer reduce large initial outlays. In addition, this direct relationship allowed Adobe to distribute updates and upgrades seamlessly and more frequently. Adobe could see how its product was being used and talk to customers directly about how they could make better use of it.

Adobe's transition from packaged product to SaaS was an arduous three-year process that required extensive planning as well as a significant investment in educating Wall Street analysts and customers to see the value of the new subscription model. By 2018, Adobe's revenues had risen to $9 billion, more than double its 2012 revenues of $4.4 billion, and net earnings more than tripled, from $833 million in 2013 to $2.8 billion.

UNCOMMON GROWTH

Disrupt or be disrupted is the mantra of the digital age. It's also a false choice. Adobe leaders chose a path to sustainable growth: Adobe products were already the clear market leaders, Adobe customers were not clamoring for a new approach, and SaaS was too new to be a credible threat, at least not yet. Adobe's leaders made choices based on what was best for their business, their customers, and the company's future. The prospect of uncommon growth, growth that could be sustained through competitive advantages that would be hard for competitors to replicate, was their goal. Disruption of the prepackaged software market was an outcome. The underlying theme of this guide is to focus on the true goal: making customers better off in ways that are sustainable, are profitable, and drive growth. In the evolving B2B world, harnessing data and technology is essential to achieving this goal.

Undertaking one or more of these digital transformations allows business leaders to take advantage of the changes in data and technology in B2B markets to drive uncommon growth. The decisions of Thyssenkrupp leaders to focus on the opportunities to remake the elevator servicing experience, Schneider Electric leaders to create a better way for electrical contractors to specify requirements on the building site, and Hilti leaders to serve construction companies with tools on demand were based on putting data and technology to work on both the customers' and the company's behalf.

Customer-first digital transformation is a tool for uncommon growth. It differs from the current technology-first transformation paradigm because customer needs are the basis for transformation. In a customer-first transformation, technologies, data, digital platforms, and analytics are enablers of the customer and the company. Digital transformation is not a choice. Failure to transform in the face of the evolution of data and digital technology makes B2B companies more vulnerable to existing competitors and to unforeseen insurgents. The choice is whether to undertake the transformation in a way that will benefit the customer and drive uncommon growth, or merely to enable the company to continue in its current position.

Seizing the digital transformation initiative is the other key theme of this guide. Taking the initiative provides the window and the urgency to develop the functional capabilities and build the employee skills, teamwork, culture, and motivation that are required. It leaves room to make mistakes and room to learn as you go in a way that reacting to crises triggered by competitive activity does not. Seizing the customer-centric digital initiative opens the door to innovation in three areas: how a company sells, the proposition it offers, and the customer experience it delivers. Innovation in any one of these areas paves the way to sustainable competitive advantage, while also building an organization that is ever evolving and future ready.

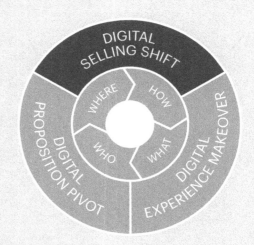

Part 1

TRANSFORMATION 1:
THE DIGITAL SELLING SHIFT

Leverage digital technologies to engage and sell more effectively

- ▶ The Digital Selling Shift challenge
- ▶ Where to Play: use cases
- ▶ How to Win: a digital selling strategy
- ▶ What to Do: demand sprints
- ▶ Who Is Needed: an analytics team
- ▶ Key Digital Selling Shift takeaways

1.1

The Digital Selling Shift Challenge

Salesforce.com and other digital natives forever changed B2B selling when they began providing (and using) digital selling and marketing tools.[1] They ushered in a transformation of such magnitude that digital marketers and analysts are now at the forefront of generating leads, cultivating decision makers and influencers, closing sales, and building relationships that fuel cross-selling, upselling, and loyalty in previously sales-force-dominated B2B industries. Although the shift began at companies with large sales teams, it has now permeated many small- and medium-sized businesses that until recently couldn't even afford large sales or technical teams to spur growth.

The Digital Selling Shift involves moving to a selling approach that relies extensively on digital marketing and data-driven selling.[2] It requires moving away from the classic but inefficient B2B sales model in which the sales force "owns" the customer relationship and marketing is relegated to a supporting role of providing content to the sales team and boosting market awareness. The digital selling shift results in an effort that can best be described as "Smarketing," the full integration of sales and marketing in a tightly linked partnership that is data driven and digitally powered.[3]

For the better part of the last century, most B2B companies, including the likes of IBM, Siemens, and 3M, relied heavily on large sales forces to drive demand and complete the sale with the support of technical service teams for systems integration, training, and troubleshooting.[4] But because the classic B2B model is so resource intensive and sales members' performance so uneven, many companies saw the need about twenty years ago to integrate the marketing and sales functions to boost revenues. However, B2B companies consistently lag their B2C counterparts in taking advantage of digital transformation and investing in customer websites, digital marketing, and digital sales enablement tools that alter the sales team's dominant role or drive measurable impact.[5]

After a long period in which B2C selling has been at the forefront of digital transformation, B2B digital selling is now starting to take hold in traditionally sales-force-driven companies. For example, GE Life Sciences, a unit of GE Healthcare that makes chemicals and biologic agents, built an extensive digital marketing operation that engages prospects through thought leadership content, allows customers to fulfill orders through an e-commerce portal, and supports researchers in seeking unique, custom biological agents.[6] Optum, the US health services company, developed an integrated marketing campaign to launch a new solution, support sales, and build thought leadership. The content marketing mix included advertorials, display ads, email, direct mail, and a campaign website. The successful campaign earned a 23.5 lead-to-conversion rate, a 475 percent increase in website traffic, 2,500-plus resource downloads, a 28 percent year-over-year increase in blog followers, and $52 million in new-business contracts—all from an investment of less than $1 million.[7]

The digital selling shift is occurring in B2B for several reasons:

- ▶ **Growing buyer demand for 24/7 digital access.** The desire of B2B decision makers and decision-making influencers to engage digitally with B2B suppliers is a natural result of their personal interaction with B2C companies as consumers, through online and mobile apps.[8] As they've seen how digital tools make their personal lives easier and more enjoyable—helping them find information online, locate products that match their individual preferences through digital apps, and make purchases—they've become more amenable to (if not demanding about) having the same ability in the buying and adoption decisions they make at work.

▶ **Advances in digital B2B sales and marketing platforms.** Over the past several years, the developers of comprehensive marketing automation platforms, such as Oracle, Salesforce, and Adobe, have consistently built in the features to enable tailored B2B efforts.[9] In addition, the development of B2B specialized marketing and sales platforms has taken off, most prominently in advanced account-based marketing (ABM) that enables sellers to tailor messages to different decision makers and influencers in a company and reach them through a wide range of digital channels. Powerful ABM platforms, such as RollWorks and Demandbase, are being harnessed to create more integrated and effective ways of engaging with potential buyers and influencers at different points in their path to purchase.[10]

▶ **The proliferation of online customer data.** Customer data is the rocket fuel of digital marketing and selling, and its access and availability are expanding fast. Decision makers and influencers are easier to identify and more reachable, thanks to B2B social platforms (such as LinkedIn) and gated professional communities (such as SERMO, the private social media network for physicians). Sophisticated tracking mechanisms enable digital marketers to see the customers' online behavior across multiple touchpoints and channels. The digital trail customers leave while they are active on social channels searching for information, visiting websites, or generally browsing is massive and rapidly growing, and represents a tremendous increase in the amount of customer data companies have collected in the past. This digital footprint can be bucketed broadly into 4Ss (social, search, site, and shop).

Data availability is also growing in intermediated industries. It is remarkable just how much data is now available on B2B customers of financial services providers, for example. But there are, of course, regulatory limits to data collection in some industries. Multiline insurers in Germany are prohibited from aggregating the data generated by, say, their property and casualty arm with the data generated by their employee health insurance arm.

▶ **The advent of artificial intelligence (AI).** AI is beginning to shift person-to-person sales interactions to digital touchpoints, such as chat bots, digitally enabled call centers, or fully automated voice assistants.[11] Advances in machine learning and natural language processing are converting complex tasks, such as matching a buyer's need for different types of services or weighing the financial risk and return of various services, into self-serve, online operations. Without a doubt, human experts will continue to be needed to assist buyers in many decisions for a long time. But it would be foolish to think that many salespeople and intermediaries are exempt from replacement by AI-powered tools.[12] For any B2B company, finding the right balance between "tech" and "touch" is critical.

▶ **The lower cost of digital sales and marketing.** The search for greater efficiency and effectiveness in sales and marketing is yet another reason the digital selling shift is taking hold. By effectively deploying digital tools for selling and marketing, companies can lower their costs as well as increase revenues. The cost/benefit ratio of face-to-face selling versus digital marketing is changing rapidly. On one hand, every company's sales team is constantly combatting the inefficiency of most of its members. Recent studies show that more than half of sales team members miss their quota each year; the bottom half is a substantial drag on the performance of the top half. [13] Moreover, it takes time to train and develop successful salespeople, and they are vulnerable to poaching from competitors.

Meanwhile, the cost of finding, targeting, servicing, and supporting customers through digital means is plummeting, as the cost of data, computational power, and access to AI tools continues to decline. The role of insurgents will also be important. With little incentive to build sales and support teams from scratch, and without the cost of converting legacy systems, these companies can invest in the optimal combination of human on-site, human remote, digital, and AI marketing. Their lower cost to serve and improved conversion rates will pressure incumbents to move faster—or perish.

Whether the shift to digital selling and integrated sales and marketing teams happens in B2B is hardly in doubt. What is uncertain is how long it will take to gain traction in any given industry. Industry dynamics and purchase-decision complexity are the best predictors. Complex, highly regulated industries with few buyers, such as infrastructure design and engineering, will be slow to adopt digital marketing, and its role will be fairly limited. Industries such as commercial insurance, with the large number of end customers, moderate regulation, extensive customer data, and AI suitability, are ripe for disruption in their selling and marketing approaches to end customers and intermediaries.

In categories where the shift is not yet fully underway—or where it has already taken hold and competitors threaten—B2B suppliers must move quickly to turn the digital selling shift into a source of competitive advantage.

CASE STUDY:
AIR LIQUIDE

Air Liquide, the world's largest supplier of industrial gases, has made the digital selling shift part of its effort to become more customer centric.[14] Air Liquide has historically focused on large customers, leaving its distributors to serve smaller ones. But rapid growth among small- and medium-sized industrial customers in general demanded a new approach. These customers are more self-sufficient and seek out expertise from blogs, social media channels, and chatbots instead of salespeople.

Air Liquide's dependence on the traditional B2B sales model made it ill-equipped to serve a more diverse customer base digitally, so in 2016 it acquired Airgas, the American supplier of industrial, medical, and specialty gases. Airgas had already offered fully integrated multichannel sales for its small and medium enterprise (SME) customers that buy online, by phone, or physically from a local Airgas store. And by acquiring five hundred distributors over the years, Airgas had also acquired a customer mindset. Air Liquide set out to adopt Airgas's digital selling capabilities in its own operations, to pursue more SME customers and to better serve its larger ones.

Air Liquide's approach is a textbook illustration of the key steps we recommend in this book for defining where to play, how to win, what to do, and who is needed to win.

- ▶ **Where should Air Liquide play?** In this first stage, Air Liquide developed a typology of customer segments and analyzed what being customer centric really means for each type of customer. This forced the company to articulate the key differences between its large customers and its smaller ones, to better understand opportunities to serve SMEs. Large customers typically had a deep relationship but infrequent contact with Air Liquide. SME customers, on the other hand, had numerous ongoing interactions with the company but a relatively shallow relationship. SME customers expected fast and reliable service, and proximity was important to them. Large customers expected trust, ease, and expertise through dedicated account teams. Both SMEs and large customers shared the desire for information, for answers to their questions, and for the ability to purchase products wherever and whenever they wanted. Customers who were able to use digital tools and apps to fill their needs felt it was now easier to procure gas supplies and thus felt empowered.

- ▶ **How could Air Liquide win?** Air Liquide identified which digital technology best fit each segment and how to deliver differentiating value at key pain points within the customer journey. The company then conducted a comprehensive analysis of each customer segment's buying process to understand which technologies could provide the most value to that segment. Different technologies were matched against the aforementioned customer needs to create a set of strategies for each key customer segment. During this analysis, Air Liquide learned that an easy, fast, and convenient omnichannel approach, where e/m-commerce plays an important role, is critical for its large as well as its small- and medium-sized customers but required skillful implementation leveraging segment-appropriate technologies. As a result, building an e-commerce platform and delivering multichannel capabilities became a more strategic objective for the company.

▶ **What should Air Liquide do?** Next, Air Liquide began implementing initiatives to make its services more tailored to segment needs and, overall, more customer centric. Some were designed primarily to generate revenue or to increase traffic, while others were intended to save money.

  ▸ *Social network initiative.* Many questions customers had could be answered in social media channels. So Air Liquide built a social media platform on its website where customers could interact with the company and other customers to resolve their issues. Air Liquide used the social platform to lower the cost to serve SMEs (by shifting traffic away from its call center) and to build brand equity through social engagement.

  ▸ *IoT initiative.* A number of IoT applications are now currently in operation or being tested in the company's operations in France and the US to improve supply monitoring, manage traceability, provide predictive maintenance, or let customers automatically reorder products. By the end of 2019, Air Liquide was monitoring the levels of more than fifty thousand oxygen and liquid nitrogen tanks on its customers' premises. This data enables the company to replenish its customers' stocks, relieving them of the need to place an order or monitor their levels themselves. In addition, Air Liquide is testing real-time gathering of stock-status data. The ability to trace cylinders using geolocation tags will enable customers to manage their stock and cylinder returns more effectively.

  ▸ *Big data initiative.* Air Liquide's "Connect" project is capitalizing on the optimal use of big data. Connect is a remote operations and optimization center that is unique in the industrial gases industry. It is able to control and optimize the production, energy efficiency, and reliability of its customers' large industrial facilities, including carrying out predictive maintenance actions. Thanks to big data analysis, the production flows of each site could be adapted in real time to the needs of each customer. The center is controlling production and energy consumption while the on-site teams will focus on the safety and availability of the equipment.

- **Who does Air Liquide need to make the shift?** Air Liquide systematically invested in understanding and building the skills, processes, mindset, and organizational changes required to execute a digital selling shift. Now, the company worked to transform itself into a learning agent.[15]

  Leaders wanted to be able to learn from customers through the company's test-and-learn experiments in digital technologies. They also flattened the organizational structure and reorganized teams to make Air Liquide better suited for a faster-paced environment where customer expectations and market conditions shift more rapidly. Airgas's experience—achieving greater agility by keeping central functions lean and pushing decisions down to the local level—proved to be a valuable lesson for Air Liquide. And although not yet world class, Airgas's effective digital marketing operation and e-commerce platform were a great starting point for Air Liquide's journey.

  The combined efforts of the Airgas and Air Liquide teams resulted in a successful digital selling shift in an environment where customer expectations and competitive dynamics were changing quickly. Air Liquide's SME customers benefited from the new digital offering, and Air Liquide benefited from incorporating a more flexible and digitally driven work culture into its operations. The lessons learned and the success of this initial selling shift have accelerated Air Liquide's digital transformation efforts to improve other aspects of the customer experience.

The Air Liquide case is a prime example of the importance of focusing on customers to determine where to play, to build a digital selling strategy that addresses how to win, to bring that selling strategy to market via a clear set of initiatives (what to do), and to establish new capabilities and mobilize the organization to answer the question of who is needed for winning.

The rest of the Digital Selling Shift section is devoted to charting an actionable path for tackling each of these four questions. To illustrate the steps required to successfully undertake the digital selling shift, we introduce a hypothetical company we'll call Acme Commercial Insurance, a composite of several real insurance companies.

Introducing Acme Commercial Insurance

Acme Commercial Insurance (ACI) provides many commercial insurance products to a broad range of industries, including property and casualty, workers compensation, liability, health, and cybersecurity. The company delivers its offerings primarily through a network of agents and brokers who range in size from large global brokers to small regional outfits.

The commercial insurance market is changing; to head off the threat of disintermediation, large brokers are turning the tables on the major insurance providers by becoming even larger. At the same time, Acme's competitors are disintermediating their own brokers and agents using digital technologies to build direct relationships with their clients, particularly in the small business segment of the market. Acme's leaders know the company needs to change and become more end-customer-oriented to succeed. They want to get going but feel constrained by their traditional B2B selling model that relies on sales teams to work with their extensive network of brokers.

1.2

Where to Play in the Digital Selling Shift

Identify and Prioritize Digital Selling Opportunities

D etermining Where to Play in the Digital Selling Shift is a multi-step process. It involves defining customer objectives, uncovering barriers the customer faces, identifying use cases to address the barriers, evaluating the attractiveness of each use case, assessing organization readiness, and prioritizing the use cases to pursue.

DEFINE CUSTOMER OBJECTIVES

Before undertaking the digital selling shift, a company must be absolutely clear about its customer objectives. That means focusing on where opportunities exist to boost the value of the customer *to the company* by providing value *to the customer*. The value of any customer is a function of their buying behavior over time. More than twenty years ago, Sergio Zyman, Coke's first chief marketing officer, identified the most important objectives of marketing and selling: "To get more customers to buy more stuff, more often, for more money."[1] In B2B commerce, these objectives often go by different terms: "more customers" becomes "customer acquisition," "more stuff" translates as "cross-sell/upsell" or "share of wallet," "more frequently" means "take-up rate" or "renewal/retention," and "more money" works out to a combination of "solution size" and "margin." Of course, the specifics will vary by industry and even company, but acquiring customers and increasing the value of existing customers are at the heart of formulating customer objectives.

To be useful and actionable, customer objectives must be specific for identifiable, targetable segments of customers and prospects. If they apply to everyone, they are meaningless. Growth leaders can take an important initial step by clarifying who they need to acquire as customers and which customers have the best potential to grow into loyal, high-value partners. Usually this requires analyzing customer data to find patterns and gaps. Often, comparisons to industry or market trends can reveal additional gaps. While it may be possible to do these comparisons via secondary data sources, they more than likely require rigorous primary research to see what the company is missing.

Acme Customer Objectives

Ann, Acme's chief commercial officer (CCO), worked with the executive team to determine where Acme's sales team should focus its resources to accelerate profitable growth (see figure 1). They examined the markets offering the greatest potential to acquire new, profitable customers, which current customers showed the greatest potential for buying more (upsell/cross-sell potential), which otherwise attractive customer segments were prone to churn, and where Acme had the greatest opportunity to increase margin per customer.

Figure 1. Customer purchase objectives

First, let's take acquisition. Analysis of Acme's book of business showed it performed particularly poorly with medium-sized service businesses, such as regional restaurant chains, law firms, and health clinics, even though Acme's service offering fit their needs well. As for upselling and cross-selling, a share-of-wallet analysis revealed that Acme was unsuccessful in selling to more than one location for multi-location businesses that were giving their business to a portfolio of insurance providers one location at a time. With its third objective, retention, analysis showed the company fell short when ownership changed hands, either to a new buyer or to the next generation in a family business. Finally, Acme's retention rates were actually too high for the medium-sized service business category. Renewal pricing analysis revealed the company failed to raise prices at renewal for those customers that had aggressively negotiated low rates when they first signed with Acme. Even aggressive negotiators will remain with a provider if they're pleased with the service, and Acme's failure to raise prices meant it had never determined who those customers were.

UNCOVER CUSTOMER BARRIERS

To accomplish any activity in marketing and selling, it's essential to understand the customer barriers that must be overcome to achieve the desired objective. We must identify, in order of importance, the biggest barriers to fulfilling the customer objectives for each segment. Established companies commonly face three key barriers, or gaps:[2]

- ▶ **Lack of understanding.** Certain segments of customer may not know about or understand the company's offering. Are misperceptions or historical associations getting in the way? What's causing the gap: a lack of access to content, or a failure of intermediaries to explain what the company does?

- ▶ **Attractiveness gap.** Some customers know about the product but don't realize it contains valuable benefits for their business. Do they recognize some benefits but miss other features such as technical support that competitors don't offer?

▶ **Purchase behavior.** For some companies, closing the deal is a problem. Is the company not addressing affordability? Is the company doing everything possible to help potential buyers overcome the switching costs of moving to a new solution? Do key aspects of the solution entail risks that customers are unwilling to shoulder?

Acme Customer Barriers

Ann, Acme's CCO, brought the finance, sales, and marketing leaders together, along with a customer research professional from outside the company, to learn firsthand about the barriers customers were facing. After listening in on a series of in-depth customer interviews, the team ranked the top customer barriers to increasing customer acquisition, upselling/cross-selling, retention, and value. They saw that the extent of the barriers varied considerably across segments, because each segment had unique needs, perceptions, and behaviors (see figure 2).

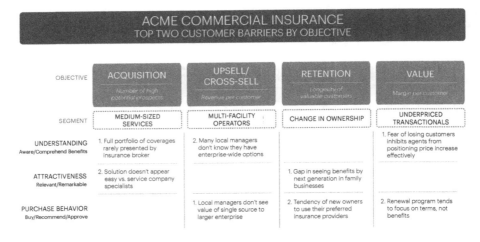

	ACME COMMERCIAL INSURANCE TOP TWO CUSTOMER BARRIERS BY OBJECTIVE			
OBJECTIVE	ACQUISITION *Number of high potential prospects*	UPSELL/ CROSS-SELL *Revenue per customer*	RETENTION *Longevity of valuable customers*	VALUE *Margin per customer*
SEGMENT	MEDIUM-SIZED SERVICES	MULTI-FACILITY OPERATORS	CHANGE IN OWNERSHIP	UNDERPRICED TRANSACTIONALS
UNDERSTANDING Aware/Comprehend Benefits	1. Full portfolio of coverages rarely presented by insurance broker	2. Many local managers don't know they have enterprise-wide options		1. Fear of losing customers inhibits agents from positioning price increase effectively
ATTRACTIVENESS Relevant/Remarkable	2. Solution doesn't appear easy vs. service company specialists		1. Gap in seeing benefits by next generation in family businesses	
PURCHASE BEHAVIOR Buy/Recommend/Approve		1. Local managers don't see value of single source to larger enterprise	2. Tendency of new owners to use their preferred insurance providers	2. Renewal program tends to focus on terms, not benefits

Figure 2. Customer purchase barriers

Acquisition. To persuade medium-sized service-business prospects to become new customers, Acme's primary challenge has been overcoming the perception that it might be hard to work with compared to the insurance companies with teams specializing in service businesses. This challenge was exacerbated by insurance brokers' tendency to rush through transactions with medium-sized customers, hitting only one or two "headlines" rather than presenting Acme's entire coverage solution—which is also one of the company's clear competitive advantages.

Upselling/cross-selling. Among companies with multi-facility operations, the barriers typically reside with the end customer. Often, local managers make purchasing decisions but don't value an enterprise-wide solution—or may not even know they have that option.

Retention. Among privately held companies, change of ownership is a major reason that retention rates drop at renewal. Younger generations who are taking over a family business often don't see the benefits of Acme's premium offering. Acquiring companies generally retain their own insurance provider and tend to consolidate their policies with a single provider.

Value. In dealing with renewals, Acme faces two barriers. Acme's brokers hate anything that might cause failure to renew. They often delay or avoid renewal discussions because raising the issue of a price increase is scary. Acme's renewal communications are a problem, too; they overemphasize the terms and conditions of renewal instead of promoting the benefits of renewal. Price increases without perceived benefits are unlikely to succeed.

IDENTIFY USE CASES

The next task is to identify the best possible application, or use case, for addressing the barriers to achieving a desired customer objective, whether through digital selling alone or a combination that includes traditional marketing and sales methods and tools. It's worth noting that digital-analog combinations should not be overlooked; approaches that integrate the sales force, the technical support team, and events such as trade shows can often be more powerful because the omnichannel strategy amplifies the impact of communications and allows prospects and customers to engage when, where, and how they choose. Digital technologies are often used to enrich, rather than replace, traditional approaches. These use cases generally fall into one of five categories:

- ▶ **Demand generation to accelerate customer acquisition.** This may be one of the most exciting and rapidly evolving areas of B2B selling. The explosion of data and a rapidly expanding set of vehicles for reaching B2B decision makers is making it possible to create direct relationships with end customers without cutting out their channel partners, their distributors, their advisors, or other middlemen. These channel and content alternatives are enabling established sellers to generate leads for their intermediaries as well as for their own sales force. Beyond generating leads, engaging in demand generation gives companies an added benefit: it creates a direct relationship with the customer. As a result, the B2B company can learn from its customers, test alternatives, and more effectively probe for new opportunities. In fact, learning may well be one of the most valuable outcomes of demand generation, as it informs and helps improve not just lead-generation activities but all aspects of the business that take place through all of the company's channels.

- ▶ **Digital sales enablement to accelerate cross-selling and boost value.** Many B2B companies have already made significant progress in this shift. Here, companies use digital tools and digitally collected data to sell more effectively. Sales engagement and relationship management platforms, including those of Salesforce.com, Oracle, and SAP, are so well established that Gartner reports that the market reached $48.5 billion in 2018 and represents a quarter of all corporate purchases of enterprise software.[3] Sales enablement platforms, networks, and apps help individual salespeople achieve more and help sales teams work more effectively together. In the past few years, these products have shifted their focus from customer relationship management to helping sales teams engage more fully with their customer's entire decision-making team. The payoff is immediate: better equipped and coordinated sales teams perform better. They generate more revenues, strengthen customer relationships, and stay with companies longer.

- **Digital relationship-building with customer decision makers.** New, more targeted vehicles, such as LinkedIn advertising, along with compelling content (such as video and virtual reality), have paved the way for ABM. ABM is more personalized and tailored to the needs of individual decision makers than traditional push email and digital advertising campaigns. As an integrated approach, it combines salesperson interactions and digital engagement for maximum efficiency and impact. Its digital components extend engagement into an anytime, anywhere experience through the 24/7 advantage of online and mobile vehicles.

- **Outsourcing routine tasks to improve efficiency.** Companies are also using digital technologies to shift more of the routine chores of selling away from the sales team, and it's little wonder: studies of sales-time utilization indicate that two-thirds of the typical salesperson's day is spent on non-selling tasks.[4] Outsourcing frees salespeople to focus on what they do best: forging and expanding personal relationships. Many early outsourcing efforts sought to target customers more precisely, improve sales resource planning, and automate routine order-taking functions. More advanced B2B companies are now using advanced AI bots and call centers to enable customers to easily order parts and accessories and get problems resolved online. Companies are also shifting their technical support and client-learning functions to digital formats. These new tools boost team efficiency and effectiveness through improved resource deployment, while freeing up the salesperson's time to develop relationships.

- **Direct digital commerce to accelerate acquisition and cross-selling.** One of the biggest opportunities digital has created for customers is allowing them to purchase services directly from companies and bypass intermediaries. Initially, intermediaries almost always saw this as a fundamental threat, so it invariably led to conflict. But as more and more customers demand 24/7 access, intermediaries' attitudes are changing. They are increasingly open to working with suppliers to support customer segments that are hard to access—for example, small, low-revenue end customers for whom it's difficult to provide one-on-one personal sales support. Intermediaries are also more willing to fulfill offers that are costly to serve, such as add-on offers that generate little revenue but that can add significant value to the customer relationship. Direct commerce can also be valuable at different points in the customer journey. Moving renewal to a direct commerce model is a good example. It's important that suppliers decide how they will integrate direct digital commerce solutions with their intermediary relationships or even with their own salespeople. Perhaps most important is deciding whether to make digital commerce an entirely separate business (which can help minimize channel conflict) or to create hybrid models of personal sales and digital commerce that may require a great deal of effort (for example, in partnering with sellers) but can also provide more integrated solutions for the end customer.

Acme Customer Use Cases

Ann, Acme's CCO, along with Chan, the head of sales, and Sergio, Acme's head of marketing, were able to identify use cases to address all of their main customer barriers (see figure 3). They did so by systematically examining each barrier and exploring which of the five selling shifts would best address it.

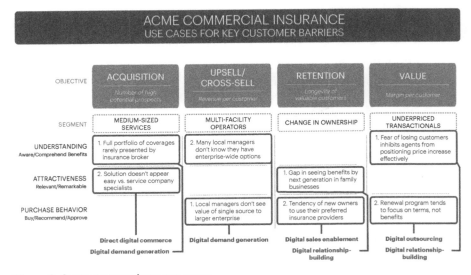

Figure 3. Customer purchase use cases

Digital demand generation appears to be a good fit with the top of the funnel barriers at upsell and cross-sell, where multi-facility customers are neglected because Acme lacks the sales team resources, and brokers have little incentive to pursue either medium-sized service companies or local facility managers. *Direct digital commerce* would serve medium-sized service companies' need for an easy way to buy and would help differentiate Acme among competitors that specialize in service companies. *Digital relationship-building* (and ABM) would be a good fit for next-generation heirs to the family business; although theirs are easy to identify and target, it is too costly to assign dedicated personnel to cultivate relationships. Digital relationship-building is also effective for bypassing brokers and creating a direct dialogue with current customers, which can also help soften the blow of price changes. Finally, by automating the labor-intensive renewal process, *digital outsourcing* will do more than save Acme money. It will allow the company to redirect resources into promoting the benefits of renewal, instead of just recapping price and terms to customers.

Most companies can identify a portfolio of use cases to consider pursuing. Each use case must include a clear customer target (i.e., segment), objective (e.g., acquisition or upsell/cross-sell), and barrier to overcome (e.g., lack of understanding), as well as a selling approach that will help the company surmount the barrier. To test whether the use case is truly customer centric, see if it can be articulated in a sentence asserting the customer benefits. For example, for Acme Commercial Insurance, we could say, "Digital demand generation can overcome midsize services companies' low understanding of insurance options that stems from brokers' neglect or inattention and can do so in a way that will attract more of these customers." The key, of course, is to not lose sight of the fact that the use case must benefit the customer and not just the company.

EVALUATE USE CASE ATTRACTIVENESS

What makes a use case attractive? Several factors:

- ▶ **Financial impact.** Financial impact, a function of the impact on the customers' needs, the size of the use case, and its growth potential, is certainly the most important indicator of use case attractiveness. Customer research can make estimating impact on the customer and number of customers who can benefit a fairly easy task for the purposes of assessment. Estimating the financial impact can be quite time consuming because of the extensive work involved in creating an incremental revenue and cost P&L for each use case. That's not usually necessary at the early evaluation stage. Instead, we've found that comparing the relative impact of different use cases is easier than attempting to make detailed calculations of the ROI for each use case. For example, it's a lot easier to get a customer who already knows you to buy more than to get a customer who doesn't know you to switch from their current provider. This fact can inform a comparison of use cases targeting prospects with one targeting current customers.

► **Strategic fit.** If the company aims to be a low-cost provider, which use cases offer the greatest opportunity to increase efficiency by shifting costs from the sales team to a more cost-efficient vehicle? If the company is pursuing a differentiation strategy, which use cases will help most in showing customers how its solutions are preferable? Companies with large market share often focus on use cases that generate more value from their existing customer base because of the greater financial impact. Insurgents and small market-share companies pursue new customers because there are more of them and their lifetime value is potentially high, even though they can be hard to attract. Most companies balance the mix of use cases, with some focusing on generating new leads and converting them and some focusing on building value among existing customers.

► **Long-term customer value.** Long-term customer value is an important consideration in choosing use cases. All too often companies fall prey to valuing a use case by the short-term improvement in transaction volume. Companies need to examine whether the target group for the use case will grow over time or if its purchasing power will grow. They also need to assess the impact of a use case on longer-term customer value, often called the lifetime value of the customer, or LTV. The rationale for pursuing a use case is strong whenever the ratio of LTV to customer acquisition costs (CAC) is high.[5] Similarly, in some use cases, such as selling post-purchase services or accessories, the transaction amount may be small but the impact on LTV may be substantial because of the significant effect multiple purchases have on customer stickiness and loyalty.[6] LTV explains why use cases that depend on subscription models or extended contracts may have a low return in the initial period because of substantial acquisition costs, but pay out handsomely over time because of the recurring revenue.

▶ **Synergy across use cases.** Adopting a set of use cases that rely on the same digital selling shift and utilize similar capabilities can drive economies of scale in deployment. These synergies can lower costs by spreading out investment in digital platforms and in developing capabilities across greater revenue. They can also serve to increase revenue by sharing learning across the board and by having the scale to undertake more test-and-learn experiments. It is also important to consider follow-on synergies. When pursuing one set of use cases enables the pursuit of more use cases later on, the value of each individual case and of the cases collectively is enhanced because of their capability-development potential.

Acme Evaluation of Use Case Attractiveness

When Ann (the CCO), Chan (sales head), and Sergio (marketing head) began assessing use case attractiveness, they focused first on comparing the use case for generating demand among medium-sized businesses with the use case for retaining privately held companies post-acquisition through sales enablement (see figure 4). The trio prioritized the demand generation use case for medium-sized service businesses because of its attractive potential for financial impact, customer value, and use case synergy.

ACME COMMERCIAL INSURANCE
ATTRACTIVENESS EVALUATION FOR TWO USE CASES

USE CASE	FINANCIAL IMPACT	STRATEGIC FIT	VALUE OF CUSTOMER	USE CASE SYNERGY
	★★★★	★★★	★★★★	★★★★★
Acquire new medium-sized service businesses by using digital demand generation to address their poor understanding of insurance possibilities	Large, growing segment; moderate insurance needs	Needs match Acme capabilities, but require different service model	High potential for new coverage lines offering moderate margins	Significant synergy with several demand-generation use cases
	★★	★★★★★	★★★	★
Retain acquired business via digital sales enablement to help overcome pattern of acquirer using their established providers	Difficult, given small number and size of businesses in segment	Needs match Acme capabilities, but are already well served	If successful, provides potential to switch coverage of acquirer	Few other use cases for this unique form of digital sales enablement

Figure 4. Use case attractiveness evaluation

On the plus side, the team's analysis revealed that, although the prospects are just medium-sized companies, there are many of them, their numbers are growing, and they buy a lot of insurance products that have good margins. On the negative side, it revealed—somewhat to the team's surprise—a gap in Acme's service model relative to the competition's that would need to be closed with some type of self-service e-commerce and claims platform. The analysis also confirmed that the use case for using digital sales enablement as a means for retaining privately held businesses that get acquired is not attractive. It would provide little financial reward, only moderate customer impact, and almost no synergy with other use cases.

ASSESS ORGANIZATIONAL READINESS

Evaluating use cases also means assessing the organization's readiness to carry out any of the five digital selling shifts. By "readiness," we mean not only the existing functional capabilities of a given team or unit; we're also referring to the skills and foundational capabilities that enable a company to integrate new data, platforms, talent, or processes needed to deliver on the use cases (see figure 5). Readiness reflects capabilities in place as well as the ability to build new capabilities and data. In reality, only a few, very mature, companies have in place most of the capabilities they need to undertake new use cases.

SELLING SHIFT READINESS DIAGNOSTIC
AREAS FOR ASSESSMENT

FUNCTIONAL CAPABILITY AREAS

CHANNEL DEPLOYMENT CAPABILITY AREAS

TEAM EMPOWERMENT
- Digital has strategic role
- Organization, process, and skills
- Reporting and governance

CREATIVE CUSTOMIZATION
- Content strategy
- Visual and verbal identity
- Content creation
- Content customization

CHANNEL EFFECTIVENESS
- OWNED: Web, mobile, CRM
- EARNED: Organic search, social, partners
- PAID: Paid search, advertising, placements

PLANNING
- Audience segmentation and scoring
- Customer journey
- User interaction design

PLATFORM ENABLEMENT
- Data strategy
- Technology platforms

CHANNEL EXTENDERS
- Geolocation
- IoT
- AR/VR
- AI

Figure 5. Selling shift readiness diagnostic areas

The organizational readiness assessment serves several purposes. For one thing, it is important for prioritizing use cases. It will also inform the strategy and the investment road map the company must devise to fill key capability gaps. In addition, it serves as an alignment tool for the organization, a way for leaders to weigh in on where the organization stands and to come to grips with the gaps and strengths related to delivering the key use cases.

It's important to assess both the functional and the channel deployment capabilities for each use case. The functional capabilities include team empowerment (such as process, skills, and governance), strategy (e.g., audience segmentation, the customer journey, designing the next), creative customization (e.g., content and visual identity), and platform enablement. Channel deployment capabilities include the ability to harness owned, earned, and paid channels. Owned channels are in the company's control (e.g., the corporate website or email campaigns); earned channels are those in which companies must compete to earn prospects' attention (e.g., social sites or organic searches); and paid channels call for purchasing media, key search terms, and ads to gain access to target prospects. Channel deployment capabilities also include channel extensions such as geolocation, IoT, augmented reality, voice recognition, and AI. Extensions are constantly evolving and encompass technologies that extend the reach and effectiveness of other channels and, to some extent, can become channels in themselves.

The basis for assessing functional and channel deployment capability is whether you have the talent, processes, tools (both data and technology), and organization in place to succeed. You want the assessment to reveal gaps where improvement is needed, voids that require hiring or wholesale change, and areas of capability that can be harnessed or extended. Externally benchmarking best practices and customer impact is also important, as is using a capability to drive results. In the readiness assessment, the basics apply: Are best practices being implemented? Are measures in place? Is the quality of execution evident? Is the channel integrated into the overall selling strategy?

Acme Readiness Assessment

Acme CCO Ann asked Ukema, the head of IT, to team up with a consultancy to undertake a readiness assessment for Acme's top-priority use case: generating demand among medium-sized businesses. But she was unprepared for the extent of the capability gaps the assessment revealed (see figure 6). Ann, Sergio, and Chan expected gaps in platform enablement but were surprised to find gaps in strategy and channel effectiveness.

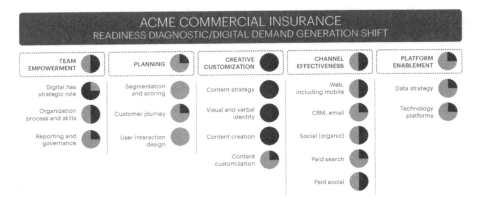

Figure 6. Selling shift readiness diagnostic example

Over the previous five years, Ann and Sergio had invested in building Acme's brand presence on the web, through email and social media, and believed this investment had given the company a fairly high level of digital proficiency. The readiness diagnostic proved beneficial in demonstrating how different the requirements for effective demand generation were from the brand-building digital activities they were already undertaking. The brand-building activities provided a foundation in brand identity, content strategy, and content creation but were of little help in customer scoring to predict the long-term financial value of customers, customer journey, interaction design, content customization, email, paid search, and data. The good news was that, although Acme would need to create new platforms, they would be relatively inexpensive to build and fairly easy to integrate with Acme's current technology. The leaders also learned that a combination of in-house talent and an external B2B digital marketing agency could fill most of their gaps temporarily and enable Acme to get started—all with an investment that Acme had been prepared to undertake.

Companies are prone to two pitfalls in these readiness assessments. One is gauging their ability to use the technology at hand rather than to produce the use case outcomes. This bias often comes from IT leaders who are confident of their ability to assemble the data and tools but who don't fully understand or else underestimate the challenges of using data and tools to achieve results in the market. Merely having digital technologies and data in place does not mean you have the ability to marshal teams to provide value to customers and to the organization. The second assessment pitfall is underestimating the value of leadership, governance, and agile work processes. These soft skills fuel the adaptability and effectiveness that are so critical to organizational change.

PRIORITIZE USE CASES

Prioritizing use cases requires weighing their attractiveness and the organization's readiness in a clear and tangible way that helps leaders determine the optimal sequence for implementation. The criteria for prioritization are also a tool for communicating to the organization why the particular priorities were chosen. In practice, prioritizing in numeric order doesn't work very well in large organizations because it ignores the need for organizations to pursue a portfolio of use cases with different time horizons, risk profiles, and impact potential. Putting all resources in one basket and waiting until one case is completed before moving on to the next priority is impractical and unlikely to succeed, given the complexities of today's marketplace. What is helpful, however, is categorizing sets of use cases into several buckets: quick wins, key focus areas, "shooting stars," and "dogs."

▶ **Quick wins.** These are typically use cases where readiness is high but the attractiveness of the case may be only moderate. Quick wins are worthwhile because they allow an organization to get moving in its digital selling shift and build momentum early on. The high level of readiness allows teams to begin immediately and to test out whether there are unexpected capability gaps that must be filled before the next set of initiatives. Because these cases are only moderately attractive, their likelihood of failure is reduced and teams are more willing to take risks, learn from their mistakes, and figure out how to move fast.

▶ **Key focus areas.** Typically, these are use cases that are highly attractive and where readiness is moderate to high. These cases provide big benefits and stretch the organization so that it can build new capabilities. Key focus areas don't take so long to show impact and a return on investment that they risk not completing the job or seeing the market dynamics change.

▶ **Shooting stars.** These use cases are highly attractive, but the organization has little readiness for them. One or two belong in a portfolio of use cases to be pursued. However, capabilities must often be developed through other use cases before the organization is ready to go after major shooting stars.

▶ **Dogs.** These use cases are unattractive, or the organization's readiness is extremely low—or both. And these characteristics are unlikely to change. Dogs burn up resources and distract the organization.

Investing in enabling capabilities is, of course, a necessity. Companies must always strike a delicate balance between waiting for the right use cases to drive the need for investment and waiting too long and having the lack of key enablers slow or even halt the pursuit of attractive use cases and growth opportunities.

Acme Selling Opportunity Priorities

When prioritizing use cases based on attractiveness and readiness, Ann, Chan, and Sergio decided to pursue quick wins in a digital relationship-building and digital demand generation use case. The capabilities they built pursuing the quick wins could subsequently be utilized in pursuing larger and more challenging digital relationship-building and digital demand generation use cases that the team prioritized as key focus areas (see figure 7).

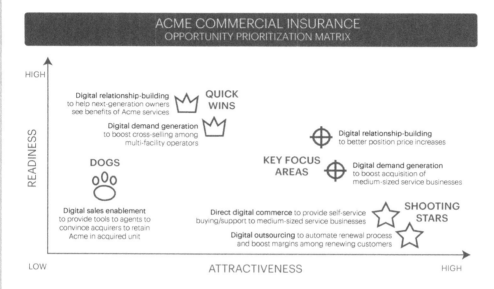

Figure 7. Selling shift opportunity prioritization matrix

Ann initially formed two quick-win teams that were chartered to deliver results within six months. After six months, these teams became the nucleus of a larger effort to tackle the key focus area use cases. Ann also asked Priya, Acme's CFO, to investigate the costs and benefits of investing in the shooting stars. Priya assigned a team that worked with Sergio and Acme's digital marketers to estimate the costs of building the infrastructure for the shooting stars. She also commissioned customer research to estimate the potential customer impact at different investment levels. Ann gained the executive team's support to fund the quick wins and investigate the shooting stars by eliminating an ongoing digital sales enablement project that the prioritization exercise proved to be a dog.

Once the use cases have been evaluated and prioritized based on attractiveness and organizational readiness, leaders are equipped with a set of promising opportunities that are informed with sufficient customer insights to drive strategy and execution. In addition, leaders are armed with information about the gaps they will need to address and the strengths they'll need to tap for the task ahead: building a winning strategy.

1.3

How to Win in the Digital Selling Shift

The Strategy for Digital Selling

The next step in the Digital Selling Shift is determining How to Win: building a customer-driven strategy to activate the use cases. The strategy should be pragmatic: it should leverage capabilities, integrate initiatives into the day-to-day work of the sales and marketing teams, and most important, create value for the target audience. Decisions about technology selection, data acquisition, and execution are crucial. However—and this is especially important—they should not drive the work to be done. It's the other way around: the work must drive those decisions.

Sales and marketing leaders often overlook the critical step of developing a digital selling strategy, under the mistaken belief that this important step can be bypassed to accelerate speed to market. Unfortunately, tech and data vendors are a part of the problem by encouraging corporate decision makers to purchase technology, then figure out how to deploy it. Leaders who pursue this path and don't build a strategy consistently report being frustrated with the results and the lack of return on investment. A study done by the MIT Center for Digital Business and Capgemini Consulting shows that many companies get seduced by new technology and fail to create value.[1] Leaders need a clear understanding of their strategy for addressing customer issues before committing to decisions about technology and data platforms.

A digital selling strategy in B2B is a four-step digital process that we call the 4Cs: *clarify* (the target), *capture* (attention), *cultivate* (interest), and *convert* (to action).

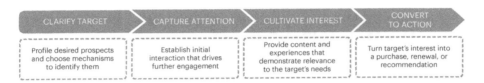

▶ **Clarify the target.** Companies must determine the profiles of the businesses to pursue, the buyers and influencers within them whom they'll need to engage, and the mechanisms by which they'll identify them for online interaction. In this step, the company builds customer data profiles and catalogs customers' needs along their buying journey.

▶ **Capture attention.** This step encompasses the act of initial engagement and directing prospects and customers into a "cultivation pathway." It includes search engine optimization (SEO) and search engine marketing (SEM), retargeting, guiding the customer's choice of initial channel, and content. It also includes techniques to encourage prospects and customers to opt-in to obtain additional content, information, discounts, or advice that may be valuable to them.

▶ **Cultivate interest.** Here, you move a prospect or a customer from expressing interest to showing intent to carry out a value-creating act—such as a first purchase, repeat purchase, renewal, or recommendation. It includes providing content that will motivate the customer, using techniques for personalizing and customizing content to make it more relevant, tracking the digital engagement path of the customer, and determining which channels and content represent the "next best move" for them.

▶ **Convert to action.** This step is all about turning intent into action. In some cases, the customer can complete the action entirely online (for example, purchasing from a web store or writing a recommendation or review). In other cases, the customer is handed off to a salesperson, a call center, or an intermediary. The convert step applies the tools and techniques that will complete the action in as little time as possible with as little hassle as possible. Techniques can also include ways to optimize the offer or entice the customer with extra services at the moment of purchase.

Prospects don't always take the steps one by one. Those who know what they want will go straight to "convert." Others will proceed to "cultivate," then disappear and need to be recaptured again. Still others may move to "convert" but find they need to step back for more cultivation. For any B2B company, the key to success is designing the digital selling strategy in a way that lets customers and prospects advance rapidly or go back a step or two while keeping them engaged.

CLARIFY THE TARGET DECISION MAKER

Targeting involves understanding who actually makes the purchasing decision and how that decision-making process works. Specifically, who within a target customer business makes the decision to try, adopt, and scale new products or services? How do decision influencers, researchers, and leaders with veto power interact with the purchasing decision makers in their organization? Which decision makers are involved in setting up a new supplier or expanding the relationship and not just placing orders through a preexisting supplier agreement?

If every company in an industry were similar and were organized similarly, this would be a fairly straightforward exercise. However, decision makers and influencers in the B2B world can vary considerably, even from company to company. To further complicate matters, decision makers' and influencers' job titles and positions in the company hierarchy can vary widely and so can the amount of time they spend on making buying decisions and the level of freedom they have to exert decision-making authority.

There are two main sources of information about the dynamics of B2B decision-making and knowing how to build profiles of target prospects:

- ▶ **Primary customer research.** This is the main information source for understanding customer decision-making. In its simplest form it involves interviewing employees and (where possible) former employees of prospective customers, the intermediaries that serve them, and your own sales force. Over time, surveys can also be used to develop a richer understanding of customer segments and uncover their decision-making patterns.

- ▶ **Observational analysis.** In this approach, you study the online behavior of decision makers and influencers to learn the main ways they seek out and delve into different types of information, content, and tools. Observational analysis usually supplements primary customer research.

In the early stages of development, your buyer profiles will usually be fairly rough. There will likely be just one or two buyer types, and you will have basic information such as who they are, what role they play in the decision-making process, and what information they are seeking at different points in the buying process. Fortunately, with a consistent effort, you can accumulate buyer data quickly. Soon you will have amassed more nuanced information: signals about when a prospect is seeking a new solution; the touchpoints and channels they prefer; their decision-making criteria; and their preferences for when, where, and how they engage with suppliers. Having this data will help your company improve its media mix and make content more relevant to the prospective buyer at each stage in their journey to purchase.

Acme Targeting Priorities

When Acme leaders Ann, Chan, and Sergio deliberated on where to play in the medium-sized service company segment, they decided that new customer acquisition via digital demand generation was a top quick-win opportunity. As the first step in building a capture strategy, Ann asked Sergio to take the lead in determining who to target and what stage in the decision-making process to address. Sergio sought to understand the typical decision-making process in three of Acme's biggest vertical segments: hospitality, professional services, and transportation (see figure 8).

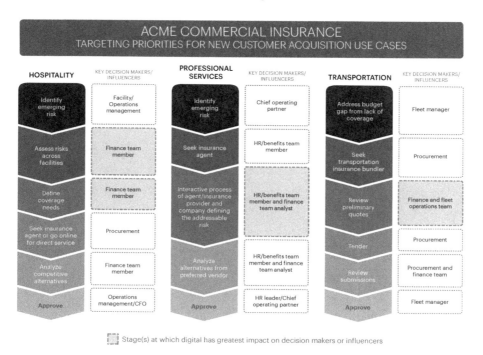

Figure 8. Customer purchase decision-making funnel

Sergio's analysis revealed that neither the key business leaders (the ultimate decision makers) at Acme's prospective customers nor the procurement managers at these companies who dealt with Acme agents drove purchasing decisions. Among prospective hospitality industry customers, it was a finance team member who was responsible for risk and insurance. Among professional services prospects, an HR manager and a finance team member framed the coverage needs and gave senior management their recommendations for insurance providers. Over time, as Sergio and the sales and marketing team probed the decision-making patterns in other industries, they learned more about how different finance departments approached buying decisions and how buyers ranked the importance of working with carriers to understand hidden risks, recover more quickly, and lower future premiums through pro-active risk management. One of the stumbling blocks analysts hit was finding a job title that readily identified their target prospect. The titles "risk manager" and "insurance manager" were rarely used. To overcome this challenge, they decided to supplement targeting based on job title alone with the targeting of finance team members who consumed insurance or risk management information online and those who attended risk management conferences.

CAPTURE ATTENTION

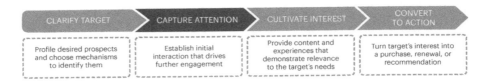

CLARIFY TARGET	CAPTURE ATTENTION	CULTIVATE INTEREST	CONVERT TO ACTION
Profile desired prospects and choose mechanisms to identify them	Establish initial interaction that drives further engagement	Provide content and experiences that demonstrate relevance to the target's needs	Turn target's interest into a purchase, renewal, or recommendation

How do you capture the customer's attention? By providing relevant content through the right channels at the right moment. Effective capture calls for strategically deploying paid media (such as banner advertisements), owned media (such as the company website), and earned media (such as interactions on an industry or third-party social platform). It also requires communicating creatively to break through all of the content a prospect encounters (not just on your platforms, but also on competitors' and in other related channels), grab their attention, and spur them to engage with you further. Most capture strategies consist of one or more of four approaches that combine these elements in different ways. Which of the four approaches you choose depends on the online content consumption behavior of the target audience:

▶ **Always-on capture** serves prospects who are already actively seeking a solution. It involves uncovering evidence of the prospect's search for assistance and then using SEO/SEM, retargeting, trigger-based email outreach, and so forth to draw their attention to a piece of content related to their need. Always-on works best in cases where it's hard to anticipate when members of a segment will be looking for help or when the segment is so small or hard to target that campaigning is probably expensive and ineffective. Management consultants face this problem in generating leads. It's very hard to predict when a trigger for seeking consulting advice, like replacing a chief technology officer or making a major corporate acquisition, will occur. Always-on marketing is effective in such cases because it addresses those looking for help instead of trying to anticipate and target in advance those with a potential need. Because always-on targets those actively seeking a solution, it is extremely efficient—which is why it is generally a part of most B2B companies' capture strategies.

▶ **Thought leadership** capture serves prospects who are seeking expertise but who don't necessarily have a solution in mind. It uses the supplier's expertise and its known experts to attract prospects who are interested in a particular topic. The key to this strategy's effectiveness is becoming a go-to place for information. The Mayo Clinic has used thought leadership successfully to build relationships with physicians who later become referrers to the Clinic's network.[2] Thought leadership is ideal for complex topics that customers want to understand better. Thought leadership can be especially effective with existing customers who already have reason to visit the supplier's site and who appreciate the added value that thought leadership content brings to their work.

Thought leadership has a downside, though: it takes time and investment to build. There is no guarantee that the company will convert the customer's engagement in content into the willingness to buy. That's partly because thought leadership often attracts students, job applicants, and other interested parties who are not potential buyers or influencers. Finally, thought leadership is a hard strategy to pull off if the supplier needs to establish expertise in a competitive arena against world renowned experts whose reputation gives them an enormous advantage.

- ▶ **Omnichannel campaigning** captures members of the target audience who are not actively seeking information but who will respond if intercepted. Omnichannel campaigning is best for presenting solutions and offers to large, well-defined target audiences with a higher-than-average propensity to buy. It has become the mainstay of digital marketing because it is straightforward: identify a target and expose them to content in the channels and through the vehicles they are most likely to use. One of the best use cases for omnichannel campaigning is launching a new B2B product or service to large populations of potential buyers such as physicians, farmers, or electricians—professionals who can be readily identified because their job titles are so unambiguous, even if they work within an organization. Omnichannel campaigns are now commonly used by the top twenty pharma companies to draw physicians' attention to new drugs or new indications for existing drugs.[3]

Omnichannel campaigns are not yet adept at distinguishing those who are ready to buy from those who are not. These campaigns must target audiences with a broad potential to purchase. New product launches in pharma are well suited to omnichannel campaigns, as most targeted physicians can choose to buy soon after capture. Because omnichannel campaigning typically requires a substantial media outlay initially, it is not suitable for reaching key decision makers in markets where buying patterns are unpredictable or simply infrequent. In these cases, it is unlikely to generate an acceptable return on investment.

- ▶ **Account-based marketing** is a rapidly growing B2B approach to capturing prospects that is ideal when it's necessary to tailor in-depth content to different decision makers and influencers. ABM capture integrates sales and marketing efforts to precisely target key decision makers and influencers inside organizations and deliver highly customized and relevant content to them. It is, in effect, a refined version of omnichannel campaigning, one more suited to reaching prospects within a company who elude normal targeting because their role in purchase decisions is hard to deduce. For example, a member of the corporate finance team may be responsible for managing employee retirement plans. But a broad omnichannel campaign from a mutual fund provider may not target them because their professional background and function are not indicators of a fund management role. ABM addresses this issue by working to deduce who in an organization plays different roles and then targeting them with the right content and media.

ABM used to be limited by the difficulties of encouraging targets to open and read emails since this was generally the only effective vehicle for reaching corporate decision makers and influencers directly. ABM has since broken free of those boundaries and is now able to intercept target prospects at different junctures in the online world, from LinkedIn to YouTube. ABM works best when the sales team participates in targeting and helps customize capture approaches based on their understanding of what's happening at the target company. ABM automation platforms enable precise targeting, integration with sales management platforms (such as Salesforce.com), and profile-based content delivery across channels. New platforms such as RollWorks and Demandbase are emerging to manage the complexity of ABM. It is now possible for a corporate decision maker to receive a banner ad tailored to their role in a company while they are checking the scores for their favorite team on ESPN, not just when they are browsing LinkedIn.

Acme Capture Approaches

Sergio and Chan determined that the best approaches to capturing the attention of their key target audiences in medium-sized service businesses were always-on marketing and account-based marketing (see figure 9).

Figure 9. Customer capture approach decision tree

Always-on looks promising because there are always prospects, either at renewal or when a major change in operations is underway, who are prompted to actively seek new insurance coverage. Even though there are many active seekers, thought leadership was deemed not worthwhile because it is hard to stand out as a thought leader amid large global giants. (Thought leadership does work for existing customers, however, where the need to stand out against the competition is not so important.) Account-based marketing was also chosen because it is suitable for attracting the attention of decision makers and influencers in Acme's key segments: hospitality, professional services, and transportation. These prospects are hard to target via omnichannel campaigning because their decision-making influence is a function of the particular role they play within their individual companies and industries. There may be a future role for omnichannel campaigning: targeting insurance advisors who can be fairly easily identified by profession, regardless of company. For now, though, Sergio and Chan decided to focus on generating demand among their end customers.

CULTIVATE INTEREST

CLARIFY TARGET	CAPTURE ATTENTION	CULTIVATE INTEREST	CONVERT TO ACTION
Profile desired prospects and choose mechanisms to identify them	Establish initial interaction that drives further engagement	Provide content and experiences that demonstrate relevance to the target's needs	Turn target's interest into a purchase, renewal, or recommendation

Cultivating interest is the step in which you shift a "captured" prospect from their initial intrigue to their serious interest in purchasing, trading up, renewing, or buying more often. But it is not about putting content, however valuable, on your website and getting the prospect to land on your home page only to leave them to their own devices. All too often, well-organized, content-rich websites end up overwhelming visitors by giving them too many options to choose from—which can actually be a key barrier to purchasing.[4]

Effective cultivation engages the user with content and tools via the channel and at a time that works for them and that will motivate them to consider buying and quash their objections. It is crucial that the appeals be sequenced properly and that you focus on the different ways that different customers want to engage. Most often, the sequence involves using paid and owned media to steer the prospect or customer onto owned digital platforms such as websites, social sites, mobile apps, and customer portals. However, in B2B the importance of engaging prospects through partnerships with other companies involved in building out a solution or through intermediaries should not be overlooked. Microsoft and Dell, for example, partner to promote and sell solutions that utilize Microsoft software and Dell hardware.[5] One example is their enterprise collaboration solution that combines Microsoft software such as Teams and Outlook with Dell servers that support this software.

Cultivation varies, depending on the prospect's starting point. Upsell- and cross-sell-oriented cultivation that provides opportunities and incentives to expand the shopping basket is warranted when prospects already know they want to buy. Consideration-oriented cultivation is warranted to help uncertain potential buyers crystalize their needs, examine their choices, determine whether to buy at all. The rule of thumb in upsell cultivation is to put the user no more than three clicks away from their destination. The rule of thumb in consideration cultivation is to provide the content and tools users need to be inspired, to match solutions to their challenges and circumstances, and to overcome their objections. These must be accomplished in ways that allow them to speed up, slow down, or retrace steps as needed.

Lead scoring is a process that helps companies determine when and how much to cultivate a prospect. Prospects who interact with paid, owned, and earned media on a topic or set of topics are assigned points depending on the nature, frequency, and intensity of their engagement as well as the characteristics of their profile. Those with low lead scores may be just casual browsers or job hunters doing background research. Those with higher scores may be ready for additional cultivation through a prompt to take a quiz, accept an invitation to a webinar, or sign up for an email newsletter. Those with the highest scores are ready for personal outreach, a one-on-one conversation, or contact by a salesperson.[6]

"Next best move" and "skipping" are two of several key practices for effective cultivation. Next best move refers to delivering content tailored to the online user's profile based on the last step they took in an online digital experience. For example, if a prospect visited the supplier's website, browsed a description of a new product, and reviewed the profile of a key R&D leader, the next best move may be to send an email highlighting a topic the prospect read about or send an invitation to chat from the leader whose profile was reviewed. The best content to be delivered is a function of testing and learning the best "move" based on the available data. When it works well, the target customer feels as if the company understands and anticipates what they are looking for.

Skipping entails allowing prospects to bypass content or navigation steps and go directly to later steps, such as making an appointment for a personal sales consultation. It may also involve skipping backward to revisit certain content. Companies should always strive to allow prospects to move at their own pace. But you want to avoid distracting the user by moving them to places in the experience where they can browse through interesting material that is not directly related to their path to purchase.

Acme Cultivation Pathways

Sergio decided to place Acme's primary cultivation path in a newly designed customer portal rather than on the global corporate website where there was a substantial risk that prospects would lose their way. He also decided to target and customize content for hospitality, professional services, and transportation verticals. He, Chan, and Ann debated organizing the path based on target company size but lacked sufficient data to identify prospects based on size. They did not want to ask prospects about company size for fear that it might turn some away. Acme initiates the cultivation sequence by directing target prospects to one of three guides, based on their industry (see figure 10).

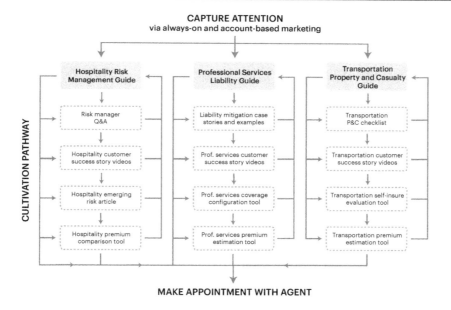

Figure 10. Customer cultivation pathway

The guide provides prospects with options to explore additional content that can help overcome the most common barriers to purchase or that can spur prospects to skip to another pathway. At any time, of course, prospects can advance to the end and connect to an agent or an e-commerce site.

To avoid diverting their attention, Acme purposely made it difficult for prospects to move to other locations on its website; it limited their navigation menu and made very prominent the buttons that encourage prospects to move to the next step in the pathway. Every element in the cultivation path—the content, format (video, text, interactive tool, Q&A), sequencing, and calls to action—is the result of test-and-learn experiments.

Cultivation works best when it is motivating and when it overcomes barriers as simply as possible. The sequence, format, and design of the content and tools represent an optimal combination that addresses prospects' needs at the right time and place in the journey.

In designing cultivation experiences, companies must make two key choices: What level of customization should we offer? And where should cultivation activities be located?

▶ **What's the right level of customization of content and tools?** This choice is determined by weighing the benefits, costs, and availability of data. In a perfect world, there can never be too much customization if it is relevant to the target. But with too little customization, the content will be too general to be relevant. However, customization comes at a cost, to both the company and its targets.

Creating customized content, keeping it fresh and up to date, and delivering it is an expensive proposition. Automated marketing technology systems can lower these costs, but the capital investment, systems integration, and training they require is not insignificant. Some B2B companies attempt to work around the delivery problem by simply putting all of the content out there for prospects to find. That's a mistake. Unless you help prospects narrow down their options, you will only overwhelm them—and deter, rather than inspire, a purchase.

For targets, the cost comes in the form of giving up personal data and time. Sometimes the company can personalize based on data already on hand, either existing customers' data or data obtained from prospects' online behavior. In these cases, the data exchange costs are minimal. Otherwise, prospective buyers will be asked to provide data about themselves, their company, and what it is they are seeking. To many prospects, time spent answering many questions is time wasted. There is also an emotional cost to a data exchange. Many potential buyers don't want to feel "sold to." They also fear that giving out their data will open them up to a steady stream of sales pitches for the foreseeable future.

▶ **How to determine where cultivation should occur?** How much cultivation should take place on the company's online turf, and how much should occur on intermediaries' assets? Our case example, Acme Commercial Insurance, chose to locate the first step of the cultivation path, its guide, on Acme's new customer platform and on the websites of key broker partners. Invitations to use the guide were placed on LinkedIn and other social media, as well as on the websites of professional risk management societies. The guide linked prospects to the remaining steps in the cultivation path, which were located only on Acme's customer portal. Acme could have chosen to put the entire cultivation sequence on its brokers' websites or exclusively on its own site. Ideally, a supplier should control as much of the cultivation pathway as possible by keeping it on a single host site; doing so minimizes the risk of losing prospects as they move from one platform to another. It also enables the supplier to establish a dialogue with prospects and build a direct relationship with them. Furthermore, it allows the supplier to measure prospects' response to the elements in the cultivation path for eventual improvement. Finally, and not least, if the company controls the site, it owns the customer data, which will be valuable for future use.

In heavily intermediated businesses, the supplier may not be able to control the cultivation path. In cases where the intermediary captures the prospect first, moves them down the intermediary's own cultivation path, and hands over the lead to the supplier only at the end of the process, the supplier can either contribute content and expertise to improve the intermediary's cultivation effort or risk being cut out entirely from the pathway. But generally, if the supplier doesn't contribute, competitors will. Despite its limitations, working with intermediaries to improve their online prospect cultivation should not be overlooked. It is an opportunity to spur growth for both parties and build stronger partnerships with intermediaries. Because improving cultivation pathways is beyond the interest or competency of most salespeople who call on intermediaries, they often fail to pursue this opportunity. Taking advantage of this partnership opportunity requires the foresight and attention of sales and marketing leaders.

Whether to transfer a cultivated prospect over to an intermediary to convert them and complete the sale, or to keep control of the entire process is often a tough decision. It's a strategic choice and one sometimes subject to negotiation. Intermediaries love suppliers that generate business for them and despise those they think are taking business away from them. But as digital continues to shift power away from intermediaries and toward the supplier and the end customer, more B2B suppliers are choosing either to cultivate the prospect first and then hand over to the intermediary, or to take the prospect all the way to a completed sale. Sometimes they do both; complicated purchases like negotiating a new contract are handed over to the intermediary, while simpler ones, such as ordering replacement parts, are completed by the supplier.

CONVERT TO ACTION

Conversion, the step that completes the sale (and converts the prospect's interest into a purchase), is well suited to optimization online because companies can test many variables: their calls to action, pricing and promotion of individual offers, the way in which benefits are described, and more. For B2B companies that complete many sales online or through an automated call center where customer conversion behaviors are observable and measurable, optimization is relatively easy. However, for many B2B companies, closing the sale remains a person-to-person effort, involving direct sales teams, intermediaries, or selling partnerships. Orders may be transmitted digitally, but the sale itself happens through people. The more complicated, long term, and valuable the contract, the more likely it is that conversion is person to person. When closing the sale involves considerable person-to-person interaction, accurate and consistent data collection is a challenge, and optimization can be slow and arduous.

Conversion in B2B is also a multistep process. It involves not only closing the initial contract but also onboarding the buyer and the users (who are often different people) and closing individual transactions within or in addition to the initial contract. Onboarding may entail installing equipment, integrating systems, training people and providing initial-stage support, and offering troubleshooting or technical support on an ongoing basis. Like closing, onboarding and ongoing support are typically multichannel experiences, combining on-site technical support and training with online tools and call-center assistance.

The digital trends we've been discussing have precipitated a shift in B2B to online conversion for straightforward and frequent purchases. For more complicated sales—highly customized, negotiated, or intermediated ones—the shift to full online buying is still early stage. AI, blockchain, and virtual reality technologies can assist buyers in making complicated procurement decisions. But these tools have not yet advanced to the point where they can replace salespeople and human intermediaries. Because companies must execute handoffs from digital to interpersonal conversion activities, B2B marketing and sales leaders face several challenges:

- **Harmonizing offers, incentives, and rewards across channels.** Digital's transparency and access to data and buying platforms has made offering a special price or incentive to a select customer or group of customers much more likely to cause channel conflict: rivalries between channels that expect the supplier to protect them from competitors that charge different prices or provide different terms and conditions for the same offering. Different margin requirements among channels can also create price disparities that, in a digital world, are far easier for customers or intermediaries to notice—and complain about. In a multichannel world, it is essential to use data and digital tools to identify and rein in sales teams that are giving out too many incentives just to close their sales. Companies must be sure to align their channel strategies for pricing, incentives, and rewards within and across regions.

▶ **Synchronizing what happens online with what happens in a personal interaction.** The prospect's front-end digital engagement related to challenges and solutions must be linked to their subsequent discussions with sales team members, call center reps, and intermediaries. To the target, this synchronization is absolutely crucial. Moreover, the onboarding and technical support teams must be in the data and contracting loop so they can deliver on the solutions that have been negotiated. The challenge in ensuring this alignment only keeps growing because, although digital content is relatively easy and quick to adapt and change, it takes more time for sales teams and intermediaries to learn about it and adapt to changes to the digital experience.

▶ **Integrating data capture and measurement.** Companies need to integrate their tracking of human conversion interactions with their broader measurement regime, which includes online data for targeting, capturing attention, and cultivating interest. Marketing technology (martech) platforms and tools such as Salesforce.com have fundamentally changed the playing field, taking measurement and tracking far beyond the sales transaction. In fact, it takes sophisticated marketing and sales leaders to work together to link all the measures to assemble an end-to-end view of the customer that drives learning and progress.

An omnichannel dashboard is a valuable tool for managing these three challenges. It can tie together the elements of the digital strategy (clarify the target, capture attention, cultivate interest, convert to action). And it allows growth leaders to spot gaps in harmonization, synchronization, or integration, as well as to track the progress of target prospects through the entire path to purchase for any given use case.

Acme Selling Shift Dashboard

Ann insisted on creating a dashboard to show critical measures for progress against each of the 4Cs (see figure 11). The dashboard can be double-clicked to view the information on a segment basis and with different date ranges. Flags highlight below-target or prior-period performance.

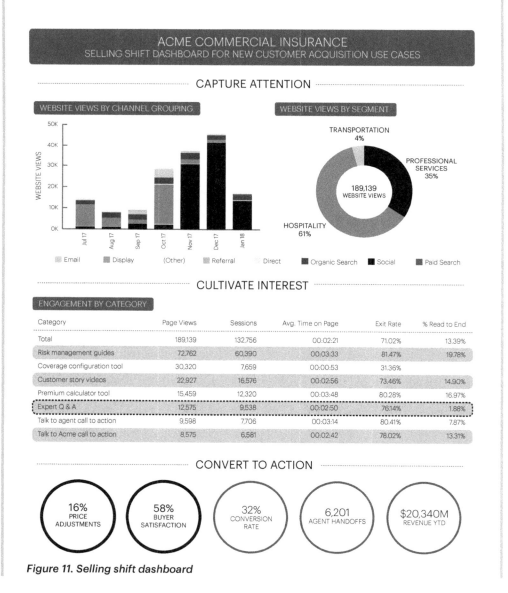

Figure 11. Selling shift dashboard

Acme's dashboard is superior to most digital dashboards because it integrates online and offline data gathered from multiple sources. "Buyer satisfaction" and "price adjustments" are particularly important. Here, these metrics are both outlined in black, indicating a lack of synchronization or harmonization between online and offline channels that is damaging customer perception and causing a higher-than-normal level of price adjustment.

No discussion of B2B conversion would be complete without addressing disintermediation. Even for companies that have already established a solid digital marketing presence, deciding with whom and how the final sale will be completed is crucial. The company must balance the advantages of forging a direct relationship with the buyer with the need for intermediary support in order to affordably access the market. Managing channel conflict is a critically important and often difficult task following the decision to disintermediate. Engendering the resistance of intermediaries is to be expected and can often be overcome. But it can also cause serious damage to the business, particularly if it is not managed well. Nationwide is an example of a company that is carefully managing channel conflict, preserving relationships with independent insurance agents while expanding direct sales channels. For small business customers, it offers the choice of direct e-commerce buying or buying through an insurance agent.[7] The company is transparent about its rationale for making this move and the parameters for serving small business customers. In this way, Nationwide has managed to expand its direct business but not at the expense of its agent relationship.

B2B companies can disintermediate part of their offerings in a variety of ways:

- ▶ **By purchase size:** Appropriate for small purchases or frequently requested items, such as replacement parts and consumables.

- ▶ **By customer size:** The supplier establishes direct buying relationships with small- and medium-sized customers and utilizes intermediaries to serve larger customers or those in unique or hard-to-serve niches.

- ▶ **By customer type:** The company handles price-oriented buyers seeking simple solutions.

- ▶ **By product line:** The company handles product lines most suitable for online buying (and least interesting to intermediaries).

Of course, the company can always choose to not disintermediate and continue handing off all digitally generated leads to agents, brokers, or distributors.

Leaders must recognize that the selling ground is shifting. In B2B, the race to control the customer relationship and gain access to their data is well underway, and few companies can afford to be left behind. Disintermediation doesn't merely change the cost/benefit calculus of a channel strategy; it can have long-term impact on the company's ability to gain access to its customer data and the benefits that access confers.

1.4

What to Do in the Digital Selling Shift

Put the Digital Selling Strategy into Action with Agile Sprints

O nce the 4Cs of the digital strategy have been determined for the top-priority use cases, it's time to take action. Unlike traditional strategies that may be too general to act on without additional planning, the 4Cs are specific enough to start right away. The 4Cs are therefore ideally suited to agile teaming approaches that can move a specific strategy rapidly to market while including customer feedback along the way. Action consists of the following steps: evaluating the agile sprint options, selecting the ones most appropriate for the challenge, planning, and executing.

INITIATE SCRUM AGILE SPRINTS

What's a sprint? Sprints are a superior mechanism for quickly and effectively bringing the digital selling strategy to life. They come from scrum agile methodology, an approach to working in teams first described in 1986 that later took hold in software development and has since spread to other applications and industries.[1] Agile is so-called because it emphasizes flexibility and resourcefulness in overcoming challenges and delivering the desired output within a budgeted amount of time. Often it involves evaluating progress every day and adjusting the work plan as required. Scrum agile is a way of organizing work through multifunctional, fairly autonomous teams of seven to ten people who use such tools as backlogs, daily stand-up meetings, and retrospectives to produce tangible deliverables. The work is organized in bursts of one to four weeks (on average, two weeks). Deploying scrum agile requires coaching scrum teams, developing a cadre of scrum captains to direct the work, and training senior leaders on how best to interact with scrum teams.

One of the most positive aspects of scrum agile is its simplicity: teams can be up and running in a matter of weeks. Organizations often see it taking hold fully across the enterprise in less than a year. It takes focus to use the methodology effectively, but the principles are not hard to master or apply, and team members enjoy the combination of structure and flexibility that it offers to spur rapid progress on complex work.

Incorporating customer feedback into sprints is another key element of scrum agile. Unlike traditional development, where market research is utilized at well-defined stage gates, scrum agile incorporates customer feedback within each step in an iterative fashion. Customer feedback can thus be incorporated quickly, which in turn allows companies to modify plans to accommodate customer needs. To make scrum agile methods effective, companies need to cultivate specific skills: designing rapid customer feedback mechanisms, learning to listen to customers, and producing customer-ready test stimuli.

Sprints based on using scrum agile methods are effective for a few reasons:

▶ They clarify objectives and outputs and provide flexibility for adjusting approaches day to day, based on continuous customer feedback and the team's ongoing progress.

▶ They create a sense of urgency and an orientation to action, inspiring team members to problem solve, work as a team, and deliver tangible outcomes at the end of each sprint.

- They promote leadership improvement because of the way scrum agile can shape leader and team interactions. When leaders understand their roles, they are empowered to contribute but also limited in their ability to interfere with or derail a project.

Scrum agile sprints are vital for any B2B digital transformation. There are a number of different types of agile sprints, and it's important to choose the right one for the job.

CHOOSE A SPRINT TYPE

The sprints required to make the digital selling shift in B2B fall within three broad types: pilot sprints, scaling sprints, and foundational sprints. Which one you choose depends on your digital strategy, use case, and organization readiness.

Pilot sprints are used to deploy a new element in the 4Cs and advance a top-priority use case. The focus of pilot sprints is delivering an in-market result that shows what's possible based on customer behavior, such as making a purchase, requesting an appointment, entering a specification, or requesting a quote. Pilot sprints help overcome the barriers to scaling a strategy across the organization and demonstrate whether the strategy is worth the investment. A key principle of pilot sprints is rapid iteration, based on putting stimuli in front of customers. Because a pilot represents new (and therefore uncertain) work, the faster you complete each iteration, the more progress you can achieve toward the ultimate goal. It's important to use existing capabilities and resources or to use those of agency partners and avoid major investment in platforms or systems before even validating the strategy. This means teams must have an agile mindset and commit to ensuring that the best does not become the enemy of the good.

Acme Pilot Sprint

Acme CCO Ann and her team leaders Chan and Sergio chose as their top-priority use case digital demand generation for acquiring new small business customers. But their only experience in generating new customer leads was through trade advertising and promotions that encouraged customers to talk to their insurance agent and request Acme products. A pilot sprint was clearly in order. Lindy, Acme's CEO, needed proof to show the board that uncovering leads directly using digital tools would be an effective way to build the business. Lindy asked Ann to avoid a large capital investment or headcount increase until the digital lead generation approach could be proven. Sergio and Chan therefore enlisted a digital marketing agency to provide the operational backbone for managing and integrating the customer database and deploying a digital marketing automation platform. They paired the agency with a cross-functional team of Acme digital marketers, communication specialists, and IT professionals.

Scaling sprints are used to scale up and expand an element of the 4C strategy that has already been validated via pilot, or that is already in use in a region or line of business. One main goal of scaling sprints is configuring digital platforms, tools, and data sets for repeated application. Another is developing employees' skills in using the platforms, tools, and data sets in similar situations. Often, scaling sprints assign a team to standardize and optimize the work of previous pilots and write an implementation playbook. Working in parallel, multiple teams then apply and adapt the playbook for different applications, regions, and targets.

Acme Scaling Sprint

Among Ann's, Sergio's, and Chan's top-priority quick wins was building relationships with agents to improve price realization at renewal. The company's Belgium team had already piloted a new renewal process that combined an improved email communication for end customers with a series of sales visits and seminars to reassure and engage agents. The program was a big success and helped Acme achieve an average 10 percent premium increase for previously underpriced customers.

Ann realized that Acme needed to conduct scaling sprints to expand the program globally and adapt it to comply with the different customer engagement regulations in different countries. With the aid of a project management expert, the Belgium team dedicated several weeks to mapping their approach to create a playbook for the company's scaling teams. Ann then commissioned scaling sprints in Hong Kong, the US, and Germany to refine and standardize the approach before rolling it out the next quarter to the entire organization.

Foundational sprints introduce a new technology, platform, or data source by putting in place the people, processes, and technologies needed to deploy them. They are typically initiated when the company identifies an important capability gap through the readiness assessment that can be neither worked around nor filled effectively by agencies. For example, adding or changing elements of what's often called the "customer engagement stack"—the set of platforms and databases that support digital selling (such as a CRM system)—calls for a series of foundational sprints to put in place the interfaces and processes that enable employees in the organization to use the platforms and databases. Like pilot sprints, foundational sprints typically need scaling sprints before the new technology can be used widely in an organization.

Acme Foundational Sprint

Acme's first demand generation pilot was so successful at generating new leads that Lindy, the CEO, won the board's approval to move ahead with investment. However, the pilot uncovered a major gap: the lack of a marketing automation platform. During the pilot, an agency partner covered for Acme, but in rolling out the program globally, it would be inefficient and ineffective to continue relying on this partner. Ann asked Sergio and Chan to charter a series of foundational sprints to select, acquire, and test drive a new marketing automation platform. They enlisted the leaders of the original pilot team to undertake the sprint, adding IT resources to support the effort. They completed the series of foundational sprints by setting up a new automation platform and using it, instead of the agency partner, to conduct a set of activities similar to those conducted in the initial pilot sprint. Once everything was up and running, the Acme team saw a 30 percent improvement in the use of Acme team resources and a two-thirds reduction in agency costs. Following the foundational sprint, the team carried out a set of scaling sprints to roll out digital lead generation globally.

The job of an agile sprint team is to creatively and flexibly surmount the challenges of bringing an element of the 4Cs to market. Those challenges run the gamut. A pilot team may never have launched a digital lead generation campaign. A scaling team might have to apply the results of a pilot to a different customer segment or apply a pilot approach to a different business unit with different data and technology platforms. A foundational sprint team might need to close a technology gap, such as the lack of natural language processing capability, when the organization is trying to put in place intelligent chat bots.

A common challenge is automating digital initiatives to reach more customers more effectively. In a pilot sprint, this may be a matter of learning to use untapped features in martech automation platforms that the company already owns. In a scaling sprint, this might entail using new data or integrating some new technologies. In a foundational sprint, this may mean installing a new martech automation platform.

PLAN THE SPRINTS

There is no single right way to plan for any given kind of sprint. The sprint plan depends on the use case, capability readiness, the complexity of the task, and its novelty. Sprint plans tend to follow two waves: the first, a set of sprints for designing, creating, and launching, and the second, sprints for optimizing traffic, navigation, and content.

- ▶ **Design.** The team roughly outlines a solution, identifies the unknowns, and sets up metrics and a test-and-learn plan to fill knowledge gaps. The rough outline is often a storyboard that describes how the customer will be engaged and how they will interact with the supplier along a path to a desired outcome, such as making an appointment or requesting a quote.

- ▶ **Create.** The team builds the solution prototype. Depending on the nature of the challenge, the team may build each module or part of a solution in a step-by-step sequence, or a number of teams might work in parallel on the different modules, finishing up with integrating sprints that put the modules together. The initial prototype is often a simulation of how technology and data will be used to bring the design to life. At each iteration in the sprint plan, the prototype becomes more lifelike until it is fully operational.

▶ **Launch.** The team puts the solution on the market, sometimes in alpha form (for employees to test), other times in beta form (for early adopters), and still other times, in final form. Launching a new solution such as a new app entails making the solution work and enticing customers to become interested in it, learn about it, and try it.

▶ **Optimize traffic.** The team tests and learns its way to improving capture by optimizing targeting, search terms, media choices, and advertising headlines. Sometimes a shift in any one of these variables can yield significant improvement in audience capture.

▶ **Optimize navigation.** The team uses navigation metrics to optimize navigation for customers in the cultivation and conversion paths. The purpose is to eliminate bottlenecks that were created inadvertently and help customers obtain the information they want in the form they want it, as easily as possible.

▶ **Optimize content.** The team tests content alternatives in the customers' cultivation path and calls to action (and offers) in the conversion path. Big improvements can often be gained by substituting video for text or one call to action (such as "sign up for a free trial") for another (such as "request a meeting with an expert").

Acme Sprint Plan

Sergio and Chan launched their sprint program by first writing a charter for the scrum team. They enlisted the help of a scrum agile coach and recruited scrum team members and a captain. Then they held a "destination session" to define success and help senior leaders understand what to do to enable it. The scrum team captain felt that the customer insights the company had gathered were not robust enough, so she asked each team member to conduct three brief interviews with target prospects to ground the team in their perspectives.

Acme's pilot sprint plan laid out the six sprints that would take them from design to launch to ongoing refinement and improvement (see figure 12).

The first, the design sprint, involved mapping out the key aspects of the lead generation approach, including how Acme would use owned, earned, and paid media. In this sprint, the team crafted a test-and-learn plan to obtain target prospects' input on pivotal choices. They also followed best practice and defined the metrics dashboard for the outcome, which would help the team and leaders alike understand what the sprint must accomplish in concrete terms.

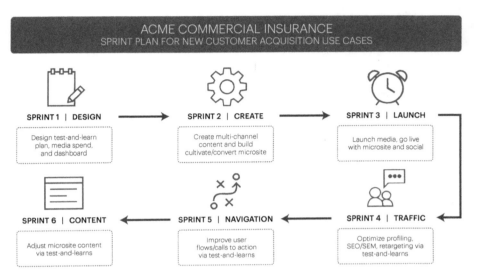

ACME COMMERCIAL INSURANCE
SPRINT PLAN FOR NEW CUSTOMER ACQUISITION USE CASES

SPRINT 1 | DESIGN → SPRINT 2 | CREATE → SPRINT 3 | LAUNCH

Design test-and-learn plan, media spend, and dashboard

Create multi-channel content and build cultivate/convert microsite

Launch media, go live with microsite and social

SPRINT 6 | CONTENT ← SPRINT 5 | NAVIGATION ← SPRINT 4 | TRAFFIC

Adjust microsite content via test-and-learns

Improve user flows/calls to action via test-and-learns

Optimize profiling, SEO/SEM, retargeting via test-and-learns

Figure 12. Selling shift sprint plan

In sprint 2 (create), the team built out content and designed a needs-matching tool. In sprint 3 (launch), the team carried out beta testing, trained the sales team about its role in the new lead generation approach, and launched communications to prospects. The team then put the lead gen engine on the market. Any sprint plan must delineate what to do after launch. The scrum captain, in consultation with Sergio and Chan, decided to focus first on improving traffic (sprint 4) and then on optimizing navigation, usability, and content (sprints 5 and 6). The team addressed traffic first because they needed enough respondents to optimize navigation and content. Content came last because, although it probably promotes cultivation and conversion more than any other element, optimizing it requires the most resources. The team wanted to make sure that navigation and usability were not impeding prospects' journey in any way before they undertook it. Before the sprints were completed, the Acme pilot team codified their results in a business case for future expansion, along with recommendations for scaling sprints that would provide meaningful follow-up.

In practice, the individual sprints described in the Acme example can be condensed, expanded, supplemented, or disregarded, as needed. Sometimes the pilot doesn't involve changing content, so that step is unnecessary. Often, the optimizing sprints aimed at improving traffic, navigation, or content take multiple iterations to achieve objectives. What's most important is to work in an agile way, put testable prototypes before your target, and learn and adapt.

Many companies neglect developing a business case and recommendations following a pilot that shows promise. In these cases, the scaling phase never gets fully funded because the pilot's impact isn't articulated in a way senior leaders can appreciate. Reporting that "we doubled the click-through rate and lowered cost to acquire new customers by 30 percent" doesn't quite resonate with senior leaders. What *does* resonate is expressing the impact in hard numbers: "Based on what we've learned, an investment of $150,000 per month in this new method can generate savings of $2.5 million per year and increase revenues at full margin by $3.7 million per year."

EXECUTE THE SPRINTS

Effective sprint execution is built on four main building blocks. The content of the building blocks may vary slightly depending on the type of sprint, but the blocks themselves cannot be omitted:

▶ **Team goals and organizing processes.** These are essential to every sprint. The team must establish goals at the beginning, track progress via daily stand-up meetings, and codify the processes it uses so that others can repeat and scale the effort. Leadership support is critical for success: it helps the team align goals with the overall strategy and ensures resources are sufficient to keep the team on track.

- ▶ **Customer feedback.** The team must obtain customer data, determine the appropriate digital action, trigger the action, and monitor the customer response. This involves actually testing stimuli by sending an email, making a banner ad appear, or triggering a response to a customer request. Customers' responses can be obtained in a number of ways, including through formal research or simple "smoke tests," where the idea is vetted in informal social channels or ad hoc polls. The key to success is having in hand a toolbox of rapid and easy research methods. When obtaining customer feedback is hassle free, teams can stay disciplined and make sure the voice of the customer is incorporated into their work throughout the sprint.

- ▶ **Content and channels.** To be pragmatic, sprints must stick to the content to be delivered to the customer and the vehicles for delivering that content. Content delivery has multiple dimensions, including developing a plan and requirements, building engines to create or assemble content, devising mechanisms to serve up the right content at key moments in the customer's path to purchase, and refreshing and updating content. Channels are either owned (such as corporate websites), earned (such as social sites where content must compete for users' attention and engagement), or paid (such as banner ads). The key to success in this building block is matching content to channel and moment in the path to purchase. When content and channel work together, the impact on the customer can be highly motivating. A good example is a video that guides a prospect through the benefits of a new solution, appearing in a channel that the prospect likes to use when sorting through what to buy.

- ▶ **Platforms and tools.** This building block is about delivering the solution: using automation tools, configuring web and mobile platforms, and setting up databases. This is often called the back end of a digital selling or digital marketing campaign. Increasingly, customer engagement automation platforms such as Salesforce.com are making the task of organizing the back end easier. Here, the key to success is to tightly link the front end (content, channels, and customer feedback) to the back end to define how the technology will be used and the data that will be required. The front end must drive requirements for the back end and not the other way around.

Acme Sprint Building Blocks

The Acme scrum team built a backlog of tasks based on goals that were determined at the first daily stand-up of each sprint. They conducted regular retrospectives, or debriefings, to assess progress, keep sprints on track, and realign the work whenever needed. They established clear goals and determined processes up front. Then, they organized their backlog into three main sets of tasks: Audience and Best-Move Strategy, Content and Channels, and Platforms and Tools (see figure 13).

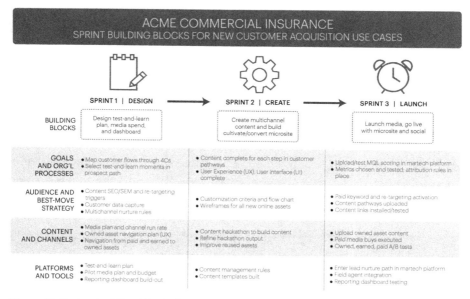

Figure 13. Sprint building blocks for selling shift sprint plan

Throughout each sprint, the team constantly asked, "What have we missed?" to avoid overlooking a major component at launch. They also routinely asked, "Is this really needed for Day One?"—an important question many companies overlook. There are many tools, platforms, pieces of content, and forms of customization that will be important over time but that are not essential for Day One. The third question they asked themselves almost daily was "Is there a piece of code, any content, any platform, any person, or any agency partner that can help us move faster?" Agility depends on reusing or tapping existing assets and ensuring the team is not trying to do everything on its own.

COMMIT TO CONTINUOUS CUSTOMER-DRIVEN IMPROVEMENT

Consistently incorporating customer insight and feedback into a program of continuous improvement is essential to making sure that the outcomes of the sprints remain relevant and become even more effective over time. It entails tracking customers' feelings, behaviors, and outcomes at each step in their path to a decision, determining those that matter most, and improving the company's performance in the 4Cs. Continuous improvement relies on a repeatable loop of *planning-executing-measuring-analyzing-executing differently*. This loop will enhance outcomes for individual customers who have not been well served, as well as optimize digital selling for each customer segment in each use case.

Acme Continuous Improvement

After the first pilots were completed, Ann, Acme's CCO, put in place a continuous improvement loop, along with governance, to ensure the recommendations were enacted (see figure 14).

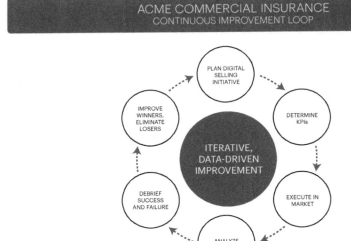

Figure 14. Continuous improvement loop

Ann insisted that the leader for each digital selling initiative, such as launching a new insurance offering or attracting new customers to an existing offering, codify their plan and KPIs in a one-page charter. The digital selling team was responsible for executing within the plan, and the analytics team, for evaluating customer impact. Ann set up a quarterly meeting of senior sales leaders to debrief them on success and failure. At the meeting, the initiative leader summarized the plan and KPIs and the analytics team leader assessed impact. Next, the regional sales leaders did their debriefings, recommending areas for improvement and activities that should be discontinued. This quarterly forum is crucial because it ensures that sales leaders "own" responsibility for improvement and that their views about what is working and what's not working are incorporated into the analysis. Charters for subsequent selling initiatives must reflect the decisions leaders made at this meeting.

Continuous improvement is a proven idea. The plan-execute-measure-analyze-do differently continuous improvement loop concept harkens back to the continuous quality improvement thinking of the 1980s and the origins of scrum agile.[2] It was instrumental in Toyota Motors' rise and its strategic differentiation based on exceptionally consistent quality (through the Toyota Way, the principles and philosophy of continuous improvement) and in Ford's comeback a decade later.[3] The digital era has taken continuous improvement from its roots as a manufacturing quality process and combined it with the use of rapid customer feedback to create a powerful way to optimize marketing and sales efforts.

The pilot, scale, and foundational sprints that are at the heart of determining what to do make up a continuous process; the learnings they generate support the next set of sprints and inform changes in the strategy (how to win) and in the opportunities identified (where to play). As momentum builds and results accrue, leaders can marshal resources to move on to other top-priority use cases and examine ways to further accelerate progress.

1.5

Who Is Needed for the Digital Selling Shift

Enabling the Transformation to Digital Selling

M ost B2B companies begin the Digital Selling Shift with a team of marketers, a sales force, customer support personnel, and an array of functions and capabilities to drive revenue and engage with customers. They often lack a customer data team that can collect and analyze the data needed to advance the work of the sprint teams and support the analysis required for continuous improvement.

ASSEMBLE THE CUSTOMER DATA TEAM

Assembling a customer data team with a robust mix of talents is crucial for undertaking the test-and-learn routines central to the digital selling shift. The team gathers the data and conducts the analysis to build the use cases that will determine where to play. It builds the customer profiles, uncovers the predictors of future customer behaviors, and determines customized next best moves in planning how to win. The customer data team are essential members of the scrum team at every step in addressing what to do.

Yet in most B2B organizations that are in the early stages of the digital selling shift, the customer data team usually suffers from the biggest talent gap. Initially, data team roles can be filled by consultants or performance marketing firms. But data skills (especially those related to unearthing customer insights) are rare and expensive to commission from outside vendors on an ongoing basis. Once the selling shift gains momentum, there is so much work for the data team to do that building a mix of in-house capability and external support is almost always a necessity.

There are six basic roles on a customer data team:

▶ The *data strategist*, who contributes client and domain expertise to help determine what kinds of data and analysis the company should invest in.

▶ The *data architect*, who understands all forms of data that affect the customer journey. This person leads the effort to optimize customer and prospect profiles.

▶ The *test-and-learn lead*, who establishes the testing approaches for audience targeting and for campaign, content, channel, and vehicle evaluation.

▶ The *data engineer*, who oversees data gathering, cleansing, movement, and storage.

▶ The *data scientist*, who heads statistical analysis and the modeling of structured and unstructured data. This person is skilled in using R, Python, and machine learning.

▶ The *data visualization engineer*, who uses visualization tools (such as Qlik, Spotfire, and Tableau) to depict the results of analysis as well as customer and campaign insights in ways that leaders and team members can easily understand (see figure 15).

In a data team the same individual, with the right skills, can serve more than one role. Certain supporting roles, such as analyst, programmer, and project manager, can work under the direction of the customer data team members.

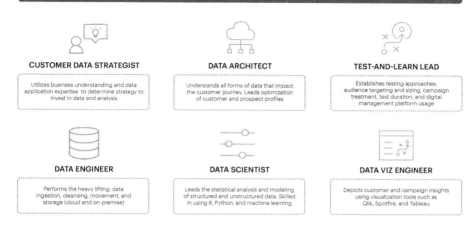

CUSTOMER DATA STRATEGIST

Utilizes business understanding and data application expertise to determine strategy to invest in data and analysis

DATA ARCHITECT

Understands all forms of data that impact the customer journey. Leads optimization of customer and prospect profiles

TEST-AND-LEARN LEAD

Establishes testing approaches: audience targeting and sizing, campaign treatment, test duration, and digital management platform usage

DATA ENGINEER

Performs the heavy lifting: data ingestion, cleansing, movement, and storage (cloud and on-premise)

DATA SCIENTIST

Leads the statistical analysis and modeling of structured and unstructured data. Skilled in using R, Python, and machine learning

DATA VIZ ENGINEER

Depicts customer and campaign insights using visualization tools such as Qlik, Spotfire, and Tableau

Figure 15. Key roles in customer data team

Acme Customer Data Team

To assemble Acme's customer data team, Ann began by hiring as its leader Nicolle, who had experience building teams skilled in customer data strategy and data architecture. Nicolle cleverly combined Acme internal talent and agency support with new hires. She sourced a test-and-learn lead from Acme's existing customer insights function, used Acme's digital marketing agency to supply the data-visualization capabilities, and turned to Acme's IT team to find data-engineering support from the consultant that helps manage Acme's marketing and selling platforms. After an intensive search, Nicolle hired a data scientist and assigned a team of analysts to work with him. Over the next year and a half, Nicolle hired a data architect, a data engineer, and several planners and programmers to support them. She continued to play the role of customer data strategist as well as team director.

PUT THE CUSTOMER DATA TEAM TO WORK

Integrating customer data team members into the work of the digital selling shift comes with its own challenges. The most important of these is assigning team members to value-adding projects related to pursuing priority use cases. Often at the beginning, team members are preoccupied with so much data cleanup and maintenance that they don't get enough time to pursue projects that demonstrate their value to the organization. Leaders who made the hiring decisions are left frustrated by the lack of return on investment, while hearing only that the team is remarkably busy.

That's where the role of sponsor or coach can help. Assigning to this role a senior leader who is savvy about the ways work actually gets done in the organization is a great way to integrate the customer data team. The sponsor can help the customer data team focus on supporting the leaders and initiatives that matter most to the company's growth strategy, while fending off time-consuming requests that add little value. They can take the heat for saying no so that the customer data team doesn't inadvertently make enemies.

ENABLE CUSTOMER DATA TEAM INTERACTIONS

Another priority is enabling the data team members to overcome cultural and communication barriers with incumbent leaders and employees so they can work together effectively. Data team professionals tend to be highly analytical technical specialists whose language and examples are new to the organization. Moreover, they often lack the communication skills to help incumbents understand what they do, how to work with them effectively, or even when to ask for their assistance.

To bridge this cultural gap, companies must help existing employees learn the fundamentals of data and analytics, as well as how to use data in their own work. Senior leaders should also proactively assign data team professionals to important, high-profile projects and sprints, where they can make a difference quickly, thus demonstrating their value to the organization. Assigning data team professionals to scrum teams is a great place to start because the work is project based and data team members' role is usually clear.

Integrating data team members in the activities related to where to play and how to win can be more difficult, because those tasks are more unpredictable. Roles may shift unpredictably, and incumbent leaders who are new to digital sales and marketing may put more stock in communication than analytical skills because it aids their own understanding. Here, the customer data strategist can be a key player in the discussions as well as a key connecting link to others on the team.

BUILD OUT THE TEAM

Many companies make the mistake of hiring an initial wave of customer data professionals, only to take too long providing them with the backup they need, such as allowing them to hire additional staff or giving them adequate funding to use contractors or agency partners. As momentum lags and the excitement of the new job fades, data professionals often begin to question whether joining the company was the right move. Customer data professionals are in such high demand that changing jobs presents little risk for them.

One way to avoid this situation is to establish up front a talent plan, with hiring and funding triggered by achievable KPIs to grow the customer data team. Make sure senior management fully fund all the resources for the first wave of employee hiring and for contractors. This will ensure that there are no hiring delays and that temporary workers can start right away and accelerate the pace of progress. Contractors can cushion the surges in demand that are hard to anticipate in the initial start-up period. Contractors can also serve as proof of the company's commitment to supporting the data professionals as they begin their work.

1.6

Key Digital Selling Shift Takeaways

A Digital Selling Shift can do double duty: it can accelerate profitable revenue growth for existing products, services, and solutions, and it can also boost the launch of new products, services, and solutions faster and more effectively than most other avenues of investment available to companies. The Digital Selling Shift has the added advantage of delivering significant cost savings and efficiencies that can justify investment. It also achieves measurable impact relatively rapidly.

The digital selling shift requires building digital marketing, sales, and data capabilities. Sales practices must change, and intermediary relationships and channel strategies will evolve. However, this shift does not generally disrupt the enterprise's operating or business model or require a fundamental change in business strategy. Dealing with channel conflict and avoiding alienating key intermediaries are the most significant challenges companies face when making a digital selling shift.

Successful digital selling shifts in B2B rely on these key principles:

► *Choose where to play* by identifying the key use cases most relevant to your business, based on two issues: attracting new customers (or generating more sales from existing customers) and understanding the barriers customers face in achieving their goals. Prioritize use cases based on their attractiveness and your company's readiness.

▶ *Determine how to win* by building a compelling digital strategy based on the 4Cs: clarifying the target, capturing the target's attention, cultivating their interest, and converting them to buy, buy more, or recommend you to others.

▶ *Accelerate what to do* by using scrum agile methods to conduct a series of sprints to pilot new digital selling approaches, scale previously piloted approaches, or build capabilities required for digital selling.

▶ *Ensure you have who is needed* by putting in place a system to undertake continuous customer-driven improvement and by setting up and promptly enabling a customer data team with the resources they need.

Once the digital selling shift is underway, B2B companies that have generated results are often ready and willing to seek a more fundamental digital transformation to accelerate growth, such as the digital experience makeover or the digital proposition pivot. The digital selling shift is generally the best place to start because it is where the organization builds its data and digital capability muscles. It generates ROI quickly (usually within a year) and does not turn the organization upside down. In reality, there is no right place to start. Companies facing disruptive change often don't get to choose—they need to transform in the area where disruption looms.

Part 2

TRANSFORMATION 2:
THE DIGITAL EXPERIENCE MAKEOVER

Leverage digital technologies to innovate and enrich customer experiences

- ▶ The Digital Experience Makeover challenge

- ▶ Where to Play: experience mapping

- ▶ How to Win: a customer experience strategy

- ▶ What to Do: prototypes and pilots

- ▶ Who Is Needed: the DERPA model

- ▶ Key Digital Experience Makeover takeaways

2.1

The Digital Experience Makeover Challenge

B2B companies that are leveraging digital trends and technologies to build customer relationships are winning in two powerful ways: they are generating competitive advantage, and they are fostering long-term customer loyalty.[1] Take Schneider Electric: by using mobile technologies to enable electrical contractors to specify their requirements from the field, the company has made contractors' work easier, less time consuming, and more reliable. In the process, Schneider has forged a deeper customer relationship. Similarly, by equipping their elevator repair technicians with digital diagnostic tools and troubleshooting software, Thyssenkrupp has cut elevator downtime by more than half—an accomplishment that few competitors can match and that keeps customers happy long after the repair.

But succeeding in digital requires more than throwing money at the latest technologies. Many B2B companies are misdirecting much of their investment in digital experiences. Instead of harnessing the potential that digital technologies offer to reinvent the experience for the customer's benefit, B2B companies waste money transposing mediocre analog interactions into equally lame digital experiences. Launching a chatbot that does nothing more than replace a call center interaction may save a few dollars per call, but it does little for the customer. Posting product manuals online may reduce printing costs but doesn't yield much of a payoff, given how infrequently they are referenced. Worse, it chews up systems and content-creation and content-management resources that could be better deployed elsewhere.[2]

So, what's holding B2B companies back? What's preventing them from investing in digital experiences that could make a real difference to customers? Mindset, primarily. Too many B2B companies and their intermediaries believe the purpose of digital experiences is to insert themselves into customers' lives, rather than offer customers a better way.

In addition, many B2B companies conceive of customer experiences narrowly, thinking in terms of discrete silos, like customer service or claims processing. They do so because they already have teams and systems devoted to these areas. But this function-by-function approach, rooted in the organizational structure, impedes leaders from seeing what's missing from the customers' viewpoint. It does not reveal gaps, such as needs-matching, onboarding, and pre-renewal engagement, that don't have an organization owner—gaps that, if filled, could make a tangible difference to customers.

Finally, B2B leaders often turn experience investment into sales conversion programs. They focus on immediate transactional outcomes, instead of considering a broader set of experiences that could promote customer loyalty and value and brand recommendation. Their narrow sales orientation may generate immediate revenue improvement but can come at the expense of long-term customer value.

Shifting the B2B supplier's viewpoint from push to pull, from tell to listen, and from sell to help is a key starting point for effective digital experience design.

Companies that appreciate the importance of end-to-end customer experiences promote adoption and loyalty.[3] They see digital experiences as an important field for innovation and a driver of competitive advantage. They use experiences to address customer frustration and dissatisfaction. They succeed because they listen to customers. They also watch and emulate improvements that companies outside their category are making and the benefits they are deriving from those improvements. They work hard to allay employees' fears about the changes digital experience may bring about, knowing that their success depends on a workforce that is on board, properly trained and skilled, and invested in the outcomes.

How can companies overcome the narrow mindset we've just described and garner coveted customer adoption and loyalty? In three ways:

- ▶ By *mapping the customer journeys* so that they surface the customer insights needed to unleash new ideas and determine where to play.

- ▶ By *developing customer-driven experience* strategies to supplant internal, silo-driven experiences with cross-functional initiatives designed to delight customers.

- ▶ By *pursuing inspired experience design* that excites employees about the possibilities for tapping outside-the-category ideas to create tangible experiences.

CASE STUDY:
MAERSK

A.P. Møller - Maersk is the largest container shipping company in the world, moving everything from blueberries and bricks to cars and clothes from one side of the globe to another. It is also a notable example of a B2B company that applied journey mapping, customer-driven strategy, and inspired design to deliver outstanding new customer experiences.[4]

In 2016, A.P. Møller - Maersk announced a new strategy. Building on its strong position in container shipping, port logistics, and container-based land-side logistics, the company embarked on a multidimensional transformation from being a conglomerate with a diversified business to a focused, integrated container logistics company that delivers digital end-to-end solutions to customers. Improving the customer experience was one of the key pillars of the company's strategy, along with cost leadership and competitive pricing. While cost leadership and competitive pricing were well established at Maersk and important in the industry, customer experience was not. The industry had no history of customer centricity. The company had always relied on scale, affordability, and reliability to compete. But in recent years, shipping has become more commoditized. Several rivals had acquired sufficient scale to deliver a good enough product, and heightened global competition made customers less willing to pay a premium for slightly better service unless they could see a tangible benefit. To maintain its leadership position, Maersk would have to shift from its operational focus to a customer-centric, experience-driven orientation so that it could identify and deliver the tangible benefits customers valued.

Søren Skou, A.P. Møller - Maersk's CEO, and Vincent Clerc, CEO of Ocean and Logistics, started with a customer-centric definition of the transformation they were seeking. "We wanted to transform our business to fit around our customers' needs instead of our assets by delivering a more personalized experience," says Clerc. To achieve this vision, Maersk needed to learn more about its customers and their behaviors and goals— and it needed to capitalize on its customer data. That meant becoming a fully digital business.

"Customer interactions are a goldmine of information," says Peter Hartz, senior director of Customer Experience and Service. "The more we digitalize the customer journey, the more data we can capture and analyze." To provide a foundation for customer data analysis and experience design, Maersk conducted one-on-one interviews with customers and prospects throughout the world. Maersk deconstructed the customer journey and identified the most important pain points customers were facing. Based on customers' different needs, the company mapped journeys for seven segments, including newcomers as well as frequent customers who thought they knew everything there was to know about the company. This segment-based view of the customer journey generated a set of insights that could be acted on right away to provide immediate customer benefits—and generate quick wins.

The notion of an end-to-end view of the customer was new to Maersk. It confirmed pain points that leaders had already suspected, but it also brought to light gaps in the experience that Maersk had been unaware of, including the most urgent problems that Maersk needed to address. The end-to-end view also revealed experiences that Maersk (or its competitors) provided that delighted customers. Maersk knew it needed to provide these "delighters" more often and to more customers, given their importance.

The end-to-end mapping exercise also helped Maersk identify opportunities to further improve what they were getting right. Leaders emphasized creating solutions that could become points of competitive advantage. But they recognized how important the interviews and mapping exercise were for instilling an outside-in view and building listening capabilities among all employees to ensure Maersk could maintain a customer-centric mindset and continue to improve experiences. All of this took hard work and focus.

Mapping pain points showed Maersk what needed fixing, but it didn't show how to delight the customer. For that, the Maersk team developed a future-oriented experience map that defined the outcomes customers sought. The forward-looking map included a blueprint of the key customer interactions for each step in the journey (for example, Find and Select, or Book). Each step noted current pain points, the desired outcome, the needs to address in the future, success measures and KPIs, value proposition differentiators, and the policy decisions needed to move forward.

Maersk was diligent about understanding what different customer segments wanted at each step in the journey. For example, in the Selection step, Segment A (newcomers) wanted to understand the range of options available and how to compare their costs and delivery implications. Segment B (frequent customers) wanted to know whether they could save money or improve delivery time by bundling shipments together, or if different routing configurations would shield them further from the risk of weather delays. Maersk project managers developed a specification chart that displayed the requirements of each segment, by journey step. This would ensure that the experience designer teams received comprehensive and sufficiently detailed customer requirements.

By rigorously analyzing customer insights and codifying segment requirements, Maersk was able to focus on quick wins; among them, addressing booking and payment issues and improving customer communications and shipping status tracking. Maersk has launched an online tool to facilitate paperless trade and a shipping information viewer that makes shipping status more transparent.

These quick wins were only the beginning. A digital experience transformation is now well underway at Maersk. A couple of years into its new strategy, Maersk started unlocking value for customers by improving terminal utilization and inland services, hub operations, joint production planning, and cross-purchases across Maersk's brands. Not long ago, an instant access and response system seemed an impossibility in container logistics. But since November 2018, thousands of Maersk customers have been able to go to maersk.com to view real-time information on the availability of routes, equipment, and resources; submit a request for shipment; and then receive instant confirmation that their cargo has been booked. Maersk.com is now one of the biggest B2B e-commerce sites in the world. Today, with the introduction of Self-Service Instant Bookings, Maersk customers can receive a booking confirmation within seconds, instead of having to wait for up to two hours, a delay that remains the industry norm. Eliminating delay is a top priority for Maersk: delays trigger customer uncertainty and extra work to manage supply chains. They also push customers to consider other shippers.

While the Self-Service Instant Booking option applies primarily to Maersk's contractual customers, the company recently introduced a new digital product called Maersk Spot, which is designed for all customers doing spot bookings. Already, more than five thousand bookings on average are being booked via Maersk Spot every day. Fully digitally enabled, the product gives customers a cargo-loading guarantee at a fixed price up front—a first in the industry. "It is not uncommon to see overbookings to the tune of 30 percent, and often this leads to rolling of the customers' cargoes since there is overbooking to compensate for the high downfall. This creates a lot of uncertainty for our customers," says Silvia Ding, global head of Ocean Products at Maersk. "With Maersk Spot, we provide full visibility of the price and terms that will ensure cargoes get on board, ultimately allowing customers to move their cargo in a much simpler and more reliable way."

Maersk took a major step to simplify its customers' supply chains by using digital tools and data to address fundamental inefficiencies and simplify the buying experience. The booking and purchase process can take up to thirteen steps offline, often involving a good deal of back-and-forth communication between shipper and shipping company and considerable paperwork. The company's Spot system has streamlined the process to five simple, integrated steps—all online.

Maersk's digital experience transformation has resulted in TradeLens, the open digital platform jointly developed with IBM, and which CMA,

MSC, Hapag-Lloyd, and Ocean Express joined in 2019. TradeLens gives supply chain parties easy access to data and the ability to share it. It also provides a platform on which participants can develop digital solutions for themselves and their customers; in effect, it's a network of logistics networks. The first two applications that Maersk has launched on the platform are a tool facilitating paperless trade and a viewer to improve visibility of the shipping information pipeline.

Maersk's rationale for building the open digital platform is that global trade is interconnected and requires Maersk, its customers, its customers' customers, and other supply-chain participants to work together to solve their challenges. Throughout the ecosystem of trade logistics—from the customer to the shipping lines, port operators, freight forwarders, and authorities—any measures that eliminate paper-based, error-prone processes speed the free flow of goods. Although still in its formative stage, TradeLens demonstrates the potential of partnering with competitors and contractors to offer new applications based on shared data and technologies.

Maersk's paperless trade tool digitizes trade documentation using blockchain technology to securely submit, stamp, and approve documents for clearance and cargo movement. Blockchain cuts overall costs and speeds shipments by reducing fraud, errors, delays, and documentation costs, all of which currently represent 15 percent of cargo value. In addition, blockchain allows Maersk and its shipping partners full visibility of shipping records, while preventing any participants in the shipping process from altering records without consent.

The company's shipping information viewer makes shipment events transparent all along the supply chain. A remote container management (RCM) system enables customers to monitor the condition of their cargo in transit. For example, it tracks more than three hundred thousand refrigerated containers, sending their temperature and location data to the cloud. RCM thus reduces spoilage of perishables such as fresh produce, which can tolerate only narrow variations in temperature and humidity.

The economic value of Maersk's RCM is significant, particularly in light of the fact that suboptimal shipping conditions account for almost half of all US fresh-produce losses. Now, when the temperature in a container of one hundred thousand bananas exceeds normal range, Maersk can quickly intervene to prevent the bananas from becoming moldy. The ability to monitor actual container conditions has also allowed Maersk to reduce the cost of and time involved in container inspection upon arrival; in fact, it has cut manual container inspection by 60 percent because the data verifies that the goods have remained in good condition throughout the shipping process. In addition, analyzing the RCM data is also proving valuable to the company. Maersk can now predict how variations in sea conditions will affect shipping conditions. This analysis informs container design, the planning of shipping routes, and cargo handling and processing. By leveraging the Internet of Things (IoT), Maersk is empowering customers to take action by altering routings, changing handling instructions, and reconfiguring offloading to safeguard the quality of their products.

Introducing Acme Distribution Software

Acme Distribution Software (ADS) is the hypothetical company we will use to illustrate where to play, how to win, what to do, and who is needed in a digital customer experience makeover.

Acme is a provider of advanced warehouse management software. Based on AI and robotics, the software determines the best location for inventory at any given time and coordinates a fleet of pick-and-pack robots to move inventory into, within, and out of the warehouse for shipment to the customer. The software manages receiving, warehousing, pick and pack, shipment, and billing and also manages the activities of all the ancillary equipment in the warehouse that scans items, labels shipping containers, and wraps pallets. Acme software is designed for large-volume warehouses whose leaders are willing to invest heavily in automation to lower labor costs, reduce employee injuries, and improve inventory management accuracy and control.

Although Acme Distribution Software is a cutting-edge software solution, the company has created a labor-intensive customer experience, delivered largely through Acme's own call center and regional systems integration companies. They are responsible for installing, maintaining, troubleshooting, and upgrading Acme software. This model is a legacy of Acme's original plug-in applications for enterprise resource planning (ERP) systems. Systems integrators sell and service distribution and warehousing software, a service vital to supply chain managers and warehouse operators, who must make multiple software programs and hardware devices work together within their distribution centers and warehouses, as well as link the warehouses and distribution centers to the software and systems in the larger supply chain.

In recent years, the warehouse software market has been changing and, in the process, threatening the role of the systems integrator. Comprehensive solutions that manage the entire warehouse with built-in integration to major peripheral devices and major supply chain players are gaining ground. These solutions require less systems integration and more understanding of how to configure the extensive code to the needs of an individual warehouse. It's easier to link these solutions to other parts of the supply chain without systems integrators, thanks to improved data-sharing standards and the wider use of application programming interfaces (APIs) to facilitate data exchange. Systems integrators are also finding it extremely difficult to match the more sophisticated configuration skills that advanced AI and robotics software developers offer to large warehouse operations. Developing these skills requires teams of data professionals and large data sets to work on, resources that are beyond the reach of systems integrators but are in the wheelhouse of advanced AI and robotics software firms.

Acme is caught in a difficult dilemma. Demand is growing quickly for its advanced AI and robotics-driven comprehensive solutions, and its systems integrators are struggling to deliver the required expertise. But creating a dedicated technical field support force to replace the systems integrators would be extremely costly and time consuming. It would also divert management's attention, which could hurt an emerging company the size of Acme Distribution Software. Acme's leaders are hoping that a digital experience transformation will solve this central challenge to their company's ongoing growth.

2.2

Where to Play in the Digital Experience Makeover

Identify and Prioritize Experience Opportunities

To determine Where to Play, we must first understand the customer's experience. Mapping the customer journey, the path from purchase to use to loyalist, is fundamental to gaining this understanding. Ideally, journey mapping should document customer behaviors and perceptions as well as experiences with competitors in a coherent map that yields insights and helps pinpoint opportunities. Journey maps depicting the current experience are a starting point for creating forward-looking maps that serve as a tool for envisioning improvements in the customer experience, operational maps that guide the building and management of platforms and data to deliver that experience, and deep-dive maps that take a specific part of an experience, such as a call center phone interaction, and break it into component parts for inspection and optimization.

Recent research by INSEAD and IBM confirms that thorough and detailed journey mapping sets successful digital experience providers apart from their competitors (see figure 16).[1]

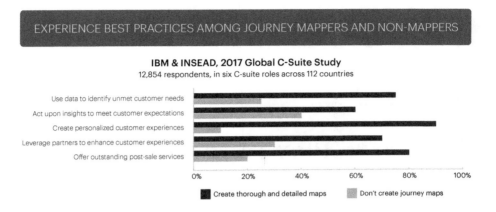

Figure 16. *Importance of journey mapping*

To make journey mapping useful (and actionable), it is vital to think of a journey map as a customer-driven model of how decision-making occurs, and not a chart of individual touchpoints. "Customer driven," because it represents the experiences customers actually have or want to have, not what you, the supplier, want them to do. A "model," because it is not based on every single possible journey, but rather depicts the most commonly taken paths that customer segments take. And about "how decision-making occurs," because it should reflect the moments that matter to customers and the inputs they need at each point to advance in the journey. Moments that matter are those that enable a customer to achieve a goal, whether it's to learn more, find assistance, upgrade, reduce downtime, or operate the product safely. Inputs to customer moments can be functional or emotional or both. An example of a functional input would be a troubleshooting flowchart available in an online customer service portal to help a customer find ways to reduce downtime. A troubleshooting video that explains how to use the flowchart is an example of an input that provides both functional and emotional support (the latter, because it eases the customer's self-doubt about their ability to fix their problem and can inspire confidence).

BUILD THE FOUNDATION

All effective journey mapping, regardless of objective, begins with a basic understanding of the customer that can be obtained only by listening to customers directly and by listening to employees who frequently interact with customers. These inputs shed light on customers' goals as they progress from purchase to use to loyalty, helping us understand the sequence and context of journey moments—that is, who is involved, what their goals are at that moment, and what channels they are utilizing. Journey maps are organized as a sequence of moments, the points where a customer receives an input or makes a choice about how to proceed.

Suppose, for example, a manager at an HVAC systems manufacturer is purchasing new thermostat components. He will start a journey so he can set up the new components. Set-up is a moment that matters in the manager's overall journey because if it goes wrong, the company's entire manufacturing line can come to a halt. Set-up involves several touchpoints, including taking delivery, testing quality, and reconfiguring the production line to include the components.

What's the context of this set-up moment? The people involved are from receiving, quality assurance, and manufacturing. Their goals are to prevent damage and ensure technical compliance and efficient operation. The channels they are using are their company's ERP system and the component supplier's customer portal. The objective of building a foundational understanding is to obtain the basics of the who, what, and why for each moment, so that later decisions about which type of journey map to create and what information it should contain are based on the customer and their overall context.

Acme Customer Understanding

To begin Acme DS's customer experience transformation, Hilke Butler, chief commercial officer, organized a customer experience task force composed of the heads of sales, customer service, tech support, and marketing. Members of the customer experience task force began their work by seeking to understand the customer basics from the customer's viewpoint. The first task Hilke assigned the task force was to conduct personal interviews with customers and gain a firsthand understanding of the challenges involved. Members chose to talk to design engineers and warehouse managers at Acme's customer companies because they were the ones who worked most intensively with Acme's software. Task force members also met with field representatives at regional systems integration companies because they handle the bulk of the interactions with Acme customers. Finally, task force members met with members of Acme's technical support teams who interact with systems integrators as well as directly with Acme customers.

With the notes from their interviews as reference, Hilke and the customer experience task force drew a simple, overarching picture of the customer experience that defined the major moments in the customer journey. It also provided basic context for each moment, identifying the customer and the channels, content, and expertise they relied on (see figure 17).

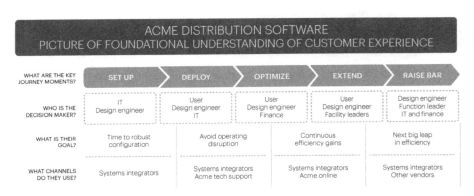

Figure 17. Foundational picture of customer experience

The initial sketch of the customer experience helped the team identify five major moments that matter: the software set up, deployment in a live environment, optimization in ongoing use, extension of the application to other warehouses and the addition of modules, and overall improvement through upgrades and enhancements to operations that required software support. As the Acme team deconstructed the journey, it became apparent that multiple customer decision makers participated in different key moments, including IT and finance professionals, process engineers, shift managers, the facility head, and the supply chain leader. Task force team members realized they needed to learn much more about the interplay among these different decision makers before attempting any further work on journey mapping.

CHOOSE THE RIGHT TYPE OF MAP

There is no single ideal map for a B2B company that's embarking on a digital experience makeover. Companies need several different types of maps—some quite comprehensive and future oriented, others more focused and rooted in the present—to accomplish different objectives over the course of their digital experience makeover (see figure 18). End-to-end maps of the current customer journey are useful for identifying gaps and barriers to meeting customer needs and for identifying where to prioritize investment. More in-depth maps of a portion of the journey, such as the steps involved in placing an order, may be needed to fix specific touch-points or design new services. Maps that show how digital platforms and data work together (the backstage of the experience) are often required for system design or technology integration. Forward-looking maps that depict a vision for new customer experiences are often needed to shift the organization from making incremental enhancements to building bold new experiences that supplant the paradigms of the present day.

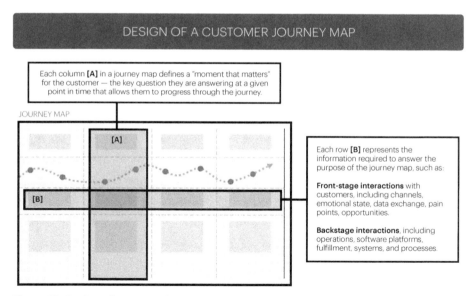

Figure 18. Design of customer journey map

Different purposes call for different maps. But the choice of map is important for another reason: the many different ways customers travel in their journey. Customer journeys are rarely linear, and different customers take different paths; even individual customers don't always take the same path in their subsequent visits. Some customers repeat steps, exit and return later, or skip steps that others find important. Some customers move through a journey in a fairly predictable path, in much the same way that a driver traveling from one city to another chooses one of several available routes that take a relatively straight line. Still other customers move through a journey as though they were spending a day at an amusement park: the entrance and exit are predictable, but the paths involve many stops, detours, and backtracks that depend on the customers' interests and the context, such as who they are with.

Customers cycle through parts of a journey and touchpoints within an overall journey repeatedly. They might loop through the claims process with their insurance provider many times in the course of a year or use an equipment provider's technical support on a regular basis. On a macro level, they loop from shopping and buying to using and consuming in the course of their day-to-day work.

So given this customer complexity, it's important to choose the right type of map to help meet customers' various objectives.

▶ *End-to-end journey* maps depict the entire customer experience at a high level, from the initial steps to becoming a customer to ongoing use to upgrades and further purchases. For example, for customers of a human resource software company, an end-to-end journey map would include the reasons prompting the customer to begin the journey; the steps for making an initial purchase, such as setting requirements, quoting, and contracting; all the steps the company must take to convert from its current software to the new software, including training employees; the different aspects of ongoing use; and all the steps involved in maintaining, modifying, and upgrading the software. Because end-to-end journey maps provide a bird's-eye view, they are ideal for identifying gaps, barriers, and pain points. The bird's-eye view also helps leaders determine where to focus their attention and resources.

▶ *Sub-journey* maps depict any given subset of the end-to-end journey. Sub-journeys can nest inside each other like Russian dolls. Sub-journeys can encompass multiple moments within an end-to-end journey, focus on a single moment in the customer journey, or delve into a customer process within a moment. In the HR software example, all of the moments it takes for the HR team to deploy the software in the organization represent a broad deployment sub-journey. Rolling out benefit enrollment is a sub-journey within the broader deployment sub-journey, and establishing a process for making benefit changes is a sub-journey within the broader benefit rollout sub-journey within the even broader deployment sub-journey. In practice, the scope of most sub-journey mapping exercises is tied to the responsibilities of the sponsor of the experience makeover effort. For instance, to identify specific ideas for improving customer satisfaction, the head of claims at an insurance company could use a claims sub-journey map to delve into narrower sub-journeys within claims, such as the claims adjustment process, where she might explore pain points that will help her redesign the claims adjustment experience. Because sub-journeys can zero in on detail and narrow their scope, they are excellent for pinpointing where meaningful experience redesign should occur and depicting the specific needs to be addressed.

▶ *Touchpoint* maps examine a touchpoint that may be part of any number of moments in a single journey or in different journeys. A corporate website, for example, may serve the needs of customers looking for buying information, installation assistance, maintenance support, thought leadership, or partnership details, while also serving the needs of investors, employees, suppliers, and job seekers. The focus of a touchpoint map is examining how customers enter and exit the touchpoint and how they engage within it. It is most useful in two situations: when an end-to-end journey map or a sub-journey map identifies the touchpoint as a bottleneck, or when an opportunity arises and detailed understanding of the customer is needed before any redesign begins.

▶ *Future-state* maps envision what could be. Future-state thinking can be applied to any type of map. Such maps are most useful for two types of objectives. One is connecting the work of different experience redesign teams in a way that builds toward a shared vision of the future and that overcomes gaps in providing a consistent and integrated experience for customers. The other is promoting breakthrough thinking and using the customer experience as a force for disruption. In this case, it's often useful to create a future-state map early in an experience makeover, just after establishing a foundational understanding. The map then serves as a beacon for experience designers.

▶ *Backstage* maps chart all of the activity, infrastructure, data, and platforms required to deliver the customer experience. As such, they are not true journey maps because they map the work the company must do to enable experiences. They are also useful in spotting gaps in backstage capabilities (in people, systems, and processes) as well as opportunities for integrating data and systems. It's most effective to tie these maps to each stage in the journey—often by putting backstage dimensions on the customer journey map so they are visible to all the experience development and management teams.

▶ *Segment* maps are variants of any journey map that focus on a single segment. For example, the sub-journey for deploying human resource software can be seen through the lens of large global enterprises, medium-sized companies, or small companies. It is best to depict segment differences whenever possible in a single journey map. That way, the teams who are managing, optimizing, or redesigning experiences can see segment differences at a glance. However, sometimes the journeys of different segments are so unique they must be depicted on their own maps. This is the case in commercial building maintenance, where the journeys of office, manufacturing, healthcare, and retail segments differ so significantly that it isn't useful to depict them in a single map.

MAP THE JOURNEY

To map the journey, you'll need to interview the employees who have the most interaction with your customers, conduct customer research, analyze online data (for example, site or search data), and study the experiences offered by your direct competitors as well as by companies in related categories. This exploratory work must answer several important questions:

- ▶ **Who do you want to target?** Which customer segments should you pursue? What is the profile of your primary target segments? Should you woo end users as well as intermediaries?

- ▶ **What are your business goals?** What objective are you aiming for that matches customers' desires: Brand adoption? Recommendation? Greater loyalty? Greater share of wallet?

- ▶ **Where should you focus?** Which part of the path do you need to understand more fully? Which touchpoints or subsets of experiences do you need to focus on to make a tangible difference for the customer? Where will an overview of the entire journey suffice?

- ▶ **What are your customers trying to accomplish?** Examine their objectives from their viewpoint. Most customers think about the work they need to do, consider how B2B suppliers can help them, and then engage accordingly.

- ▶ **How do your customers currently behave?** Which digital and non-digital touchpoints do customers use, and how do customers move from one touchpoint to another? How often do they use your channels? How deeply do they engage with you? How valuable are your touchpoints and content?

- ▶ **Where are the pain points?** What frustrates customers in their current journey? What confuses them? What takes too much time? Because customers cannot (or won't) always tell you what might improve, it's important to observe the points where they abandon their journey.

- ▶ **What's working?** What do customers find most helpful or most useful about your journey moments? Do you know what makes customers loyal?

- ▶ **How do customers vary by segment?** When delving into customer behavior, do you see variations by segment? Are the journeys themselves among segments different, or do customers follow a similar path but just need different information at specific moments in the journey?

Acme Customer Journey Map

Alison, Acme's CEO, and the customer experience task force focused their journey mapping efforts on the post-purchase—the stage of the customer journey that includes installing, configuring, deploying, maintaining, trouble-shooting, optimizing, and upgrading the software. They made that decision after initial customer interviews showed that the post-purchase represented Acme's biggest vulnerability. But Alison also sensed opportunity here: the task force interviews revealed that Acme's competitors struggle with many of the same support challenges and face similar limitations in their heavy reliance on systems integrators.

Developing the post-purchase journey map helped Acme's customer experience task force pinpoint aspects of the warehouse customer journey that left substantial room for improvement (see figure 19).

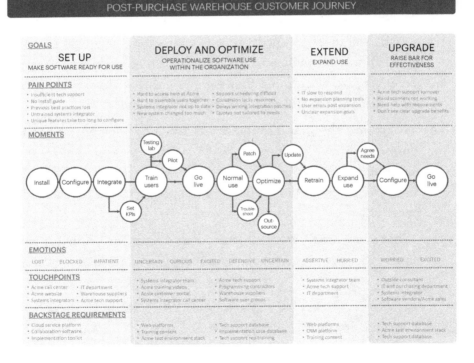

Figure 19. Customer journey map for post-purchase experience

Customer goals. At each major step, Acme was missing the mark with customer goals. For example, the task force was surprised by how much time it took from first use of the Acme system to achieving normal and predictable operations. They observed that exception management and offline expediting were far too common in the early stages—a clear danger sign in any logistics operation.

Touchpoint engagement. Customers' warehouse IT managers, design engineers, and to some extent, shift managers visited Acme's two primary touchpoints, the online portal and call center, frequently at many moments in the journey. But customers did not feel that either touchpoint delivered the depth of expertise they needed. So despite the high cost, customers found they had to rely on systems integrators for assistance.

Pain points. The task force found several customer pain points where parts of the experience were confusing, time consuming, or simply not helpful to them. This was the case with the entire set-up and initial deployment steps. Acme failed to offer services or benefits that competitors and companies outside the category offered. One important gap for Acme (and the category as a whole) was user and leader training and consulting services on warehouse operations improvements beyond software use.

Segment differentiation. The ability to see differences among customer segments was revealing for the customer experience task force. They charted separate maps for end customers and systems integrators and within those maps charted the journeys of four different segments: brick-and-mortar retailers, direct-to-consumer retailers, manufacturers, and distribution/transportation companies. Brick-and-mortar retailer journeys differed because they needed to move large shipments between stores as well as from the warehouse to the stores. Direct-to-consumer retailer journeys differed because of the need to send small packages to individual homes and businesses. Manufacturer journeys were different because they involved shipping to the distribution facilities of retailers and distribution companies. Distribution company journeys were the most complex because they involved all of the activities of the other segments.

Gaps in backstage capabilities. The task force found that many of Acme's systems and resources were poorly matched to journey moments and barely integrated from a customer viewpoint. For example, the software configuration tool was useful in the test environment but not once the software went live. A software management tool could have overcome this problem, but it was not linked to the configuration tool. This example and others like it reinforced the notion that many experience challenges did not require new systems; they could be solved by using existing systems and technologies better. In many cases, all it would take was adding new data sources or getting systems to work together more seamlessly.

No company can complete a customer journey map in one go. Generally, it takes three drafts to ensure the right level of detail and level of customer input to serve the needs of experience managers and designers.

▶ The *hypothesis draft*, or the first draft, can be created by company and intermediaries' personnel who frequently interact with customers. It serves as a framework for undertaking customer research and typically depicts the moments in the journey, touchpoints, known pain points, and backstage requirements.

▶ The *insight draft*, the second draft, is a working draft designed for strategic problem-solving. It takes existing data about the way customer segments flow through the pathways and combines it with field research to understand what happens and why. This draft fleshes out details about customer goals, pain points, and navigation from one point (or moment) to another and notes elements of the journey that the hypothesis draft missed.

▶ *Deep-dive drafts* are subsequent drafts that dig deeper to understand in more detail particular subsets of experiences. For example, you might create a deep-dive draft within onboarding to understand the steps in the product registration process or to focus on an important touchpoint such as an installation guide microsite. These maps provide more nuance and clarify what matters most to customers. They also highlight segment differences more clearly.

UNCOVER OPPORTUNITIES

The goal of any makeover is to make the experiences within the customer's journey more relevant, more motivating, and more engaging. Through customer experience mapping, you identify a set of opportunities to serve as the basis for the digital experience makeover. Opportunities generally fall into three categories: fixing what's broken, enhancing experiences that are working, and launching new experiences (see figure 20).[2]

TYPES OF CUSTOMER EXPERIENCE OPPORTUNITIES

FIX

The experience drives participants to abandon their journey, find another supplier, or tell others about how dissatisfied they were with their interactions.

ENHANCE

The experience functions as intended. Customers don't complain. Enhancing the experience can boost purchase intent, engagement, or loyalty.

LAUNCH

There are gaps or white spaces in the current experience. Launching new experiences to fill the gaps will meet important emerging needs and expectations.

Figure 20. Customer experience opportunity types

▶ **Fixing broken aspects of the customer experience.** This is the most straightforward type of opportunity. Here, you want to convert negative experiences into positive experiences—all the points that frustrate customers, all the places where they seem to stall—and fix the "dead spots," the touchpoints that generate little interest. Analytics can help identify pain points because they indicate where customers abandon an experience (or "bounce"). But there is no better way to uncover the source of pain points—and what can be done to fix them—than by talking to customers. Dead spots may be easy to detect, but they're not so easy to fix. (In fact, fixing them is often a fruitless task; it may make more sense to move on to something more interesting and relevant to customers.) Around 80 percent of all mobile health apps are abandoned within a month of being downloaded.[3] They never even get the chance to disappoint customers because there's not a compelling enough reason to use them.

- ▶ **Enhancing experiences.** This type of opportunity requires the ability to recognize the chance to take something that's already working and improve it enough to make a big difference to the customer. In 2008, Zurich Financial, one of the world's leading commercial insurance carriers, upgraded its well-functioning Swiss help desk into a truly differentiating touchpoint for business and consumer customers. The company changed its simple call routing function that directed the customer to the right person into a broader service called HelpPoint that quickly connects the customer to the information, tools, or people that match their needs. The initiative was so effective that Zurich's European operation trademarked the service and has showcased it as a proof point in its advertising and communications for the past twenty years.[4]

- ▶ **Launching new experiences.** Opportunities to launch new experiences that fill gaps in existing experiences (white spaces) can be more difficult to identify than areas to fix or enhance, because, by definition, one must recognize what's not there. Because gaps are often prevalent among all the companies in a category, competitive analysis rarely unearths them. The best way to uncover gaps is to examine experiences outside the category and see if any could be applied within the category. For example, after making a purchase, many B2B customers don't completely understand how to use what they bought. Onboarding that occurs within the first 120 days after purchase has been proven to fill this gap so well that it can spur double-digit increases in additional purchases and inspire lasting loyalty. However, few B2B companies have an onboarding team to identify, let alone fill, that white space.

Salesforce.com is an example of a company that's had great success building a customer onboarding program. In July 2019, Jason Lillie, a business analyst on the company's journey-building product team, broadcast the story on YouTube. He described how his team built an onboarding program for administrators that helped cut the time it took for them to generate measurable value for their companies.[5] The results were impressive: in just three years, the team increased account penetration, measured by the number of administrators actively engaged and generating value, by 500 percent.

Acme Customer Experience Opportunities

In its search for opportunities, the Acme customer experience task force assembled a multifunctional group of customer-facing employees. With the help of a facilitator, they explored the company's customer journey, uncovering insights and identifying improvement opportunities. They used the Fix, Enhance, and Launch model to think through ideas, noting segment differences to identify opportunities specific to the individual segments (see figure 21).

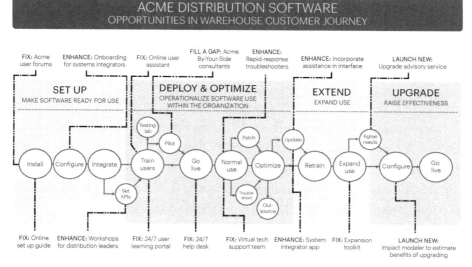

Figure 21. Customer experience opportunities in the customer journey

Fix broken experiences. As expected, the task force found several fix-it opportunities, such as improving set-up guides (there was no installation guide, for example), beefing up the 24/7 help desk (it was hard to know who could help), strengthening the user learning portal, and hiring more tech support people.

Enhance experiences. Several promising opportunities to enhance the customer experience emerged. Most involved helping customers use the software more effectively on a day-to-day basis. One idea: creating a rapid-response team for system integration challenges. Another: changing the software interface so users could receive more help while using the software, such as by adding pop-up dialogs. Yet another: improving the onboarding program for systems integrators to bring their new employees up to speed faster.

Launch new experiences. Alison, Acme's CEO, was most excited by opportunities to launch altogether new experiences. One was creating an in-house consulting service to help customers set up and launch a new warehouse, not just the software for it. The service could be accessed online at any time or, for a fee, an advisor would travel to the customer for on-site assistance. Another opportunity was building a modeling tool to analyze the impact of hardware, process, talent, or software upgrades on a warehouse and estimate their costs and benefits. Still another idea was developing a team of authorized software partners to provide accessories, peripherals, or data analytics to customers to enhance their use of Acme applications.

Several of these customer experience improvement opportunities could potentially help Acme build a more direct relationship with the customer and bypass systems integrators. Acme found that possibility attractive, recognizing that the company could learn more firsthand and gather data directly to monitor progress and adjust its offerings more readily.

FILTER OPPORTUNITIES FOR IMPORTANCE

A successful B2B customer journey satisfies customers' and suppliers' objectives well enough that it makes both want to do more business together. But B2B business leaders must be wary of seeking perfection with every experience. Certainly, some improvements will resonate with all or most customer segments, and some will matter to only a few. The key to building ideal customer journeys is to invest in meeting expectations in all the important parts of the journey. When you let the customer down in some area that's important, you leave room for a competitor to replace you.

Preserving resources to invest in moments that matter requires companies to be disciplined about not squandering them to pursue experience opportunities that are unimportant to customers. The trouble is, organizational silos often muddy allocation decisions. Among the large commercial insurance carriers we've dealt with, for example, we have yet to find one in which the leaders in every major area of operations—claims, risk management, underwriting, renewal, and segment relationships—did not believe the company should invest substantially more in improving customer experiences in their area. They all worked tenaciously to increase their budgets each year.

Customer experience investment decisions should be made based on what is most important to the customer that will also drive business impact. So how do you first define "importance" and how it will be measured? Generally, importance comes down to whether taking advantage of an opportunity will drive customer satisfaction or loyalty. These two outcomes are similar, but they are not the same. Satisfaction is an immediately measurable and fleeting attitude, while loyalty reflects sustainable, multiple-purchase behavior that can take years to measure.[6] Customer behavior researchers have an ongoing debate about whether changes in satisfaction drive greater loyalty; some studies show a link between the two, and other, equally respected, studies show the link is tenuous or nonexistent.[7] We've found that it's best to forgo the debate by looking at both satisfaction and loyalty in a pragmatic way. With satisfaction, consider the experience improvements with the potential to relieve customer "heartburn"—the worries about an experience that keep a manager or leader up at night. Research shows a strong link between high dissatisfaction and low purchase behavior.[8] Conveniently, heartburn relief is immediately measurable through surveys. Regarding loyalty, consider whether the improvement could move customers to become more engaged. Would it slow abandonment? Research shows clear links between customer engagement and future purchase behavior.[9] And engagement is immediately measurable via user testing.

CEMEX, the global building materials company, represents a good example of focusing on what's most important to a specific customer segment. It launched CEMEX Go, a first-of-its-kind, fully digital, multi-device offering that provides a seamless experience for order placement, live shipment tracking, and managing invoices and payments for CEMEX's main products, including bagged and bulk cement, ready-mix concrete, aggregates, and multi-products. It addresses customers' needs to get more done in less time and have more control over their businesses by delivering real-time, detailed information. CEMEX Go has changed the experience of more than twenty thousand customers in eighteen countries, who represent approximately 60 percent of CEMEX's total recurring customers worldwide. Currently, those customers are placing around a third of their orders—or about 20 percent of CEMEX's global sales—through the platform.[10]

Acme Experience Opportunity Filtering

To screen the list of customer experience improvement opportunities the Acme task force had generated, Acme's sales team shared the list with customers for their input. Apart from refining the list, Acme wanted to understand how important each opportunity could be to customers (see figure 22). For warehouse customers, the greatest source of heartburn was their failure to make complete, on-time, and error-free shipments to their customers. Such failure makes their customers angry—and leads to additional shipping and labor costs and often fines that far outweigh the potential labor savings and productivity gains that Acme's software solution could generate. The greatest risk of delivery breakdown comes from transitioning from legacy systems to Acme software and from upgrading software. With the widespread use of systems integrators (whose quality and expertise vary), all warehouse customers face this problem, regardless of their software provider.

Figure 22. Customer experience opportunities by opportunity type

The high incidence of customer heartburn across the category is precisely what drove Acme to prioritize opportunities for improving the customer's transition to and integration of its software solution.

Opportunities to fix. The most important of the potential improvements were those that would give customers direct online access to Acme's knowledge and expertise, and repair the poor support they were receiving from systems integrators. Improvements included converting the help desk to a 24/7 operation, providing an online channel to improve technical support team access, and changing software set-up guides from static downloads to interactive online tutorials. Some larger companies and distribution center customers were interested in more do-it-yourself offerings, such as a self-help learning portal and a toolkit for expanding the application to new warehouses. The feedback clearly showed that the systems integrators, who are customers' primary interface, are stretched thin and that customers are becoming frustrated by their lack of support.

Opportunities to enhance. The top-ranking "enhance" opportunity, according to the customer survey, was a rapid-response systems integration team. The business disruption that integration causes provokes tremendous anxiety in warehouse leaders. Incorporating user assistance into the software user interface was particularly important to customers who were experiencing high employee turnover. These customers saw the features as efficiency boosters that would be particularly helpful to new employees.

Opportunities to launch new experiences. The opportunities in this group most interesting to customers were those involving making the warehouse operate more efficiently, not just making the software work better. A consulting service dedicated to warehouse efficiency improvement appealed in particular to segments of medium-sized operators who, unlike Amazon or other industry giants, lacked internal consulting teams. High on every customer's list were warehouse performance analytics and a modeling tool for planning and assessing the impact of warehouse labor, process, and equipment changes—a reflection of customers' thirst for more data and analytics to improve operations.

The astute reader will note that certain considerations that are typically part of the initiative prioritization process—namely, time to market, cost, and synergy with existing assets—were not used to filter the customer experience improvement opportunities. Although these are important considerations, they should come later, when exploring design options. By including them at this early stage, you risk discarding potentially promising ideas. In the next chapter, How to Win, we describe the process of developing a strategy for turning opportunities into initiatives.

2.3

How to Win in the Digital Experience Makeover

The Digital Experience Makeover Strategy

O nce leaders have selected the most important customer experience improvement opportunities, they can turn to building a customer experience strategy. The strategy will address how to convert important opportunities into experiences that enable customers to achieve their goals and enable the B2B company to win in the marketplace. The customer experience strategy is also important for aligning and galvanizing employees, because so many parts of the organization and so much of employees' core work are involved in delivering customer experiences.

The customer experience strategy must also encompass three time horizons: today, when the organization focuses on running the experience and making it work for customers; tomorrow, when the focus is on building and launching new experiences and the capabilities and platforms to support them; and the future, when the focus is on conceiving and testing new ideas to advance the experience (see figure 23).[1]

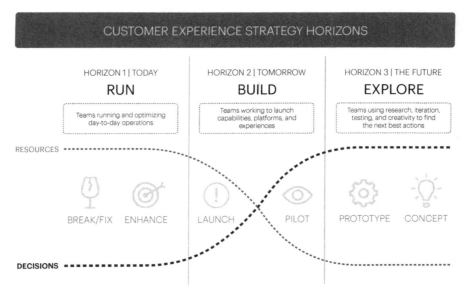

Figure 23. Customer experience strategy horizons

The level of resources needed and the intensity of decision-making will vary by horizon. Running the experience requires the maximum resources, but the scope of decision-making is minimal, primarily about finding ways to fix and enhance the current experience. Building new experiences through pilots and launching them in the market also uses resources intensively and calls for a broad scope of possible decisions. Exploring the future through concepting and prototyping expands the range of decisions and possibilities but requires more limited resources—resources focused on innovation and technology.

Leaders charged with crafting the customer experience strategy must determine what should be in the portfolio of opportunities for each time horizon. They then need to allocate sufficient resources and decision-making expertise to enable all the fixing, enhancing, launching, piloting, prototyping, and concepting work.

What should the strategy itself address? We believe every customer experience strategy must address five important challenges:

▶ Where should you seek competitive advantage by delivering distinctive value beyond customer expectations (advantage drivers), and where should you achieve expectations on a par with, if not better than, the competition (fulfill essentials)?

▶ Which design approach is best for creating and delivering the advantage drivers versus the essentials? For example, for a given opportunity, do you design a single touchpoint, build a service, create a new product, or make it part of redesigning the end-to-end experience?

▶ What design and delivery principles should you adopt to guide experience designers and developers? Design principles must be in sync with the brand and align with customer preferences on engaging with the company.

▶ What level of customization and personalization should you offer now and in the future? In the digital age, these are becoming major determining factors for how customers judge experiences and rate their value.

▶ How should the experience connect to the company's supply chain ecosystem? How will data be exchanged with customers and suppliers? How will partners be involved? And how will members of the supply chain ecosystem exchange information and assistance?

Let's consider these five important challenges in more detail.

DECIDE WHERE TO EXCEL

A key aspect of any experience strategy is deciding where in the experience a company will seek to set itself apart, build competitive advantage, and promote growth. Leaders must determine those areas where they simply want to meet customer expectations as well as or slightly better than competitors, and where they want to provide distinctive value that exceeds customer expectations.

Fulfilling customer expectations as well as competitors do is usually a matter of repairing the malfunctioning parts of the journey and enhancing or optimizing what already works. Being number one is not always necessary, but losing out to the competition is not an option. If the gap grows too large, customers may turn away from the experience or, worse, competitors may take advantage of your weakness to usurp the customer relationship.

Generally, providing differentiating value—the kind that truly sets a company apart (or even causes disruption)—calls for launching new experiences or significantly redesigning an existing one. New, signature experience moments and touchpoints that provide differentiating value reinforce brand distinction. Distinctive value inspires customers to recommend you and motivates them to buy more, more often. While it's tempting to seek excellence in every moment that matters for every customer segment, pursuing such a goal takes tremendous resources. The most successful companies don't try to be great at everything; they excel at a few critical things and are good enough at the rest. The key strategic questions you must ask are, What are those critical few things? Where do we strive for excellence, and where is it acceptable to be good and simply keep pace with the competition?

The idea of creating distinctive value in the customer experience is illustrated well by American Airlines' experience with its Sabre reservations platform.[2] In 1957, American Airlines hired IBM to build Sabre, the first automated, digital airline and travel reservation system. Sabre initially offered travel agents a way to reserve tickets and obtain prices on demand at a time when it took multiple phone calls to book a travel reservation. American actively promoted the use of Sabre and enhanced its features and benefits to make it the dominant travel reservation system throughout the '70s and '80s, beating out rivals Apollo (United Airlines' system) and Datas (Delta's system). The more travel providers that joined the Sabre booking network, the more valuable it became to travel agents.

In providing distinctive value to travel agents, Sabre also delivered competitive advantage to American Airlines. Customer research showed that the flight indicated at the top of the screen was chosen by travel agents more than half of the time. American had the ability to optimize the algorithms and the profiles of its own flights to appear in the top three lines more often than flights from rival airlines, much as brands today succeed in appearing at the top of a Google search results page. American had an added advantage: it not only became proficient at managing flight characteristics such as departure and arrival times to enhance the algorithm's performance (the equivalent today of excelling at search-term optimization), but it also owned the algorithm and could adjust it to favor the characteristics of American's flights. American's experience advantage lasted for more than forty years and withstood the prohibition of screen bias by the federal government in 1984. American's competitive advantage only disappeared at the turn of the millennium, when it spun off Sabre as a publicly traded company.

Providing an experience that is both differentiating for the company and valuable to customers is always a challenge. After all, if it were easy, the competition would have already thought of it. Areas of the customer journey undergoing rapid change or uncertainty are often ripe for such efforts. Sabre capitalized on the explosive growth of airline travel in the early '60s and the changing demands of travel agents. IBM is another example of a company taking advantage of rapid change in the supercharged growth area of cloud services.[3] IBM zeroed in on B2B customers' trepidation about transitioning to cloud services and integrating them into their IT infrastructure—fears that were delaying the move to the cloud in spite of its many benefits. So IBM began offering customers guidance by a team of specialists to help them adopt the company's Cloud Storage solution, guiding them not only through their functional issues but also in optimizing their use of the cloud. The IBM team promotes customer engagement with the product; as a result, the company has won more contract renewals and customers have purchased more.

Acme Experience Opportunity Priorities

Acme's customer experience task force eagerly set out to choose where best to seek competitive advantage (see figure 24). Earlier, members realized that reducing customer heartburn over the failure to ship complete, on time, and error free was a source of distinctive value to customers. In the migration to new software or during software upgrades, none of Acme's competitors were meeting this burning need because of systems integrators' growing inability to support AI-driven software. Alison, Acme's CEO, and the task force believed addressing this challenge through online set-up, a 24/7 help desk, a virtual tech support team, and a rapid-response team could give Acme an immediate competitive advantage. Over time, this advantage might shrink as competitors caught up and leveled the playing field. By that time, Acme could move on to other opportunities.

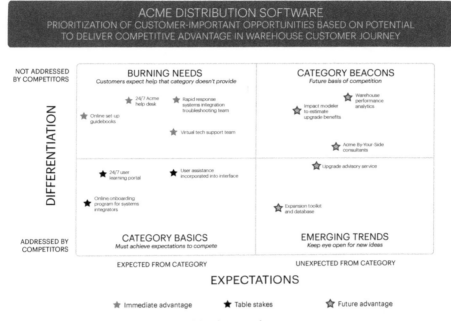

Figure 24. Customer experience prioritization matrix

The Acme team also identified several basic improvement opportunities in areas that competitors were delivering well. Because these were important to customers, Acme could not let a substantial competitive gap remain. Most of these opportunities involved ongoing learning and training through a 24/7 user learning portal, assistance built into the user interface, and onboarding training for systems integrators. For these basics, the Acme team set a goal of pulling close to even with the competition to eliminate the gap. At the same time, the team did not want to overinvest because the potential for gaining advantage was small.

The task force found four customer experience improvement opportunities related to warehouse optimization that could be the basis for future competitive advantage. They believed that these optimization opportunities were beacons of Acme's future, representing its next wave of growth, because they were important areas that customers did not expect from the category and were not the focus of Acme's competitors. Warehouse performance analytics would give customers a view of their entire warehouse, enabling them to manage all of the inputs—labor, processes, equipment use, stock locations, and delivery scheduling—to optimize performance. Another opportunity: an impact modeling tool that would help customers evaluate the benefits of upgrading facilities, equipment, or software and assess the impact on costs, efficiency, and safety. Acme By-Your-Side consultants, a third opportunity, would be of particular interest to smaller warehouse operators that, unlike Amazon and other giants, lacked in-house expertise for optimizing operations. When linked with the performance warehouse analytics, this could become an important value-added service and revenue driver for Acme. Finally, the team conceived an advisory service to help customers manage their facility, equipment, and software. Like the operations optimization consulting idea, it targeted smaller warehouses. Combining the advisory service with the impact modeling tool could beef up its distinctiveness; no other supply chain consulting firm offered anything similar.

CHOOSE A DESIGN APPROACH

To transform any important improvement opportunity into a tangible customer experience, you need to choose a design approach. Doing so sets parameters such as scope, cost, and resource requirements with which to brief the team, measure progress, and determine success. There are four basic design approaches to experience makeover opportunities: touchpoint design, service design, product design, and end-to-end experience design. Although there is overlap in terminology with the discussion of journey mapping in the Where to Play section, the scope of the journey map does not determine the design approach. An end-to-end journey map may identify the need to make over one or more touchpoints, services, product experiences, or the entire journey. A sub-journey map, by virtue of its detail, provides deeper insight into how to redesign the touchpoint, service, or product.

Touchpoint Design

B2B companies have built an array of touchpoints that serve an important role and deliver distinctive value to customers. Through repeated use, these touchpoints become signature experiences for their brand. Touchpoints vary considerably by industry; among them are the following:

- ▶ Digital tools that help B2B users configure complex equipment, software, or services, tailoring them to users' specific needs.

- ▶ Technical support navigators that direct customers to important online resources, such as operating manuals and troubleshooting routines, as well as help them gain access to live support via a call center, scheduled appointment, live chat, or other avenue.

- ▶ Direct e-commerce touchpoints that allow customers to easily find, choose, and order the spare parts, accessories, software upgrades, or value-added services they need.

Touchpoint design applies to designing (or redesigning) the customer interaction point, such as a website, mobile app, customer portal, or call center. The launch of a chat-bot-powered customer care application, an insurance policy configuration tool, and a mobile spare-parts ordering app are all examples of touchpoint design that enhance or fill gaps in existing experiences. Sometimes a touchpoint needs to be redesigned because it has become a roadblock for the customer. This frequently happens on the corporate website of many B2B organizations. Over time, website managers are asked to meet the needs of so many stakeholders (including current and prospective employees, regulators, shareholders, suppliers, and partners) that the sites grow into behemoths that quickly confuse and alienate customers. Creating navigation improvements and routing stakeholders to tailored landing sites is usually part of the design solution.

Service Design

To improve a set or a sequence of customer touchpoints (for instance, all customer onboarding touchpoints) or to launch a new service (such as consulting help), service design is in order. More disruptive than touchpoint design, service design can also yield bigger benefits. Years ago, for example, GE revamped its entire contracting process to make a set of touchpoints simpler and easier to adapt to the needs of different types of customers. As a result, the company cut contracting time (a key barrier to customer onboarding and cross-selling) by more than two-thirds. Often, service redesign encompasses all the steps in a particular customer journey, such as the claims process in insurance or loan writing in banking.

Digital tools and data can create new services in B2B in so many ways that it's impossible to categorize them all. To cite just a few: digital fleet management services for supply chain participants; predictive risk management and mitigation services in insurance; data-driven patient care management in large hospitals; analytics and data-driven optimization for virtually any operation. These types of services involve multiple touchpoints; as a result, they have the ability to extend and deepen customer relationships while also creating new sources of revenue, such as fee-based services. Service design is blossoming because data driven analytics are a powerful engine of service creation for services directed at improving and optimizing customers' operations. Digital platforms also make delivering these services less costly and easier for customers to access.

Many services are owned by functional leaders, such as the head of commercial lending at a bank or the director of field service at a facilities management company. These leaders are often champions of digitally driven service redesign, which involves reevaluating all the different touchpoints and customer interactions to streamline, reorganize, and improve them for the customer's sake. Redesigning them can also help lower costs as well as improve customer service. But owned services are subject to two pitfalls. Process redesign can become internally oriented, instead of customer focused, particularly when cost reduction is the primary reason for the redesign. In addition, siloed thinking can take over. For example, redesigning a loan service experience may present opportunities to help commercial customers with their payroll or with money transfers, but these opportunities can easily be ignored because only the loan team is involved in the redesign effort.

Product Design

Products and solutions are, of course, the biggest component of the customer experience. For most customers, using a supplier's product or solution—from learning how it works to enjoying its benefits—takes more of their time and attention than any other part of the customer experience. The design of a product or solution can also affect other aspects of the experience, such as delivery, set-up assistance, support for changeovers, training, spare-parts ordering, and technical support. The supply of manufacturing robots to automotive manufacturers is a great example of how the product design makes an enormous impact on the car maker's customer experience. The design of the robots has a profound impact on how the automaker runs and manages important operations, such as painting and assembly: it affects the speed of the operation, the number of changeovers it can handle, the functions that can be automated (and those that cannot), and the time and effort needed to reconfigure an assembly line. As these robots have become smarter, they have a greater ability to convey information and respond to their surroundings. They have become agents in operator training; they anticipate the need for changeovers and correspond with factory operations to schedule key preparation activities; they conduct quality checks using built-in sensors; and they even monitor their own function, requesting maintenance and ordering their own spare parts.

IoT, AI, robotics, augmented reality, voice interfaces, and data sensing and collection are changing the face of product design, turning many products into solutions. These technologies are not just affecting physical products and equipment; they are also extending the reach of software in many different ways. At one extreme, we're seeing software that smartly controls the environment inside offices and commercial buildings; at the other, we're seeing software that serves the place of the buyer to explore alternative suppliers or compare prices.

The challenge of product design is ensuring that it is experientially as well as benefit driven. So much has been written about the topic of customer-driven design and design thinking that there is little we can add except to encourage companies to put as much energy into seeking customer input in product design (including via test-and-learn experiments) as they do in touchpoint, service, and end-to-end customer experience design.

End-to-End Experience Design

Few company leaders are willing to undertake a complete end-to-end over-haul of the customer experience. That is a costly and disruptive endeavor. End-to-end design is usually pursued by new entrants in a category—small players intent on disruption, or large companies bold enough to embark in a new direction. (End-to-end experience design often goes together with a business model innovation or pivot that we will explore in more detail in the Digital Proposition Pivot section of this book; see pp. 169–237.)

FedEx is famous for revolutionizing the business model of the pack-age delivery business and, with it, fundamentally changing the customer experience. Before FedEx, shipping a vital spare part to a manufacturer could take days, even weeks, if it had to travel far.[4] Typically, it involved visits to the internal shipping department, transfers by multiple carriers, no tracking, and no delivery-time commitment. With its next-day service, FedEx didn't just change the timeline; it changed the whole experience, with ready-to-use packaging, direct pickup that bypassed the customer's shipping department, no handoffs between shipping companies, item tracking, and guaranteed delivery windows. It is hard to remember that FedEx was once the insurgent. UPS had been the shipping leader—and could have reinvented its experience from end to end but did not—until forced to by FedEx's overwhelming success.

Disintermediation is one of the most common catalysts of end-to-end experience redesign. It forces the redesign of most, if not all, of the cus-tomer experience, even if the company's or the end customer's business model doesn't fundamentally change. In B2B, the widespread disinterme-diation of regional and local distributors for equipment, parts, and sup-plies is a good example. Often, it has fueled direct relationships between suppliers and their end customers, thanks to advances in online ordering and the advent of low-cost package delivery. Elsewhere, it has moved the locus of the experience from a distributor to a different type of middleman, as has been the case in building supply, when local contractors began using building-supply retailers instead of a mix of lumber, plumbing, and electrical specialty distributors. The entire experience had to be recon-ceived, with the purchase and sale occurring simultaneously at a single site and much of the technical detail that a distributor used to offer now the responsibility of the supplier.

Acme Design Approaches

The design choices that Acme's customer experience task force faced made the team reflect not only on their impact on the individual improvement opportunities but also on how they could work together to strengthen the customer value proposition (see figure 25).

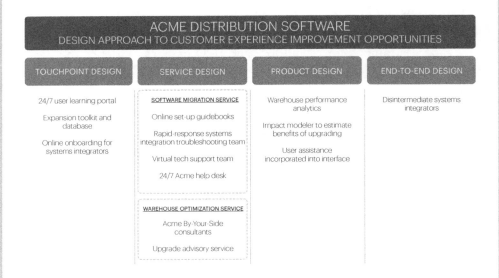

Figure 25. Customer experience improvements by design approach

Touchpoint design. The task force chose to redesign the existing learning portal so that it could address 24/7 user learning, online onboarding for systems integrators, and the information needs of managers who wanted to expand the use of Acme's software to other facilities. It would shift from a portal for downloading user manuals to a learning environment for users, managers, and systems integrators to engage with a variety of learning content, including videos, simulations, Q&As, and case studies to address their needs.

Service design. The task force saw an opportunity to bundle multiple touchpoints (such as the online set-up guidebooks or the 24/7 help desk) to provide two broader services: a software migration service to address customers' anxiety over migrating to new software or upgrading programs, and a warehouse optimization service, which the team believed could be a future source of competitive advantage. This meant making a change to the entire process (steps, roles, information exchange, services provided) of seeking assistance or optimizing performance. It also meant redesigning the touchpoints used in the new services, such as the help desk and the online interface for the virtual tech support team.

Product design. The task force decided to tackle warehouse performance analytics and the impact modeler by building a software product for each opportunity. Each software product, they reasoned, would be a valuable tool for the new warehouse optimization service. The software could also be valuable for very large customers such as Amazon that had their own internal consulting services. By addressing these two opportunities through product development, Acme could provide value as part of a service and as a freestanding tool for its large customers. Incorporating user assistance into the software interface was an easy choice, since it was already in Acme's product development pipeline.

End-to-end design. As the team delved into the software migration and warehouse optimization opportunities, it began to grasp the opportunity inherent in disintermediating the systems integrators. Shifting to a direct delivery model for Acme Distribution Software solutions was a step the company was not ready to take at the time, because it would require redesigning the entire customer experience. And that, in turn, carried the risk of lost sales during a transition and a major investment in bolstering the Acme field sales force and software installation team. So the task force added disintermediation to the pipeline of future opportunities. First, members wanted to better understand the costs, benefits, and risks and perhaps run a small pilot.

INSTILL CUSTOMER EXPERIENCE PRINCIPLES

Two B2B companies in similar situations can design and deliver very different customer experiences, depending on the experience principles they apply. In providing surgical implants for trauma care, J&J Medical Devices competes for the same hospital buyers, with similar solutions offered through similar experience touchpoints, as its major rivals. However, its principles, which reflect and bring the company's credo to life, set J&J's customer experience apart.[5] The principles promote an experience that is more consultative, more relationship oriented with surgeons, more education based, and more clinical evidence based than rivals' experiences. These principles have enabled J&J to maintain its leadership in a category in which product differences are hard for buyers to distinguish.

Experience principles guide design and delivery and are useful for experience developers and any employees who interact with customers. The principles must reflect the brand, its purpose, and the essence of the company so that they are authentic and meaningful to customers. They should be limited in number—a handful suffices—so they can be memorable to all who must abide by them. Experience principles must also be broad enough to apply to many types of experiences, yet differentiating enough that the experiences demonstrate what is special about doing business with the company.

Experience principles play two roles: (1) they boost the performance of every experience by making it just a bit more engaging for the customer, and (2) they integrate all the experiences in the customer journey, so the customer sees that the experiences are unified and have a logic and that, when taken together, all the moments of engagement add up to a valuable and comprehensive experience.

Acme Experience Design Principles

Alison, Acme's CEO, took an active role in crafting the Acme experience design principles. She wanted to make sure that Acme's new brand and its association with cutting-edge technology development came to life in a unique and engaging way for customers. Each of Acme's experience principles serves a concrete purpose, while also reflecting what Acme Distribution Software stands for and what makes it special (see figure 26).

EXPERIENTIAL FROM START TO FINISH

Sustainable engagement requires engaging people's heads and hearts. We make sure we design highly collaborative interactions that make the engagement personal and meaningful for every participant.

SLIGHTLY DISRUPTIVE

We're genuinely curious, slightly irreverent, and just disruptive enough with our customers. We dial up energy and encourage customers to incorporate a digital mindset to challenge traditional thinking and break down rigid paradigms about how a warehouse operation should work.

LOOK AT MORE STUFF. THINK ABOUT IT HARDER.

LAMSTAIH is our core philosophy. A visit to the facility floor, an online competitive exploration, lessons in item sorting. Inspiration creates inputs that drive insight . . . and, ultimately, ingenious software solutions and system integration.

OPTIMALLY VISUAL AND DIGITAL

On mobile devices, in charts that wallpaper an entire room, using visualization software, or deploying smartphone cameras, we design customer interactions with a visual and digital sensibility, knowing the more senses we engage, the more people will retain knowledge and take it forward.

UNEXPECTEDLY DELIGHTFUL

Whether we include a cookies and milkshakes break, bring in a demonstrator, or offer a cutting-edge mobile app, we find opportunities to elevate the event by adding a personal touch.

Figure 26. Customer experience design principles

The principle "Experiential from start to finish" has been a guiding light for Acme's software development since the company's founding. Alison wanted to extend it to the broader experience of customer-employee interactions, so that customers and Acme would focus on improving warehouse operations together, ensuring that customers participate in building solutions they will ultimately use.

The "Slightly disruptive" principle reflects Acme's role as industry insurgent. As the company grows, Alison wants to be sure to preserve the energy and creativity this principle promotes. The principle "Look at more stuff. Think about it harder" is core to Acme's problem-solving approach to major challenges. This principle helps prevent the tunnel thinking that threatens innovation in all engineering-oriented companies. "Optimally visual and digital" is a new principle for Acme. The more AI-driven and complex Acme solutions become, the more important it is to use every available tool to help customers understand what makes Acme special. "Unexpectedly delightful" is self-evident, but Alison felt it was important to state explicitly. It has always been a part of Acme employee interactions but hasn't always been as evident as it could be.

CALIBRATE THE LEVEL OF CUSTOMIZATION

The level of customization to offer customers is an important decision in any digital customer experience strategy, not the least because customization is a moving target: it keeps advancing as data accumulates and as the technologies to deliver it keep evolving. This dynamic requires settling on an initial starting point so the organization can get to work, establish a base, and then extend the level of customization over time. The basic customization criteria are fairly similar across most B2B industries:

- **Company profile:** That is, industry characteristics, firmographics, and consumption history.

- **Need:** What customers are seeking or the requirements for their solution.

- **Trigger or application:** What started the journey; for example, opening a new plant or a cost cut.

- **Journey moment:** The context of the customer journey and the customer's observable behavior within that moment (for example, do they browse, interact, search for more information?).

- **Decision makers' profile:** Role, title, and area of responsibility (for example, procurement versus design).

Ideally, every experience would be customized in detail by every criterion that meaningfully distinguishes one experience participant from another. But in the real world, that's not practical, either because the necessary data is unavailable or because creating and managing all the possible content and experience permutations would be too expensive. Advancements in martech platforms that automatically customize experiences have made customization easier and less costly, as long as data is available. Although customization technologies are becoming more advanced and affordable, customization is valuable only to the extent that it favorably shifts customer behavior or attitudes. Customization is not a goal in and of itself.

A company doesn't need to be data rich in order to customize. A robust customer database makes for a great start, but companies can acquire data in a number of ways:

- ▶ **Through self-customization.** Provide options that users select for the content and interactions they want. Their choices indicate what's important to them.

- ▶ **Via Q&A.** Ask the user for personal data while interacting with them. The data you request can be simple, like what industry they are in, or it can be presented as a set of questions they answer in order to operate an online tool. Contact information is not necessary.

- ▶ **By last move.** Capture the last move the customer made within your online environment. Test-and-learn experiments and AI are powering the predictive abilities of this approach, based on variables such as where the cursor lingered while the user was browsing or whether the user scrolled to the end of the page.

- ▶ **Through opt-in.** Gather information as part of a registration or opt-in process.

- ▶ **Via storage.** Store and reuse information about the customer based on their prior offline behavior, their online behavior, or both.

- ▶ **By purchase.** Procure data from third parties to enrich the existing customer database.

Over time, customization should continue to grow in depth and level of detail so that it keeps offering customers value while providing a positive ROI. Increasing customization over time is not a strategic choice; in a digital world, it's a given. Customers expect it. The only strategic choice is how much customization is required at the start to make the experience valuable and relevant to customers.

Acme Experience Customization

The Acme customer experience task force decided to base customization on customers' systems requirements and the profile of the experience participant. Systems requirements were available in Acme's customer database, and participant data could be easily obtained by asking the participant directly at any one of several touchpoints. Because launching a service to help customers migrate seamlessly from their legacy systems to the Acme software was Acme's top-ranked opportunity, the task force anchored its customization choices on it. The original purchase trigger (the reason the customer purchased Acme software in the first place) and the company profile (industry, customers, company size, and so on) were only slightly helpful in tailoring the experience. The most important customization drivers related to systems were legacy system configuration, the new configuration requirements, and systems integration requirements. Among the other important customization drivers were the user, including their role (programmer, data architect, and so forth); level of experience; and position in the company hierarchy (senior leader, manager, or team member).

CONNECT TO THE SUPPLY CHAIN ECOSYSTEM

A customer experience strategy is incomplete unless it resolves how other entities in the supply chain—whether suppliers, the customers' customers, intermediaries, regulators, experts, industry associations, and at times, competitors—will link to the customer experience. Most often this involves how other entities will share data that is used in the customer experience undertaking the makeover. Connecting to the ecosystem also includes how the experience will rely on or utilize the expertise of other entities in the ecosystem. A pressing question for companies undertaking a makeover is, How will other stakeholders in the ecosystem (other suppliers, intermediaries, influencers, and customers) be involved? This question influences important decisions, such as whether to pursue an open versus proprietary data-sharing strategy or a channels strategy (direct, via captive intermediaries).

Open versus Proprietary Data Control

One key ecosystem consideration is how open or proprietary the platforms for data sharing should be. How much of the customer experience will the supplying company control, and how much will be under the control of customers and other entities in the ecosystem? For example, several of the largest medical device companies offer inventory management solutions that reside on their own proprietary software. The hospital customer logs onto the medical device company's system to manage their inventory. Rival medical device suppliers link their device inventory to hospital inventory management systems that are under the control of the hospital. With permission, the device supplier logs onto the hospital system to make a transaction. A few device makers support both paths. The proprietary solution provides great benefits to smaller hospitals that lack advanced inventory management systems and allows the medical device company to erect a barrier that limits rival supplier access to data. But larger hospitals with advanced inventory management systems in place avoid proprietary medical device inventory management systems because they pose integration maintenance challenges.

The IoT has made the choice of integrated, open systems and data platforms versus proprietary ones particularly important. The data that IoT sensors collect has to go somewhere to be useful. Sharing protocols, standardized data formats, data security technologies, and blockchain have made safe data sharing easier. However, the applications to turn data into productive information or action are embedded in all sorts of systems, and control of these systems has become a big issue.

In our experience, large B2B companies often leap to the conclusion that they should create proprietary customer platforms, hoping that their platform will emerge as the dominant choice of customers and that competitors will be put at a disadvantage. In effect, they are engaging in the same type of race to dominance that American Airlines' Sabre won against Delta's Datas and United's Apollo travel reservation systems, or that Google, Apple, and Microsoft are still battling out for control of mobile operating systems.[6] The prospect of becoming the dominant industry data platform is so enticing that companies often don't recognize how hard, costly, time consuming, and often fruitless the pursuit can be. B2B companies used to competing on the basis of product differentiation underestimate how valuable it can be to open up systems or cooperate with competitors to create shared platforms designed to deliver outstanding customer experiences. They ignore the powerful examples—the consortia that standardized internet protocols, mobile telephony, and copyright protection, all of which provide access to and take input from rivals and competitors.

Intermediary Relationships

In B2B, many interactions in the customer journey occur through intermediaries. Until the advent of digital, customer interaction with source suppliers was limited in many industries. There, intermediaries controlled most of the customer interaction points, and circumventing the intermediary was time consuming, difficult, and likely to provoke an angry response from the intermediary. But in the digital world, with heightened transparency and direct access to the supplier, customers hold them to account and expect their help, even though an intermediary may still play an important role in certain situations.

This added burden of fulfilling customer expectations for an integrated and seamless experience can be an opportunity if the supplier makes clear choices about when and how they will partner with—or bypass—intermediaries. The best practice in this regard is to build a tiered approach that defines which intermediaries will be close-knit partners, which ones will be respected cooperators, which ones will be transactional agents, and which ones can be bypassed—all, of course, within the limits of business values and regulation.

These choices regarding intermediary participation in the customer experience abound in a digital ecosystem. Specifically:

- ▶ What are the rules for sharing customer data between suppliers and intermediaries and among different types of intermediaries?

- ▶ How will codevelopment and piloting work? Will intermediaries who are development partners be entitled to advanced deployment of the innovations they help create? If so, for how long?

- ▶ How do you tier services and solutions by level of partnership? How do you handle this when a very large customer or intermediary is not a close partner?

- ▶ How do you keep the focus on serving the end customer?

Acme Supply Chain Ecosystem Connection

The choice of data-sharing model—whether open or proprietary—and the scheme for intermediary partnerships was not one that Acme's customer experience task force felt it could make on its own. This decision required input from the senior leadership team, because a misstep could have major repercussions for many important stakeholders in Acme's ecosystem, as well as for Acme's future.

Leaders decided their best option was to follow the prevailing practice in the transportation ecosystem of sharing data among customers, suppliers, shipping and logistics companies, and peripheral devices using standard protocols (see figure 27). Plugging in to a small set of dominant systems was not an option because there is no dominant logistics platform in the industry. Despite the lack of a dominant data-sharing platform, Acme's leadership team wasn't interested in creating a proprietary system. The company's position in the ecosystem as a supplier to warehouses and distribution centers made this too costly and too difficult, especially given the presence of a few global transportation companies that are actively striving to gain share for their systems. Finally, because the supply chain can be vulnerable to hacking, Acme decided not to pursue the path of an entirely open system with easy data access.

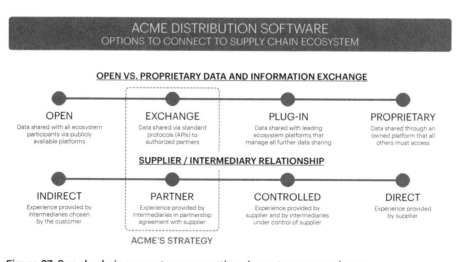

Figure 27. Supply chain ecosystem connections in customer experience

Acme's intermediary relationships with systems integrators presented Acme's senior leadership team with a tough set of choices. Systems integrators have not been handling the migration to AI-driven systems well because they lack expertise. This is likely to become a more acute problem as AI-based warehousing management and robotics become ubiquitous and more sophisticated. For this reason, Acme's leaders were tempted to fundamentally change the customer experience by disintermediating systems integrators entirely. The customer experience task force had already added an end-to-end experience redesign to the portfolio of improvement opportunities and was planning to study and possibly pilot this opportunity with one or two customers.

Acme's senior leadership team decided to follow the task force's lead and delay the decision to fully disintermediate systems integrators for at least another year. They felt that warehouse customers were still loyal to their regional systems integrators and were not yet cognizant of how ill-prepared systems integrators were to support the next wave of AI-driven software. Leaders also wanted more time to bolster Acme's technical support team and to launch the software migration service; both would be needed if the company proceeded with disintermediation. Instead, the senior leadership team decided to switch from using a wide network of systems integrators chosen by the customer to forging top-tier service and support partnerships with ten large, more sophisticated systems integration companies throughout the world. Acme would reinforce these partnerships by investing in its own technical support and launching its software migration service.

Building a customer experience strategy should yield a number of outputs: a portfolio of customer experience improvement opportunities that reflect strategic choices about when to pursue competitive parity as opposed to competitive advantage; what type of design to use (touchpoint, service, product, end-to-end) to pursue the opportunities; the experience principles with which to authentically boost customer engagement; answers about the level of customization; and a position on how your company should connect to the supply chain ecosystem through data sharing and intermediary relationships. These components of the strategy answer the question of how to win and prepare the company for addressing what to do.

2.4

What to Do in the Digital Experience Makeover

Building Digital Experiences

xperiences are created. Designers conceive them, engineers build them, user experience and user interface experts construct their interfaces, coders make them operate, data experts feed them, and platform experts deliver them. The four types of experience design (touchpoint, service, product, and end-to-end) require different team structures, talent, expertise, and innovation approaches. In this chapter, we focus on touchpoint and service design. Not only are they similar in their requirements, but they also account for the most prevalent shortcomings in most B2B companies' experience-building capabilities. We've chosen not to cover product design because so many B2B companies have advanced product development capabilities and because the subject has been written about extensively. End-to-end experience design is discussed in the next section of this book, the Digital Proposition Pivot. Most end-to-end experience makeovers demand a new business model and a fundamental shift in the customer value proposition, both of which are better addressed by thinking through the value proposition and working out how to implement it in the market.

Building a minimum viable experience (MVE) helps touchpoint and service design teams mobilize and focus on the essentials.[1] An MVE ensures that time and money are not squandered on building frills and extras until the value of the core experience has been proven among customers. The minimal nature of an MVE improves development and customer feedback gathering by enabling the iterative loop of build, try, and test to go faster, and by making the results easier to interpret. Most important, an MVE sharpens the development team's focus on what matters most from the customer's point of view.

To build a successful touchpoint or service MVE, the company must

▶ *crystallize* the initial design concept;

▶ *prototype* rapidly by quickly iterating from rough draft to progressively improved versions, with the aid of customer input all along the way; and

▶ *pilot* the experience in-market to identify real-world challenges that were not anticipated and to ensure it operates as intended in complex situations.

Speed, feedback, and iteration are crucial. They allow experience designers to start out with ideas that are directionally correct and weed out flaws and defects through feedback and iteration. However, real-time or in-market pilots may not be appropriate for every category. In highly sensitive or critically important categories such as healthcare or aerospace, MVE development must skew toward extensive prototyping and premarket testing because there is zero tolerance for error once a product goes live. But in many more categories, customers will grant considerable latitude to those developing new experiences and can often be enlisted to try them out and provide feedback to help refine them.

CRYSTALLIZE THE CUSTOMER EXPERIENCE CONCEPT

There is no secret formula for innovating experience concepts. Before we delve into the how-tos of experience concepting, it's important to dispense with a few prevailing myths.

- ▶ **Customer insights reign supreme.** Wrong. While immensely valuable, customer insight does not tell you, as the provider of an experience, what to do. Insights are key to understanding the problems that need to be solved and what matters most. But customers are not inventors, nor should we expect them to be. Most people cannot imagine what doesn't yet exist, so it's unreliable to base innovation on their notion of what they think they might want or like.

- ▶ **Only creative gurus can create experience concepts.** False. Research has consistently shown that there is no single profile of the inventive person or a best model for innovation.[2] What has been proven is that assembling teams made up of different types of thinkers with different backgrounds and expertise and arming them with tools to work together is a far more reliable path to success than depending on "creatives" to come up with a winning idea.[3]

- ▶ **Brainstorming is all you need.** Not so. Merely throwing people together in a room rarely gets it done. Brainstorming can be effective, but it is just one among many innovation-spurring tools. It works well only if stimuli are prepared in advance, session participants are given appropriate tools to work with, and the outcomes are evaluated and prioritized for their practical value.

To develop innovative touchpoint and service design concepts, companies must properly equip multidisciplinary development teams. They do so by providing teams access to rich sources of inspiration, relevant innovation-igniting tools, and stimulating forums for concept creation.

Six sources of inspiration can put touchpoint and service experience development teams on the right path to innovative ideation and concepting:

▶ *Customer needs and trends* are always the most important source of innovation ideas. They are particularly vital when needs shift or emerge due to changing market dynamics. The insight that physicians need a safe environment to freely engage in social sharing enabled Sermo to build the world's leading physician social site that limits participation to members-only physicians and excludes life science companies and consumers.[4]

▶ *Ideas percolating within the company* are a go-to source of ideas. It is not just current ideas under development you want to consider; it's also ideas that have been set aside and ones in the minds of employees that were never documented.

▶ *Technology and data trends* are a valuable source when innovators think through the different implications of technological change. For example, fully self-driving cars imply that drivers' licenses may no longer be needed, which in turn implies that we might see major changes in verifying personal identification.

▶ *Hidden assets* are company capabilities that can be applied in new ways. These can be an unexpected source of innovation because they can turn a mundane or overlooked strength into something exciting. Stericycle, a leader in the US hospital medical waste recycling market, realized their logistics expertise, hospital relationships, and transportation network were a hidden asset that could provide a new service to pharma and device makers: they could facilitate product recalls by retrieving recalled products and replacing them with new products.

▶ *Analogous company innovations* from direct competitors and similar companies outside the category are one of the first and most productive places that teams can look for inspiration. Seek experiences that almost worked so your team can try to crack the code.

▶ *Businesses you can't ignore*, specifically their disruptive business models and experiences, are great at forcing development teams to look outside their comfort zone. Tesla's approach to regular remote updates and upgrades is an inspiration for just about every B2B equipment maker.

Acme Sources of Design Inspiration

The Acme customer experience task force formed a multidisciplinary customer experience development team to tackle their top priority—designing a software migration service. The development team went to work by tapping into the six sources of inspiration as they began to build concepts (see figure 28).

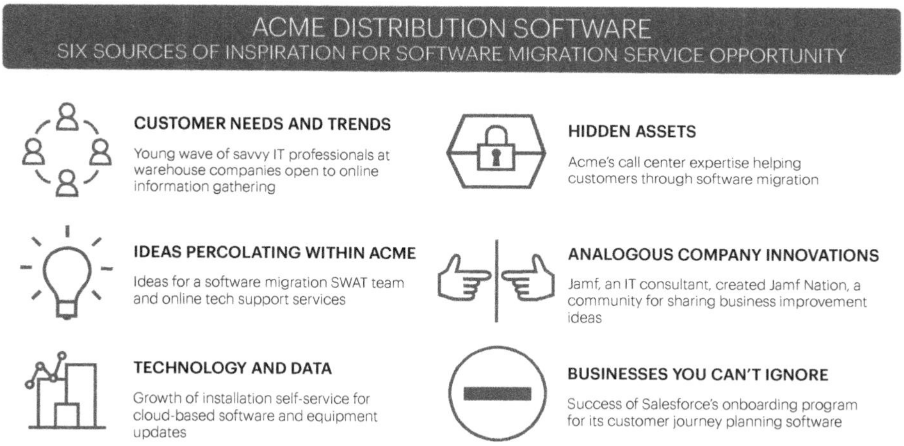

ACME DISTRIBUTION SOFTWARE
SIX SOURCES OF INSPIRATION FOR SOFTWARE MIGRATION SERVICE OPPORTUNITY

CUSTOMER NEEDS AND TRENDS
Young wave of savvy IT professionals at warehouse companies open to online information gathering

HIDDEN ASSETS
Acme's call center expertise helping customers through software migration

IDEAS PERCOLATING WITHIN ACME
Ideas for a software migration SWAT team and online tech support services

ANALOGOUS COMPANY INNOVATIONS
Jamf, an IT consultant, created Jamf Nation, a community for sharing business improvement ideas

TECHNOLOGY AND DATA
Growth of installation self-service for cloud-based software and equipment updates

BUSINESSES YOU CAN'T IGNORE
Success of Salesforce's onboarding program for its customer journey planning software

Figure 28. Sources of customer experience design inspiration

The Acme development team thought it was important to put themselves in the mindset of a new generation of IT professionals at warehouse companies who were more used to online information gathering than their senior leaders. The development team also conducted interviews within Acme and uncovered an abandoned project to create a software migration "SWAT" team. Many of the ideas they unearthed were useful. In technology trends, the growth of cloud-based updating of installed software struck them as something they needed to consider for the service they were building. A visit to the call center revealed that three Acme programmers were go-to resources for

Acme call center reps when they received customer calls for migration help. The way they worked together was an inspiration to the development team. Jamf, a company that helps small businesses manage their Apple product infrastructure, inspired a new way to think about community building. Jamf eschewed forming a user group in favor of a more vital and valuable community that tackles business issues.[5] Salesforce.com's rigorous approach to onboarding was another source of inspiration. The development team was impressed by an online case study Salesforce posted that was by the company's onboarding project leader.

Relevant Innovation-Igniting Tools

Customer experience development teams need innovation tools to help them shed their preconceptions, prejudices, and mental models so they can effectively tap the sources of inspiration. An innovation toolkit is an important resource because it enables team facilitators to pick tools that are most relevant to their team's particular challenges and mindset, as no single ideation or concepting tool will be applicable to all groups in every situation (see figure 29).

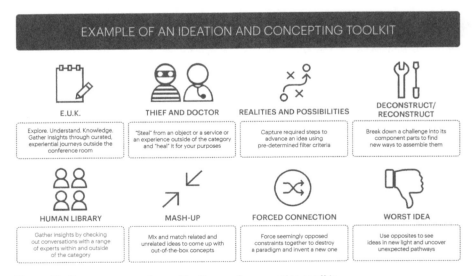

Figure 29. Customer experience ideation and concepting toolkit

To grasp how well these tools can work, consider a simple experience innovation at Acme that could result from the use of the tool called "Worst Idea." Imagine that Acme innovation team members get stuck while trying to come up with new ideas for experience improvements to their distribution software. They decide to brainstorm the worst possible things they could do to a warehouse operation. One item on their list might be sending a truck filled with customer shipments out in the midst of a natural disaster, such as a flood, hurricane, or blizzard. From this springs the idea of tracking cargo while in transit and using Acme software to sync the routing of the shipments based on weather and traffic.

Stimulating Forums for Concept Creation

Stimulating forums are an essential way of putting the sources of inspiration and the ideation and concepting toolkit to work crystallizing touchpoint and service experience concepts. What do you need? A mix of diverse, multidisciplinary participants; agendas specifically tailored to the challenge at hand and to the forum participants; facilitators who are adept at deploying inspiration sources; and a set of innovation tools. Successful sessions never go according to plan, and the facilitator's ability to adapt and improvise, while keeping things on track, is pivotal. Moreover, a single forum is not a process; you can't expect big results from only one session. Rather, a series of appropriately timed and facilitated forums can accelerate the process tremendously, by providing a space and time where participants have the stimulation and freedom to create together. Such forums are not only a powerful way to develop experience concepts but also help align and galvanize participants around the ideas at the same time.

Companies can hold forums to stimulate exchange throughout the concept creation process. Their success relies on following several key practices:

- Ensuring participants are thoroughly prepared before the event, so session time isn't wasted downloading and uploading information or in orientation.

- Conducting "ice breakers" at the opening of the session, such as having participants share a favorite customer experience from outside the category or an example of the best customer service they have ever received. These exercises signal to participants that they will need to think differently during the session and have some fun in the process.

▶ Establishing clear goals each day and allowing participants to have a role in setting them. In order for people to buy in to objectives, they need to have a say in shaping them.

▶ Providing stimulation from the outside, drawing from the six sources of inspiration. Participants need to be equipped to think differently.

▶ Holding a "lightning-round" exercise in which participants apply a number of innovative concepting tools in rapid succession. The idea is to spur improvisation and creativity with intensity to keep the energy flowing.

▶ Reserving time at the end of the session to bring the ideas together. It's important to build and refine concepts so that the forum can meet objectives and participants feel a sense of accomplishment.

▶ Setting a collegial, collaborative tone by dividing the group into small teams. For actual brainstorming and ideation, small teams of three to four people work well. People shed their self-consciousness and bond more quickly to tackle a joint task.

▶ Assigning lots of work to the teams. Don't be afraid to be demanding. People will readily work hard when the work is stimulating and valuable.

▶ Cultivating fun even when the work gets serious. Small touches— candy on the tables, engaging stories from facilitators, and rapid-fire, thirty-second exercises—help participants actively contribute and overcome the shyness or reluctance to share that they'd have in a normal business setting.

The goal of all the touchpoint and service ideation and concepting exercises is to devise an innovative, customer-relevant concept that can be the basis for prototyping and further development. What's most important is clarifying how the idea will address an important customer insight. Details about the concept's workings, the underlying data and platforms needed, and channel delivery options should wait for the next phase, experience prototyping.

Acme Experience Concepting Forum

Early on in their concept creation work, the software-migration service-development team hosted a forum of Acme personnel whom they believed could provide meaningful perspectives. They did not shy away from inviting senior leaders, including Alison, the CEO, or restricting participation to managers. Their agenda covered all the fundamentals—ice breakers, clear goals, stimulation, innovative concepting exercises, allocating time to bring all the ideas together—along with hard work carried out in a fun and engaging environment (see figure 30).

ACME DISTRIBUTION SOFTWARE
CONCEPTING FORUM AGENDA FOR SOFTWARE MIGRATION SERVICE OPPORTUNITY

INTRODUCTIONS AND WELCOME
8:30-9 am | Detail the day's objectives, review agenda, and participate in brief ice-breaker around a surprising service.

GOALS
9-10 am | Participants discuss drivers of outstanding service design and what they want to achieve.

GALLERY WALK
10-10:30 am | Participants review current thinking, trends, and research about services in B2B.

LOOK AT MORE STUFF (LAMS)
10:30-12 pm | Facilitators guide teams through unique examples of B2B services and delivery already in market.

HUMAN LIBRARY (HL)
12-1:30pm | Outside experts in reliable and consistent service delivery hold a panel discussion.

THIEF AND DOCTOR
1:30-2:15 pm | Using inspiration from LAMS and HL, list CX service ideas that could be stolen, tweaked, and applied to Acme.

RUN THE GAUNTLET
2:15-3:15 pm | Teams travel to a station every 15 minutes where they apply a different innovation tool with help of a station facilitator.

DEFINE IT, SELL IT, EVALUATE IT
3:15-4 pm | Small teams further detail the unmet customer need and CX concepts and present to the larger groups.

MARKUP AND REFINE
4:15-5:15 pm | CX concepts are visualized on walls for forum participant voting. Teams refine top-voted software migration service concepts

WRAP-UP AND NEXT STEPS
5:15-5:30 pm | Thank participants and align on next steps.

Figure 30. Customer experience concepting forum agenda

The agenda incorporated several unique team exercises. For example, in the Look at More Stuff exercise, each team participated in a video conference with a company outside Acme's category that demonstrated a B2B service it had developed that is now on the market. In the Human Library session, unexpected experts—an air traffic control planner, the president of a hazardous waste disposal company—explored the underpinnings of service reliability and consistency when it really matters. The Thief and Doctor exercise—in which teams "steal" an idea from outside the category and "doctor" it to adjust to their company's particular challenge—was chosen for an afternoon session. The development team felt it was appropriate, given the many service ideas from outside Acme's category that could apply to the software migration service.

PROTOTYPE RAPIDLY

Build it, build it fast—but don't necessarily build it. The challenge in digital prototyping is to quickly make the touchpoint or service concept manifest so that users and developers can work with it and developers can apply feedback to rapidly shape it into a real experience. Beware of attempting perfection or completion with early prototypes. A simulation, mockup, and customer demonstration is sufficient for kicking off the iterative loop of testing, learning, and refining that will ultimately result in a completed service. The goal here is to make it work well enough for customers to provide feedback.

Creating a prototype blueprint can speed development of the initial prototype. The elements of a blueprint include a clearly articulated customer insight, along with a description of the service, how the touchpoints would work together, a user "flow" (or pathway), and the platforms needed to support the service.

Acme Experience Prototyping

Acme's software-migration service-development team felt a blueprint would help speed the prototyping of the proposed service, providing a clearer view of the service's components and of how touchpoints would work together (see figure 31).

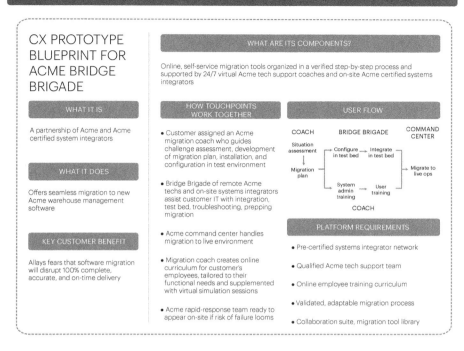

ACME DISTRIBUTION SOFTWARE
PROTOTYPE BLUEPRINT FOR A SOFTWARE MIGRATION SERVICE

CX PROTOTYPE
BLUEPRINT FOR
ACME BRIDGE
BRIGADE

WHAT ARE ITS COMPONENTS?

Online, self-service migration tools organized in a verified step-by-step process and supported by 24/7 virtual Acme tech support coaches and on-site Acme certified systems integrators

WHAT IT IS

A partnership of Acme and Acme certified system integrators

HOW TOUCHPOINTS WORK TOGETHER

USER FLOW

COACH   BRIDGE BRIGADE   COMMAND CENTER

• Customer assigned an Acme migration coach who guides challenge assessment, development of migration plan, installation, and configuration in test environment

Situation assessment → Configure in test bed → Integrate in test bed → Migrate to live ops

Migration plan

WHAT IT DOES

Offers seamless migration to new Acme warehouse management software

• Bridge Brigade of remote Acme techs and on-site systems integrators assist customer IT with integration, test bed, troubleshooting, prepping migration

System admin training → User training

COACH

KEY CUSTOMER BENEFIT

• Acme command center handles migration to live environment

PLATFORM REQUIREMENTS

Allays fears that software migration will disrupt 100% complete, accurate, and on-time delivery

• Migration coach creates online curriculum for customer's employees, tailored to their functional needs and supplemented with virtual simulation sessions

• Pre-certified systems integrator network

• Qualified Acme tech support team

• Online employee training curriculum

• Validated, adaptable migration process

• Acme rapid-response team ready to appear on-site if risk of failure looms

• Collaboration suite, migration tool library

Figure 31. Blueprint for customer experience prototype

Developing the blueprint really helped break down the service into its core components. The team quickly saw that Acme would need to partner with systems integrators to deliver the service. It also became clear that onsite support would be essential, because the interface between robots and peripheral devices can sometimes require physical manipulation. Once the decision to postpone disintermediation was made, the best option appeared to be to work with the top systems integration companies to provide on-site support when needed. But a certification process would be needed to ensure that these companies would be able to fulfill their role.

The core solution consisted of four components: (1) assessment and planning, led by an Acme coach, (2) test-bed configuration and integration, overseen by the new Bridge Brigade, (3) employee training, curated by the coach and delivered by an Acme online learning system, and (4) go-live migration managed by a new Acme control center. Based on this blueprint, the team realized that building a complete service prototype would be too complicated and time consuming at this stage. Instead, it divided the effort into four smaller prototype efforts, one for each main component of the service. These prototypes could be developed by building a mock-up demonstration that customers could see and use to provide feedback.

A demo is often the ideal first form of a prototype. It usually has no code or data. It consists of mock-ups of scenarios based on assumptions about how a target user with a given profile and in a certain context would use the experience for a specific purpose. It typically walks through the user's experience step by step, simulating what the process looks and feels like through a series of drawings or photos that are sequenced in a video or demonstration-building app.

The demo serves several purposes. Most important, it provides the initial version of the idea so users can react, ask questions, and evaluate it. In this regard, it is effective for identifying gaps in the planned experience. The demo also helps the development team break the experience into logical steps that must work together to make the user experience functional. These steps can be programs, subroutines, or data exchanges that make a part of the experience happen, such as logging in. Finally, the demo is an alignment tool that enables members of the team and senior leaders to rally around the initial idea and show their support as well as their concerns.

Generally, the next step consists of creating a module prototype. This is where the component parts of an experience come to life in code (when delivered via software) or in processes (when delivered by people). Module prototypes solve any one of an array of specific challenges in the experience, such as registration, serving personalized content, helping the user navigate the service, and running reports. They aren't always built from scratch; they can be adaptations of subroutines or processes borrowed from other programs and systems. The feedback customers tend to give about module prototypes is usually related to usability. At this point, the key is to focus on the piece parts that will be crucial to the MVE and not worry about programming, data, or process challenges. Distinguishing between nice-to-haves and essentials is a constant challenge.

The first functional prototype combines the modules into the initial working example of the service or touchpoint experience design. Often, it is only partially functional and can handle only limited data. However, this prototype effectively uncovers what it will really take to get the experience to work. Data, privacy, technology, and integration barriers are often revealed. This prototype also serves as a platform for launching the iterative improvement process through customer usability testing.

From here, the prototypes advance in completeness, functionality, and the design and look of the user interface. In scrum agile processes, new prototype versions can be delivered every one or two weeks. The final set of prototypes provides ample opportunity for user input as well as for adaptation and improvement. These prototypes lead to a market-testable version that's often called the alpha or beta version, depending on its launch readiness.

To speed prototype building, experience developers can also hold a hackathon—a tool borrowed from the software development world. Participants with different backgrounds, such as coders, user-interface designers, graphic designers, copywriters, data specialists, and systems architects, gather in one location for one or more days at a time and, in the spirit of friendly competition and idea sharing, "hack" their way to working prototypes at a piece-part, larger component, or solution level. Multiple teams can be assigned the same challenge to discover alternative approaches. The teams report out regularly by demonstrating what they've actually made up to that point and asking for help when they get stuck. The competition and the sharing generate impressive levels of energy and urgency that can turn prototype-building efforts that would otherwise take weeks into overnight success stories.

LAUNCH THE PILOT

The pilot tests late-stage prototypes in real-world situations. Like prototyping, piloting is an iterative, test-and-learn process. Its goal is to take a prototype that works in controlled environments and make it work consistently, reliably, and predictably in actual situations, with all of the uncertainties and unexpected events that happen in working environments.

To illustrate the difference between testing and prototyping a pilot, consider the example of experiences designed to teach customer employees a skill or provide them with important information. The learning proto-type examines how the experience works when employees are paying attention to the application. The pilot must confront the challenges of employees not having enough time, getting distracted with other tasks at the same time, speaking another language, not being able to read at all, being unaware that the training tool is available, working with equipment or peripherals that were never intended to be integrated with the touch-points in the service—and a litany of other challenges, from weather to labor disruptions. Companies run pilots because the only way to uncover the myriad realities that can limit the effectiveness of an experience is to encounter and deal with them.

Another major benefit of pilots is the way they are evaluated. Deter-mining their effectiveness goes beyond examining the innate features of the experience and encompasses all of the steps leading up to and imme-diately following it. As a result, piloting ensures the new experience inte-grates and works with other parts of the experience in real time, accounting for all the device-related, bandwidth, and user constraints that are hard (if not impracticable) to anticipate in prototype form.

Piloting is all about understanding what is happening and why—and what can be done, through design and content changes, to improve the experience. For these reasons, companies often ramp up pilots in scale and scope. At first, pilots may be limited to small groups of employees, and then expanded to larger groups of customers as the service grows more robust, until it is rolled out to all potential cus-tomers for whom the service or touchpoint can add value. Considering all of the valuable information that pilots can yield and the need for customer feedback, rigorous measurement and analytics are critical to the effort. Indeed, they are as important to success as the service or touchpoint design itself.

Acme Prototyping Plan

The prototyping and piloting plan that the Acme migration-service develop-ment team put together called for breaking activities into four main work-streams, one for each of the service's major components (see figure 32). The team set up a weekly progress-sharing routine, along with a backlog and deliverables site to provide transparency and avoid unnecessary delays or hiccups when the workstreams came together at the alpha version stage.

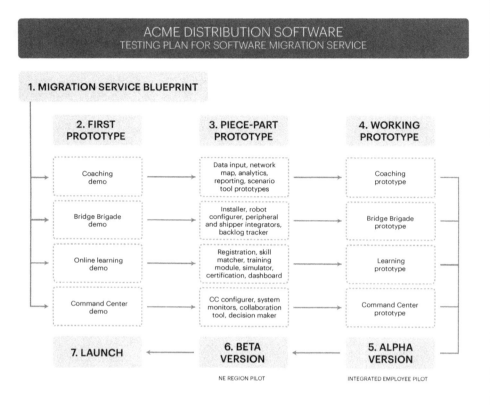

Figure 32. Testing plan for customer experience prototype

The development team realized that the number of piece parts that needed prototyping was likely to increase as they delved further into development. Because the customer experience task force wanted to launch the service in one year, significantly more development resources would be needed for the piece-part prototyping and working prototyping parts of the development plan. Acme began recruiting a team of contractors to help create the prototypes simultaneously and keep the overall project on schedule. And because coordination and talent recruitment would be a major challenge, the development team set up a dedicated talent manager, Marian, whom they enlisted from HR, to keep the effort on track.

2.5

Who Is Needed in the Digital Experience Makeover

Enabling the Digital Experience Makeover

t takes five core capabilities to develop and manage customer experiences: design skills to conceive the solutions, engineering expertise to build them, research proficiency to uncover customer needs and spot new technology trends, experience management capabilities to guide the team and the experience development throughout its lifecycle, and data science and analytics expertise to fuel the experience and identify ways to improve it (see figure 33). Best practice companies build these capabilities using a mix of in-house leaders and experts, in-house implementers in each area, and a network of contractors and agency partners to supplement and augment where needed. The internal-external mix can be adjusted based on talent availability, the need for flexibility (engaging more contractors usually provides greater flexibility), and the company's growth trajectory. The faster the company grows in an area that requires one or more of the core capabilities, the greater the need for in-house talent to plan and coordinate the next wave of growth.

CUSTOMER EXPERIENCE (CX)
DEVELOPMENT AND MANAGEMENT CAPABILITIES

DESIGN	ENGINEERING	RESEARCH	CX PRODUCT MANAGEMENT	DATA SCIENCE AND ANALYTICS
Develop insights. Generate experience prototypes. Design user interfaces. Build online tools and touchpoints.	Full-stack software development, including UI/UX, middleware, integrations, and back-end systems development.	Reveal current and emerging customer needs, wants, attitudes, and pain points. Investigate new technologies or applications.	Create an experience vision, business case, roadmap. Quarterback ongoing delivery across the team from MVE through launch and the service lifecycle.	Develop the infrastructure to collect, store, and utilize data and deliver analytics about how an experience is being used by customers. Build models and AI algorithms for customization.

Figure 33. Key types of customer experience capabilities

Through his research on organizational design among diverse companies developing digital products and experiences, Prophet Partner Tony Fross developed the DERPA maturity model.[1] The model, which stands for Design, Engineering, Research, CX Product Management, and Analytics, pinpoints the elements essential for successfully developing and managing digital experiences. The DERPA model is based on two key insights:

▶ Development teams require extensive support and the right mix of talent. As we've described, creating today's digital experiences calls for a wide array of core capabilities along with management skills to align and orchestrate teams and individuals across those areas. But team members cannot easily play these roles without support from each other and the larger organization. This support must come from senior management, in their willingness to invest in capabilities and fill important capability gaps; from functional leaders, in their willingness to share resources, promote top talent, and break down silos; and from team members themselves, in their cooperation, collaboration, and orientation to problem-solving, which includes seeking help outside the company. Equally import-ant are a robust set of development tools, access to resources, a sup-portive culture, and incentives that promote and reward effective development and innovation.

▶ Experience maturity should determine how digital experience development teams are organized. There is no one-size-fits-all orga-nizational structure for experience development teams. They all need design, engineering, research, experience management, and data science and analytics capabilities. However, the number of employees on a team and the mix of capabilities on each team will be largely a function of the maturity of the given customer expe-rience. For example, a newly launched customer experience needs to be constantly revised and refined until it demonstrates that it is consistently delivering value. Here, too much specialization and too big a team can hinder the rapid improvement, and the flexibility of team members who can cover more than one capability area is essential. As the experience matures, and delivery becomes more predictable, headcount will grow and team members' roles will become more specialized.

Fross found that successful experience builders proactively manage team capabilities, adjusting team structure and leadership as the experi-ence matures. The founder of a major experience-development company shared with Tony his view of flexible organizational design. Corporate leaders, he noted, must be utterly conscious of the need to evolve and adapt team structures on an ongoing basis. "We flex around what's being developed, and around the customer—regularly."

CONFIGURE TEAMS BY EXPERIENCE MATURITY

The DERPA model depicts five phases of experience maturity: start-up, market fit, validated, scaled, and mature (see figure 34). Each requires a different mix of capabilities for development team success.

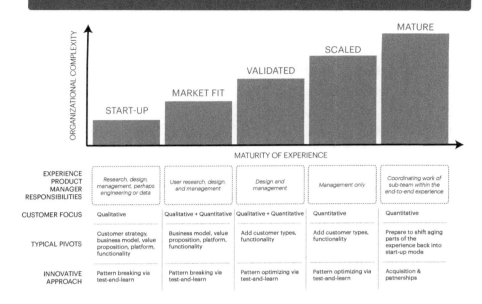

DERPA MATURITY MODEL

EXPERIENCE PRODUCT MANAGER RESPONSIBILITIES	Research, design, management, perhaps engineering or data	User research, design, and management	Design and management	Management only	Coordinating work of sub-team within the end-to-end experience
CUSTOMER FOCUS	Qualitative	Qualitative + Quantitative	Qualitative + Quantitative	Quantitative	Quantitative
TYPICAL PIVOTS	Customer strategy, business model, value proposition, platform, functionality	Business model, value proposition, platform, functionality	Add customer types, functionality	Add customer types, functionality	Prepare to shift aging parts of the experience back into start-up mode
INNOVATIVE APPROACH	Pattern breaking via test-and-learn	Pattern breaking via test-and-learn	Pattern optimizing via test-and-learn	Pattern optimizing via test-and-learn	Acquisition & patnerships

Figure 34. Experience design maturity model (DERPA)

▶ **Start-up phase.** Start-ups are new ideas or pilots that haven't yet been validated by the market. A start-up team is tasked with finding what matters most to customers and turning it into reality. In this phase, innovation focuses on creating new patterns and breaking old ones. Creative design and innovative problem-solving skills, the ability to deal with ambiguity, and rapid development expertise are qualities essential for iterating on the design to bring it closer and closer to the ultimate product. At this incubation stage, the DERPA team is typically small, made up primarily of "makers"—designers, programmers, and engineers experienced at building prototypes from scratch. A product manager (who may even be a "maker") has general oversight of all functions, and team members often wear many hats.

Teams must be proficient in drawing implications from observational research, such as physical and digital ethnography, so that they can uncover and exploit underserved customer needs. Often, they must pivot by altering (if not abandoning) the experience improvement idea, shifting the customer target, or changing the delivery model or experience functionality. Team members who can discard a problematic idea and readily move on to the next one are prized.

▶ **Market-fit phase.** In this phase, there's evidence of early traction. The CEO focuses on adding new customers or further engaging existing ones. An experience manager must concentrate on commercial realities, such as integrating the new experience into a larger ecosystem or refining the business model to achieve financial and customer-growth targets. Adaptation and refinement skills are highly prized in this phase. At this stage, you want designers and engineers to be not so much inventors as editors who take a creation and shape it into a useful form. The team typically acquires more members in this phase, and designers and engineers predominate, even as researcher roles become more important.

Because greater rigor is required in this phase, the company adds quantitative customer research to the qualitative research that began at start-up. The ability to interpret and apply quantitative research to make rapid adjustments is valued. Major pivots are still possible, but most changes are narrower and involve tailoring the core idea established at startup to serve more customer segments in more relevant ways.

▶ **Validation phase.** Here, the emphasis is on accelerating growth. This means adding new use cases and design functionality to support new customers or improve benefits for existing customers. Team members' roles become more specialized as the experience manager hands off research and engineering supervision work to dedicated teams. Coordination and operational skills are critical in this phase, because team leaders must get increasingly specialized groups to work with each other and with all of the functions and regions in the enterprise. In this phase, the emphasis shifts away from "makers" and toward design- and engineering-team technicians, managers, and experience management personnel. There is also a greater overall emphasis on research, data, and analytics, as the search for customer improvement opportunities—new ways to serve the market, new types of customers, and greater function-ality—becomes more important. Teams are increasingly focused on quantitative inputs and measures, and innovation centers on improving customer interactions: streamlining log-in, account set-up, and steps within critical activities.

▶ **Scaled-experience phase.** By this point, many customers have demonstrated that they trust the new experience, and it is already having an effect on customer satisfaction and market share. While adding new customers remains important, the team's role shifts to continuous optimization, personalization, and configuring the experience to the needs of different segments. Customers are gen-erating massive amounts of real-time data, and research is increas-ingly aimed at analyzing behavioral data. Unlike the start-up phase, the scaled-experience phase calls for considerable specialization. Skills prized in this phase include the ability to gather new forms of data as well as techniques for incorporating new data. Additional data and analytics talent is brought on board to augment the opti-mization bench. For engineering tasks, technical and data skills are important for meeting customization requirements.

▶ **Mature phase.** In this phase, the team has two roles: managing the experience and forging the longer-term road map by recognizing when it's time to bring one or more parts of the experience back to the drawing board. Most of the team focuses on optimization and the rollout of the next feature, and a few future-oriented leaders begin preparing those who head the digital experience makeover to return parts of the experience to start-up mode, enlisting the help of designers and engineers. Particularly with large, complex multi-stakeholder experiences, such as those of Salesforce.com and Adobe, the optimization and improvement teams will have layers of management and teams within teams managed by junior experi-ence product managers. Team members see customers face to face less often and usually engage with them only online or in confer-ences. Data and analytics remain front and center.

In the mature phase, the approach to innovation changes as well. Because mature experiences are more likely to be threatened by competitors, leaders might want to consider accelerating their readiness by acquiring new capabilities, rather than rebuilding internally—that is, relying on acquisition and partnership investments for innovation.

APPLY THE DERPA MODEL

Applying the DERPA model involves thinking through new roles, organizational structures, and skills—not to mention recruiting fresh (and frequently hard to find) talent. Leaders looking to up their game right away can start by addressing these few fundamentals:

- ▶ **Gauge maturity.** Conduct a review of the current experience development pipeline and the different elements of the experience makeover. Determine where each experience sits on the maturity scale. Is the business case proven? Does it still have good market fit?

- ▶ **Identify what's important.** What's required to get to the next level? Younger experiences may need more technical and commercial sharpening and development. Mature experiences may need to be more customized or personalized. Prioritize the capabilities that can best elevate the experience to the next level.

- ▶ **Assess each team's skills.** Do teams have the right mix of skills? Is the span of DERPA capabilities properly covered? Highlight gaps and identify near-term and long-term strategies to resolve them.

- ▶ **Right-size the teams.** Having an abundance of resources can be as challenging as having too few. Small teams assigned to successful experiences lose market traction as they stretch too far too often, and large teams slaving away on digital products and experiences without a true market fit are a proverbial money pit. Determine the roles and team sizes appropriate for the maturity of the experience, and make whatever changes are necessary to the team's structure.

- ▶ **Build in continuous improvement.** Organizational change is hardest when it's needed most. Introduce self-organizing (or reorganizing) mechanisms for teams little by little, based on the roles and ways of working they find are most successful. Scrum teams, for instance, typically conduct a retrospective after each sprint to reflect on what worked and what didn't, tweaking processes and organization going forward. Empowering teams to adapt roles, structures, and processes incrementally may prevent more disruptive changes down the road.

Acme Experience Development Talent

The Acme customer experience task force applied the DERPA maturity model to its plan to develop a software migration service. Working through the model revealed several important talent gaps. Team members spotted data and analytics gaps that could stall development in the early phases. They feared that mounds of valuable customer data generated over the past year would be useless without the analytics capabilities to turn it into insights to inform development. They also realized that the intense need for "maker" type designers and engineers was greatest in the first year. They sped up their recruiting plans by focusing on attracting experts in key "maker" areas who had access to a network of contractors and agencies. Contractors and agencies could be mobilized in a short period of time and help Acme through the first-year surge in talent demand. The team's skill assessments revealed a gap in market research talent that could not be filled internally. Most important, the DERPA model helped Acme create a plan to evolve the development teams and put in place a clearer organization and governance model to guide them.

2.6

Key Digital Experience Makeover Takeaways

T he Digital Experience Makeover is the most flexible of the three transformations that B2B leaders can undertake because it can be applied to a single aspect of the customer journey or to the entire end-to-end journey. Effective digital experience makeovers are at the heart of building customer relationships, enhancing customer value, and growing customer loyalty because they forge more intimate, more customized, and more engaging interactions with customers. And because customer experiences touch so many employees within the organization, leaders can look to digital experience makeovers as an enabler of broad culture change, a way to become more customer centric and digitally capable.

The risks that accompany a digital experience makeover can be substantial or minimal, depending on the extent or the nature of the makeover. Extensive makeovers or those reliant on new technologies come with operational risks: something new might break down, or a customer supply chain could be disrupted. However, these risks can be mitigated with strong contingency planning. When the experience involves fundamental changes in the customer relationship, such as cutting out middlemen to interact directly with customers, the risks and the rewards are greater, but harder to anticipate. Customers may not change how they interact; competitors may introduce alternatives that make customers feel safer; intermediaries may fight back by cutting a company out of their book of business. However, the opportunity to create direct, customized, 24/7 interactions with customers usually far outweighs these risks.

As we've explained, successful digital customer experience makeovers in B2B rely on these core guidelines:

- **Choose where to play.** Map the part of the customer journey that will enable your company to make a meaningful impact on customers. Use the journey map to uncover opportunities to fix, enhance, or create new customer experiences. Assemble a portfolio of customer experience improvement opportunities by identifying those that are most important to customers at the moments in the journey that matter most to them.

- **Determine how to win.** Build a digital customer experience strategy to bring the portfolio of improvements to life. This means making customer-driven choices about when to excel, which design approach to utilize (whether touchpoint, service, product, or end-to-end), which experience principles they will embody, what level and type of customization are best, and what mechanisms to deploy to connect to the supply chain ecosystem.

- **Accelerate what to do.** Crystallize customer experience concepts through diverse sources of inspiration, relevant innovation and concepting tools, and collaborative forums that can accelerate progress. Make the work of turning concepts into in-market experiences successful through rapid prototyping and pilots that incorporate customer feedback at each step in the path to launch.

- **Ensure you have the talent you need.** Apply the DERPA model to organize your current experience development teams based on the maturity of the experience you are endeavoring to build. Adapt the organization, skills, and roles of the team as the experiences mature.

The time to undertake a customer experience makeover is when emerging digital trends reveal an opportunity to serve customers better in some area of the experience.[1] It's also when you see competitors using technology within the customer journey in a way that could expose a weakness in your experience delivery or, worse, put your company at a disadvantage.

Because of its flexibility, a digital experience makeover can precede the digital selling shift or a digital proposition pivot. More often, though, it follows a digital proposition pivot because pivots (which we describe in the next section) change the nature of the customer value proposition. That, in turn, triggers the need for different customer experiences and interactions. Because digital experience makeovers usually include several quick wins in the portfolio of opportunities, they help cultivate development teams that can deliver initial impact quickly and are then equipped to follow up with even larger-scale makeovers.

Part 3

TRANSFORMATION 3:
THE DIGITAL PROPOSITION PIVOT

Leverage digital technologies to pivot to data-powered solutions

- ▶ The Digital Proposition Pivot challenge

- ▶ Where to Play: the demand landscape

- ▶ How to Win: the go-to-market proposition

- ▶ What to Do: growth moves

- ▶ Who Is Needed: a transformation management office

- ▶ Key Digital Proposition Pivot takeaways

3.1

The Digital Proposition Pivot Challenge

At the foundation of every B2B buyer-seller interaction is the value proposition. The value proposition represents the customer's understanding of all the ways in which the supplier delivers value to them: not just through its offerings and pricing but also in its incentives, services, support, access points, experiences, innovation, reputation, and expertise. For the supplier, the value proposition answers the question "Why buy from us?" At the individual offer level, it answers the question "Why buy this particular service, product, or solution from us?"

Thinking in proposition terms is useful because it focuses a B2B company on the things it does that add or detract value for customers. It's useful for another reason: it encompasses what a company actually does and what it promises to do to help the customer. In the B2B world, where purchasing decisions, especially large capital expenditures, can have major long-term consequences for the customer's business, this promise of future intention is as important as what the company does today.

Buying enterprise resource planning (ERP) software is an example of the future-oriented nature of a value proposition. ERP software is used to manage all the internal processes of a company, such as keeping track of orders, scheduling work, billing customers, and paying employees. The choice of one comprehensive ERP system (like SAP or Oracle) versus another, or whether to buy a comprehensive system or best-of-breed modules from different providers, is partly a function of the full system's current features, benefits, and limitations. We say "partly" because ERP feature sets are often fairly comparable. What separates one ERP from another is the "future" part of its value proposition: what's next, and what's next after that. Buyers ask themselves, "Is the supplier of ERP software advancing their solution in a way that will meet our needs, not just today, but in the future? And will it be able to provide the tech support, upgrades, training, service, and systems integration that we'll need long after we've made the commitment to purchase?"

Most B2B companies are actively innovating in their R&D and IT departments to make their offerings more digital. Agricultural suppliers are tailoring seeds and fertilizers to farmers' fields based on geo-location and satellite imaging. Manufacturing equipment suppliers are incorporating sensors and AI into assembly systems. Packaging manufacturers are incorporating radio frequency identification (RFID) technology into labels and containers. As a result, farmers' seeds are more productive, manufacturing lines are more flexible, and packaged goods are more traceable.

However, the lag between digital invention and customer adoption can be substantial, and early adopters often represent a sliver of the potential customer base.[1] That's largely because sales, marketing, and other market-facing functions (including the pricing department, distribution, and technical support) typically fail to adapt their portion of the value proposition that relates to the digital innovation. Technical support doesn't keep up with the technological changes required, such as system integration. The sales team doesn't shift to consultative selling and struggles with how to explain the benefits of data, analytics, and ecosystems. Marketers don't adjust their targeting to a new set of decision makers or craft messaging that touts the potential of their solutions to share data or help customers improve and learn over time. The pricing team doesn't recognize the opportunity to capture ongoing revenue from subscriptions or value-added services. The customer training team doesn't adapt to the onboarding challenges of new technologies for the customer's employees. The list of oversights is long.

So most B2B organizations remain stuck upholding an outdated product proposition that doesn't advance digital. B2B customers, however, want digitally powered solutions and experiences, not products. As the famed Harvard Business School professor Theodore Levitt wrote in 1960, when technology was just beginning to disrupt modern business, "Customers don't want to buy a quarter-inch drill; they want a quarter-inch hole."[2] In today's data-driven, rapidly evolving world, customers need more than technology innovations; they want new solutions to their challenges, which these innovations can provide. Marketing and selling these solutions effectively depend on pivoting all of the elements that support a digital or data-based innovation: pricing, channels, selling, technical support, learning, analytics, and on and on.

Take, for example, the IoT-enabled devices that deliver data to building management platforms and enable offices and plants to operate more efficiently and securely. Initial adoption was slow, in part because suppliers had not built solutions that address the organizational barriers to adoption. For example, the security benefits of the data remain limited unless human resources departments adopt data security and privacy policies and train departments in how to use the technology to control access, secure the facility for emergency protection, and so forth. When the devices are first installed, energy savings surge. But that savings won't last unless facilities management personnel are trained in how to analyze, test, and discover new practices for lowering energy use.

The medical devices industry is one of many examples of an industry that, despite abundant digital innovation, remains stuck in an old product orientation—and one that is hurting business. Insurgent makers of increasingly high-quality devices are becoming a competitive threat: they're augmenting their offering with digitally delivered sales and service support that reduces the cost to serve, thus allowing them to offer their product at lower prices. Incumbents, on the other hand, are undermining their innovation in device design with their snail's-pace response to digitizing the customer proposition and shifting to providing data-driven solutions. Incumbents have also been slow to recognize that portions of their portfolio are no longer differentiated and need to match the lower-cost delivery model of their competitors. By failing to shift to higher-value solutions and moving to a low-cost model where appropriate, incumbents are seeing margins shrink in one therapeutic area after another—and enabling commoditization. Companies in similar circumstances are prime candidates for the digital proposition pivot.

CASE STUDY:
MICHELIN SOLUTIONS

Michelin Solutions' Effitires is a prime example of a successful digital proposition pivot.[3] This comprehensive tire-management offering for transportation fleets changed Michelin's B2B proposition so fundamentally that it is no longer about selling tires.

With Effitires, Michelin Solutions (a unit of Michelin Group) provides the tires for free—the customer pays for their use, based on a per-kilometer fee. Customers win cost savings and Michelin benefits from the value-added services it offers and the access to customer data it gains, which will help it develop additional services in the future. The incentives of both Michelin and its fleet customers are aligned through a new business model, in which digital sensors track tire travel and performance, and feed the data into a platform that bills the customer per kilometer. This proposition pivot converted Michelin's fleet management unit from a product-driven to a data-driven solution company.

Michelin tires offer superior performance. However, superior product performance is not terribly differentiating in the traditional, purchase-based business model because many customers don't properly maintain their tires. Michelin's customer research revealed that the operating cost per kilometer of its tires, if properly maintained, was significantly below the actual cost per kilometer customers logged. Yet Michelin was unable to do much about controlling or changing tire management of its traditional, purchase-based model. Michelin Solutions' pivot is both differentiating and appealing to fleet customers. It provides proper tire management that extends product life, improves fleet fuel consumption, and reduces dangerous blowouts and accidents, which also cause downtime.

Like many digital proposition pivots, Michelin Solutions provides the promise of future as well as commits to current benefits. This value proposition builds customer relationships and makes customers "stickier" and more loyal over time. The offering entails working more closely with customers, which helps Michelin gain an intimate knowledge of their transportation and logistics operations. The insights Michelin has gained have inspired further digital fleet management services that are not confined to tire performance management. Many of these solutions rely on a combination of sensors, IoT, and real-time data analytics and data visualization to provide significant new value that extends Michelin's fleet impact far beyond tires. One is Effifuel, a comprehensive solution that includes sophisticated vehicle telematics, training in eco-driving techniques, and the Effitires optimized tire management system. Effifuel improves fuel efficiency and servicing and maintenance, which lead to savings that can boost per-vehicle profits.

In 1999 Michelin began preparing for the launch of its first major digital fleet management solution by first determining where to play. This involved mapping the landscape of needs and challenges for the different types of fleet customer segments: transit, motor coach, garbage trucks, package delivery, freight, and refrigerated vehicles for small, medium-sized, and large operations. The landscape map surfaced the gap between optimal and actual tire and fleet performance. It also uncovered other problems, such as the high up-front cost of purchase, the dissatisfaction with tire leasing programs, and the overall lack of fleet management tools, particularly in medium-sized fleets. The landscape map also accounted for the trends in the automotive industry and digital trends in general, including the use of sensors and IoT, and how aggregating data is generating operational value.

In determining how to win, Michelin's fleet business leaders were very conscious of the need to differentiate—and break through—in a crowded marketplace with many high-quality competitors. They considered a product-based approach that used smart (sensor enabled) tires but dismissed the idea because it didn't really address the core tire management challenge; it could be copied, and it wouldn't create stickiness in fleet customers. Instead, Michelin set up a separate digital unit to drive the initiative. The unit was directly attached to the Group's senior management team, who gave it license to thoroughly reshape the value proposition and business model.

One important part of the proposition was deploying an ambitious customer engagement management and marketing automation system, first launched in the US. This system was the basis for improving the company's understanding of the customer and for working with customers more closely. Another part of the proposition was the move to real-time data, which is crucial to successful fleet management operations. Michelin sensors control the temperature, pressure, and condition of its tires. Michelin introduced Michelin Tire Care, a solution designed to help fleets of fewer than twenty trucks better manage their tires, regardless of brand. In exchange for entrusting Michelin with their data, customers receive predictive control and maintenance services. In just eighteen months, the owners of sixty thousand vehicles signed on, demonstrating customer confidence in the value of this data exchange.

Figuring out what to do to make the digital proposition pivot took determination and a test-and-learn mindset. Although this pivot promised many advantages to Michelin and its customers, it took time to make it a success. Undertaking a proposition pivot from products to solutions was not easy for customers or company employees to understand or embrace. In the beginning, many customers didn't grasp the value of the new business model, and there was no comparable point of reference for them in the tire market. Michelin needed to find ways to educate its customers and its distribution partners while it experimented with how to configure the proposition itself for different customer segments and different regions. It took Michelin a few years to make its contracts profitable—yet further evidence of the complexity of a proposition pivot. Getting the right mix of services, pricing, and support resources for each target segment took experimentation and time.

The organization and people change at Michelin was also significant. Michelin Solutions embraced a new culture and organizational structure. Leaders realized that to sustainably compete with the new proposition, they had to transition from a materials science company to a digital technology company. The customer engagement program, Engage, was an important first step in this transformation. Launched in 2016, Engage provides sales, marketing, and customer services teams with a 360-degree view of the customer, helping them generate deeper insights for customers on how to become more efficient, improve safety, and decrease vehicle downtime. Michelin implemented a governance structure in which the Group's executive committee serves as the "digital board," ensuring that each business line or corporate director is involved in shaping Michelin Solutions' digital transformation road map.

Michelin's proposition pivot from a product-driven business to one that includes solutions with performance guarantees or fuel commitment has helped the company achieve higher customer satisfaction, increased loyalty, and greater EBITDA margins. It is a striking example of how important it is to focus on a key growth opportunity by figuring out where to play (for Michelin, by understanding the needs of fleet operators), by determining how to win (through a strategy built on a data-driven solution), by addressing what to do (by launching new services, such as Effifuel), and by taking action to address who is needed (through the Engage employee learning program and the formation of a digital board). Throughout the Digital Proposition Pivot, we will discuss how these best practices can be applied to other B2B businesses.

Introducing Acme Medical Devices

Before we address the elements of the digital proposition pivot, let us introduce Acme Medical Devices (AMD). This hypothetical company (like the previous sections' Acmes, a composite of actual companies and their experiences) will serve as a vehicle for illustrating our frameworks and approaches in action, highlighting the key choices a company must make in undertaking the digital proposition pivot.

Acme Medical Devices makes surgical implants to replace damaged bone, nerves, and tissue. Its product portfolio covers a broad array of devices, including heart stents and pumps, hip and knee replacement inserts, inner-ear devices, sutures, bone replacements, new limbs, and an equally broad range of performance-monitoring devices that can be worn on or inserted in the human body. Acme MD delivers its offerings primarily through its own sales force, which calls directly on hospitals, surgeons, and specialists around the world. A large technical support team (twice the size of the sales team) works with surgeons and specialists to help them implant the devices when they are just learning a procedure or adapting to a new device. Acme also has an extensive learning program featuring seminars and talks for healthcare teams to help them adopt best practices.

The implant market has changed dramatically since its beginnings. For more than three decades, the market grew rapidly as materials and biological-compatible technologies for implants were developed, tested, and applied to an expanding array of uses, including heart stents and hip replacements. Today, the market is maturing and starting to commoditize; new market entrants offering low-cost, high-quality products are putting pressure on the operating margins for product applications that are no longer new. Hospitals and health systems are encouraging commoditization in their attempt to slow the growth in healthcare spending. Innovation-focused leaders continue to improve product performance, but the costs of improved device performance are hard for hospitals and health systems to justify when the benefit improvement is hard to measure—and when existing inserts already perform so well. At the same time, digital insurgents are emerging, with new ideas and solutions that add data to the competitive mix. Meanwhile, large digital companies, such as IBM, Google, Epic, and UnitedHealthcare, are becoming major players in the use of data to develop new drugs and devices or to reduce costs inside the hospital.[4]

Acme's leaders are well aware of the digital disruption in healthcare and its potential to profoundly change the medical device industry. But they are uncertain about the path forward. Some advocate returning to the product-innovation orientation that made the company an industry leader in the past decades. They also support expanding product innovation and improving the company's consultative selling as a means of restoring its competitive edge. Other leaders recognize that, while the future depends on innovation, it cannot be limited to product innovation. The entire proposition, they contend, needs to become more digital—and it needs to be more differentiated in a market pressured on one end from low-cost competitors and, on the other, from the insurgent disruptors. Leaders want to move forward but worry about endangering the bottom line.

3.2

Where to Play in the Digital Proposition Pivot

Identify and Prioritize Growth Opportunities

o determine Where to Play in a Digital Proposition Pivot, you need to look ahead to predict the sources of future demand and identify the most promising territories. In *The Disruption Mindset*, a 2019 book about leading digital transformation, author Charlene Li emphasizes the need to identify and seek out the future customer.[1] She argues that companies must learn to anticipate future customer needs and preferences by understanding how their work is changing in a more digital world. Li quotes hockey legend Wayne Gretzky, who said, "I skate to where the puck is going to be, not to where it has been." Gretzky's words apply to business leaders who must understand the emerging context around them, anticipate opportunity, and try to reach it as swiftly as possible.

SEGMENT THE CUSTOMER UNIVERSE

Customer segmentation identifies the main groups who will drive demand, along with their needs, motivations, and aspirations. It is an essential tool for understanding customers because it is predicated on the idea that individual customers are not alike. Based on their behavior patterns and characteristics, they can be divided into groups that can be best served by addressing their specific needs.

One complicating factor in B2B segmentation is that in any given supply chain, there are potentially multiple types of customers to segment:

▶ *Direct customer segments* consist of segments of current customers and potential prospects for the existing value proposition. These include decision makers, influencers, and intermediaries. Companies tend to know their immediate or direct customers fairly well, but because their knowledge is based on past experience, they can often be blind to changes that might be taking place within a particular segment.

▶ *Adjacent customer segments* are segments of prospective customers who are not currently direct customers but who may be interested in one or more aspect of the current value proposition. For example, medical research laboratories are an adjacent customer segment to hospitals in the market for CT scan machines. Because laboratory purchase criteria differ from those of direct hospital customers (and the channels serving them are also different), they are not the same as direct customers. In the biometric sensor market, home-security-system makers are an adjacent customer segment to human-monitoring-device makers. Although home-security and human-device-monitoring systems often use similar underlying technologies, these segments have different purchasing criteria and use different distribution channels and applications. In the CT scan example, the degree of adjacency is fairly close; there is considerable overlap in what a radiologist in a medical research laboratory and a radiologist in a hospital require. In the biosensor example, the adjacency between home security and medical testing is not nearly as close. The degree of "stretch" at the outset of a proposition pivot is a judgment call for senior leaders: stretch too far, and the pivot takes on too much added risk because the purchase criteria of potential new customers may be too far afield; stretch too little, and important growth opportunities could be missed because large potential customer segments were ignored. It's best to have a clear hypothesis on where stretch may be attractive, based on a unique and sustainable capability or technology.

▶ *End customer segments* are segments of the customers' customers. In the medical devices industry, patients are the end customer, because they are the physicians' and the hospitals' customers. Sometimes there are opportunities to reconfigure the existing proposition to make it more attractive to end customers and engage them in the decision-making process. For example, 3M holds design forums, demonstration events, and customer workshops with designers at end customers, such as airlines, construction companies, and government agencies, who buy components from suppliers that use 3M materials to fabricate the components.[2] At other times, there may be end-customer solutions that are entirely new and are sold directly to the end customer. For example, AMD, the chip maker, sells specialized graphics chips and boards to OEMs and computer makers but also sells graphics cards, based on the same technology but an entirely different value proposition (in terms of price, service, and channels), to end consumers looking to upgrade their desktop computers.

The underlying criteria for B2B customer segmentation can vary. The most commonly used are firmographics (the company's industry vertical, size, location, number of employees), customer motivations (needs, perceptions, attitudes, intent), and behaviors (buying behavior, online behavior, degree of loyalty).

In segmenting their customers, B2B companies should follow a few helpful guidelines:

▶ **Build hybrid segmentations.** Whenever possible, combine customer motivations, behavior, and firmographics. Segmentations based purely on firmographics offer no insights, those based purely on motivations lack actionability, and those based on behavior can't help predict what customers will do the next time.[3]

- **Talk to members of each key segment.** Segmentations built from existing data or from new quantitative research need conversations to bring them to life.

- **Pay attention to decision makers and influencers.** Firmographics are a good starting point; they describe the right target companies. But companies don't make decisions; people do. Decision makers and influencers generate demand, have applications in need of improvement, and will change their requirements as the forces of disruption affect them.

- **Understand the "what" and the "why."** Understanding current customer behavior is important, but without an understanding of the motivations underlying it, it has little predictive value.

- **Gauge the use of intermediaries.** View them through the user's lens. How and why do different segments use intermediaries? What value do they add?

- **Consider their technology orientation.** Look at technological maturity, receptiveness to digital innovation, and willingness to make digital investment.

- **Learn what gives leaders heartburn.** What are the challenges in their business? What do they do to improve their P&L? What keeps them up at night?

Acme Customer Segments

Mats, Acme MD's chief strategy officer (CSO), wanted to explore pivot opportunities by looking at segments within all three customer types: direct, adjacent, and the customers' customers (end customer) (see figure 35).

ACME MEDICAL DEVICES
KEY CUSTOMER SEGMENTS

DIRECT CUSTOMER SEGMENTS	ADJACENT CUSTOMER SEGMENTS	END CUSTOMER SEGMENTS
• Teaching hospitals • Hospital groups • Regional hospitals and specialty clinics	• Health device companies • Health data companies • Animal health companies	• Surgical patients • Chronic condition sufferers • Health-savvy consumers

Figure 35. Key customer segments in proposition pivot

Direct customers. Acme MD's direct customers fall into three main segments: surgeons and administrators in teaching hospitals, surgeons and purchasing professionals in hospital groups, and surgical leaders in regional hospitals and specialty clinics. Although all are hospital based and their surgical applications are the same, each segment has different purchasing criteria and a different decision-making process.

Adjacent customers. The most promising adjacent customer segments consist of rivals that might be interested in licensing Acme's biosensing technologies, health-data and platform providers serving hospitals and insurers that may be interested in an anonymous form of data that Acme's devices generate, and animal healthcare providers who may have surgical uses for some of Acme's human solutions.

End customers. Patients who are about to undergo a surgical procedure and might utilize an Acme solution are prime potential end customers. People suffering from chronic conditions who are interested in tools for managing them, as well as health-savvy consumers who seek tools to monitor and manage their health, are also promising end customers.

UNCOVER EMERGING DEMAND DRIVERS

Emerging demand drivers are the trends, new technologies, and changing expectations that shift the decision-making criteria of customer segments. For example, several emerging demand drivers are reshaping the commercial-facility heating and cooling business: a growing desire among property owners to lower their carbon footprint; new digital technologies that monitor a facility in real time and adjust heating, cooling, and lighting systems as needed; and new sensor technologies and data-sharing protocols that allow companies to monitor for potential dangers in the environment, such as hazardous gas emissions or flooding. These developments are altering the dynamics of decision-making in purchasing; instead of searching for the most reliable mechanical systems, companies are now looking for digitally enabled management solutions that can monitor and control multiple facilities from a single control room.

When considering emerging drivers, it's important to recognize their aggregate impact. In trucking fleet management, for instance, you wouldn't just examine the availability of electrical charging stations, improvements in battery technologies, and advances in semi-autonomous driving software. You'd want to factor in existing demand drivers, such as road safety, gas mileage, and minimal downtime in order to fully understand how fleet managers think about modernizing their delivery services.

Emerging demand drivers can have different impacts on individual segments that are at first hard to spot. Often these factors must be dissociated and dissected in order to determine the underlying ways in which they are changing decision makers' thinking. Doing so helps us distinguish between short-term fads and longer-term trends and, in turn, understand how to capitalize on their potential benefits while avoiding their worst effects. It's particularly helpful to identify emerging drivers early on, when they are just beginning to have an impact on the market, so the company can get ahead of competitors to reshape its value proposition and be prepared when the impacts become more widespread.

In our work with companies, we've identified ten sources of emerging demand drivers (see figure 36). It's rare that all ten apply in any given case, but together, the sources provide a fertile field for unearthing the forces that are shifting demand and buying behavior.

Figure 36. Sources for emerging demand drivers in proposition pivot

- **Company innovation.** What innovations are on the drawing board at your company or already in the innovation pipeline? Is there a new technology, customer application, or business process in development or under consideration that could transform the solutions the company currently provides? Dash Hudson is an example of a retail analytics company that pivoted into social media analytics for leading consumer brands by using elements of the technologies it developed through a series of new business launches, including an Instagram shopping app.[4]

- **Users.** Are you seeing important changes in how users evaluate and deploy your products and potential solutions? The shift to cross-functional cancer treatment teams fundamentally changed how pharma and biopharma companies run clinical studies, launch new offers, and support ongoing patient treatments in oncology.

- **Competitive dynamics.** Bust paradigms. Ask questions like "What if we adopted a technology or an application that our competitor is testing? Could we take it to another level? What if everyone adopted it—would it change the market structure?" One example is the use of drone and satellite imaging, which has fundamentally changed the nature of competition in the crop-forecasting and yield-improvement consulting businesses.

- **Industry ecosystem.** Is the ecosystem itself changing? Have new competitors entered the market? Is technology changing how customers perform their work? Are digital tools automating workflows? Take the graphic design industry: in just a few years, the low cost of personal computer memory, the shift of CAD programs onto affordable PCs, and the emergence of online file sharing propelled the entire design world online. Sales at design supply stores for small business dropped precipitously, forcing many out of business.

- **Outside the category.** Forces that have taken hold in other categories but have not yet reached your own are potentially a powerful source of emerging demand. But it takes work and creativity to pinpoint cross-category parallels. For example, the professional supply division of appliance maker Electrolux was able to learn a lot from Sephora, the beauty retailer, about configuring solutions for individual customer needs.

▶ **Regulation.** Try to discriminate between regulatory changes that will have a marginal effect on cost or delivery and those that will have more profound impact. Scrutinize those changes that affect data access and usage rights. The 2019 Open Banking regulations set by the European Union affect both access and use.[5] Keep in mind that governing bodies and trade agreements can have impacts as great as those imposed by individual governments.

▶ **Technology trends.** This is rich territory, but be skeptical of technology experts' bias. Of course Amazon promotes deep-learning AI as the greatest revolution of all time; it's in the company's interest to say so. Seek out consultants and academics who don't have a hidden agenda or monetary incentive.

▶ **Data access.** In B2B, the rise of data as an asset has been dramatic in scope and speed. However, data availability and use vary considerably by industry, segment, and region. The drivers of demand are not just what's available and possible now but also what's next.

▶ **Monetization.** Follow the money. Changes in the ways companies monetize their offerings are often disruptive; to wit, the shift to SaaS models for hosting and delivering software on the cloud. These have profoundly changed the dynamics of enterprise software competition.

▶ **Leaders' heartburn.** Most senior leaders have a set of things they worry about and a set of things they dream about. Use these worries and dreams as the basis for what-if scenarios, where technology and data make them happen (or prevent the worst from happening).

Acme Demand Drivers

Acme Medical Devices identified ten key demand drivers (see figure 37).

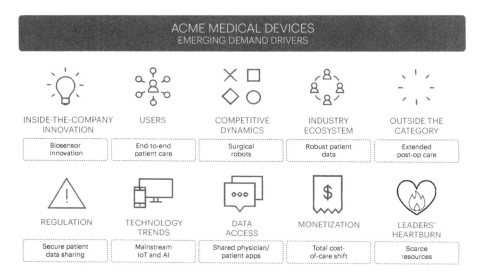

Figure 37. Emerging demand drivers in proposition pivot

Company innovation. Acme's R&D labs have proven the viability and marketability of biosensors that can report digital data and survive within the hostile environment of the human body.

Users. Research found that hospitals that broke down silos and handoffs between preoperative, operative, and post-op patient care focused more on end-to-end patient care, which boded well for biosensors.

Competitive dynamics. Major announcements by leading medical device companies of their plans to launch surgical robot programs have initiated a race to turn surgical robots into the digital hub of the operating theater through which all ancillary intelligent digital surgical tools, devices, and sensors will interact and provide data.

Industry ecosystem. More robust patient data is becoming more available as patients increasingly interact directly with life science companies and Acme through digital channels.

Outside the category. Increasingly, postoperative care is being extended from surgical recovery to the home environment to improve outcomes and minimize complications.

Regulation. US and EU regulatory agencies are studying regulatory reform to allow secure patient data sharing via anonymized patient data to support research and development.

Technology trends. The application of IoT sensors and data-sharing technologies and AI has accelerated in a wide range of healthcare applications.

Data access. Clinical studies show that digital apps that allow physicians and patients to share data have greater levels of engagement and efficacy than patient-only digital apps.

Monetization. Hospital purchasing departments have begun launching pilot programs that measure the impact of devices on the total cost of care.

Leaders' heartburn. Hospital leaders admit to losing sleep over allocating scarce resources that are being stretched thin by escalating demand from the growing geriatric population.

MAP THE DEMAND LANDSCAPE

The purpose of mapping the landscape for demand is to develop a list of high-priority growth territories—those reflecting the opportunities to deliver the growth and profitability that shareholders demand. A crucial part of this effort is examining how emerging demand drivers will impact individual segments.

By mapping the demand landscape, leaders can anticipate how emerging demand drivers might disrupt different parts of the market, much in the same way that a landscaper tries to anticipate how major storms and environmental changes might alter different parts of a physical landscape. Mapping improves their chances of investing time and resources in the territories most suited to a new climate and helps to protect assets that are most vulnerable to change.

Useful demand landscapes are developed by identifying territories at the intersection of the customer segments and emerging demand drivers that we've described in the two previous sections. The customer dimension of the landscape depicts a segmented view of direct, adjacent, and end customers who generate demand. The emerging demand drivers dimension represents how trends throughout the ten sources compel segments to consider new approaches, change suppliers, or alter their buying behavior.

Mapping a landscape entails imagining scenarios that result from the impacts of the demand drivers on segment needs and behaviors. It is a visioning and strategic exercise; by examining how different demand drivers work in combination (either magnifying or conflicting with each other), companies can get a sense of strategic directions or territories worth exploring. For example, the intersection of cloud computing (technology demand driver) with the needs of many business segments to upgrade major parts of their IT infrastructure opened up the B2B web services demand territory that Amazon, Google, and Microsoft have turned into multibillion-dollar revenue businesses.[6]

The best way to identify potential demand territories is by holding working sessions that bring together company leaders with agency partners and external thought leaders who are skilled in applying outside-the-category analogies to solve industry problems. The major question to consider is, What would it look like if varying combinations of the emerging demand drivers were to take hold in our market? This approach usually generates a list of several major potential territories to which the business might pivot. At this stage it is more important to generate several viable candidates than to evaluate and vet each one in detail. That comes next.

Acme Demand Landscape

Mats, the chief strategy officer for Acme Medical Devices, convened the entire senior leadership team, including Alison, the CEO, to consider the demand landscape his team had mapped. Three demand territories interested them in particular (see figure 38).

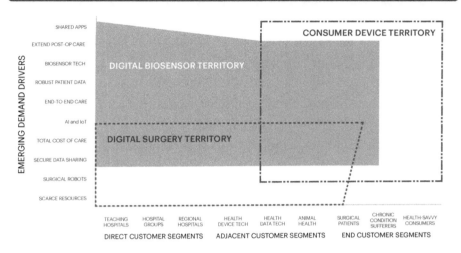

Figure 38. Customer demand landscape

- *Digital surgery*, through the use of AI-powered, advanced surgical robots that enable surgical teams to implement the best practices of the most advanced practitioners. The goal is to improve implant surgeries by helping surgeons and surgical teams emulate the best practices of the world's most successful surgeons. In doing so, the total cost of care would drop significantly because of fewer infections, fewer complications, and faster recovery times.

- *Digital biosensing solutions* that bring Acme's advances in biosensors and inside-the-human-body IoT to medical inserts. This opportunity could entail remaining a supplier to hospitals and surgeons or expanding to supply sensors to other device makers. This territory also includes opportunities to extend Acme's relationship with patients after surgical recovery. Biosensing and data reporting technologies could be used to monitor insert performance and provide repair alerts.

- *Consumer devices*, such as skin patches or more advanced smart watches, use biosensing and IoT technologies that could improve consumer health, with or without surgery. Small devices or sensors embedded under the skin could monitor all sorts of situations and needs, such as the patient's adherence to a prescription drug regime, glucose levels, blood characteristics, and fitness levels. This territory could also open up the possibility of building a direct-to-consumer business model and improving Acme's margins.

CHOOSE A GROWTH TERRITORY

Mapping demand landscapes will generate more growth territories than most companies can pursue at one time. Senior leaders should apply their strategic insights to the concrete data their teams have assembled to choose the growth territory that offers the greatest promise, the best odds of winning, and the least uncertainty. Doing so will help senior growth leaders decide where to focus their growth investments. In determining where to play, growth leaders should assess the potential growth territory from several perspectives:

- **Its attractiveness.** How big are the customer segments that fall within the territory? How important are their unmet needs, and how much value is there in addressing those needs—to customers as well as to the company? It is important to avoid classic industry analysis, which sizes segments only according to current sales and profitability. Such analysis tends to overvalue mature segments that are loyal to current solutions and undervalue emerging segments with significant, but as yet not well-served, needs.

- **The ability to win.** The key criterion in determining a company's ability to win is how unique its capabilities are relative to the competition. Are there gaps in any of the foundational capabilities required to stay abreast of the market? This is not a game of absolutes ("I have it, and my competitors don't"). Instead, it is an assessment of how close the enterprise is to building the right capabilities by integrating what it already has, by investing in building capability organically, or by acquiring capabilities. Be sure to evaluate the capabilities from the perspective of both users and intermediaries.

Current market position, brand reputation, sales support, management's skill in executing change, and an adaptable workforce are all important factors to include in the assessment. These factors are frequently not included by technologists, who often limit their assessments to business model, technology platforms, and data capabilities.

▶ **The level of uncertainty.** All predictions about future opportunities are likely to be wrong to some degree. One way to think about uncertainty is by asking how likely it is that barriers limiting a growth territory will be overcome. Among the most common uncertainties in digital transformations are the degree of data access, new technological developments, and organizational change:

  ▸ *Data access.* In B2B, the barriers to data access are rapidly falling. Even industries such as financial services and healthcare, where privacy regulation is prevalent, have been enjoying greater access to customer data. One reason is the growth in technologies that anonymize personal data by stripping away sensitive information. No one knows to what extent regulators can keep up with these new technologies, or how willing they are to permit their use.

  ▸ *Technological developments.* The uncertainties associated with new technologies spring from one of three types of advances: those that require an entire ecosystem to support them (such as battery-powered trucking fleets, which need refueling stations), those in which the underlying science is not fully understood (and the unintentional consequences to the customers' business may be hard to foresee), and those whose path to completing development is not clear or contains important unresolved challenges.

  ▸ *The organization's ability to adapt to change.* Fear of change is debilitating. Most organizations embrace major changes in their value proposition not because they want to but because they have to. After working to establish deep expertise in their industry, leaders can be reluctant to abandon the practices they have so successfully leveraged. The perceived risk of the new, in particular digital investments (which leaders often don't fully understand), may also contribute to the resistance to change. The preference to stay with "the devil I know" captures the sentiment. Even when disruption is evident and competitive challenges abound, leaders may be reluctant to act in the face of new and uncertain potential solutions.

Acme Demand Landscape Assessment

Mats and Alison had a lot to think about when they reviewed the landscape assessment that Mats's strategy team put together (see figure 39). All three demand territories looked attractive, with high levels of customer need. Because the consumer device territory is more mature, it is larger and has a faster growth rate. But willingness to pay is higher in the digital biosensor and digital surgery territories, because the reimbursement model for breakthrough healthcare innovation is so attractive.

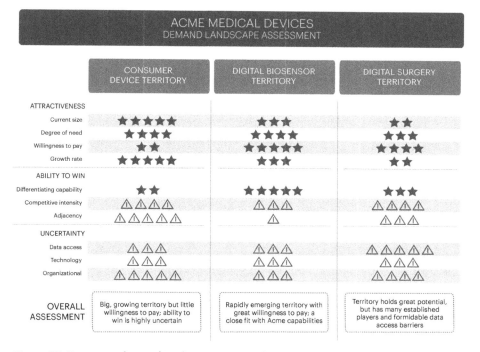

Figure 39. Customer demand territory assessment

Differences emerged in the assessment of "ability to win" and "uncertainty." In the consumer device territory, ability to win is challenging and uncertainty is extremely high because the territory represents a huge stretch for Acme. It would involve transitioning from being a supplier to hospitals and surgeons to being a consumer products company. The competition, along with the business model and organizational commitments, was far too hefty in a business whose success would depend on much greater scale and lower margins.

The digital surgical territory was at first glance enticing to Alison and Mats, because it would put them in the familiar position of competing against other medical device and robotics companies to win among hospital administrators and surgeons. They could see a path to entry: through the acquisition of a robotics company. Acme's in-the-human-body IoT technologies could be combined with robots in several ways beneficial to patients and surgeons. However, the more the two leaders considered it, the more challenging this territory appeared. It was clear that a race was already underway to put robots at the center of a digital surgery system. Hospitals would need to make a major capital investment at a time when resources are growing scarce. The competitive dynamics have winner-take-all characteristics similar to those that played out in Epic's battle for leadership in electronic patient records. Ultimately, success in the digital surgery territory will depend on hospitals' ability or willingness to share patient information—a condition that is highly uncertain.

At Mats's recommendation, Alison, the Acme board, and the senior management team decided to focus on the digital biosensor demand territory. Even though developing such sensors for internal body use is an uncertain endeavor, Acme's R&D department had already made substantial progress. Although the timeline for launching the solution depended on several unknowns, the materials technologies central to sensor development were far enough along in development that leaders felt confident of eventual success. Acme's head start in R&D gave it a significant advantage over competitors in completing the development of viable biosensors. Other aspects of the territory looked promising as well. Acme would need to carry out a major transformation in order to pivot from product manufacturer to digital solution provider. But Acme leaders understood the customers, the channels, and the reimbursement mechanisms that constitute a big part of success.

Once company leaders complete the assessment and choose a demand territory, the next task is crafting a customer value proposition. This helps reinforce senior leaders' confidence that they are pursuing a territory with real promise—one based on an objective assessment of customer needs and important emerging demand drivers. They can proceed with a clear-eyed understanding of the territory's attractiveness, the constraints on their ability to beat the competition, and the risks involved in overcoming important uncertainties.

3.3

How to Win in the Digital Proposition Pivot

The Strategy for a Digital Proposition Pivot

A value proposition is a powerful way for a company to define How to Win. It does double duty by playing both a strategic and a communication role. In its strategic role, it lays out the company's destination and keeps teams dedicated to growing the company and on track to reach that destination. It forces leaders to make choices about what they will do in the demand territory that they've decided is most important. As a communication device, it articulates what the company is offering its customers today and what it intends to deliver to them in the future.

The value proposition keeps communication focused and sharp by laying out the essential choices, the ones that remain at the heart of a winning strategy even as individual tactics evolve and change.

It's worth noting that in the digital age, the present and the future are bound together far more tightly than in the past. Because the features of digital solutions evolve and expand rapidly, prospective customers want to make sure that the supplier's vision of the future and commitment to investment will support their ongoing needs. It's a well-known fact that when Jeff Bezos pitches Amazon Web Services to prospective customers, he tells them what's next for the service, where investment is going, and why his vision of the future is attractive. The value proposition of Amazon Web Services addresses what the service can do for a customer today, and what it will do tomorrow. Customers also want assurance that their supplier will have sufficient market longevity to support their own software when it becomes legacy software, so their data remains accessible.

A digital value proposition is different from an analog-era product value proposition. That's because of the unique feature that data adds: the ability to learn and improve. Digital propositions don't just describe benefits a customer will receive; they also show how the solution's design will improve over time through data collection. They show the way the solution will learn to adapt to change by using data and how the solution will deliver greater impact as it serves more customers in more situations. The AI features of Amazon Web Services offer a good example of the ability to learn and improve.[1] AWS's image-recognition software improves over time, as more images are used to train it. As the number of companies using the software increases, so does the number of images it processes. Each time a user corrects or labels an image, the data refines the image recognition algorithm with this new information. A cycle of improvement is built into data-driven solutions. This also means that digital value propositions must support data analysis and data-driven improvements by the supplier, the customer, supplier-customer partnerships, and in some cases, partnerships across the ecosystem.

We've found that the best way to craft a digital value proposition is to work through a distillation process that converts the value proposition building blocks into a unique and motivating value proposition for the chosen growth territory.

ASSEMBLE THE PROPOSITION BUILDING BLOCKS

The first step in this distillation process is to assemble the building blocks common to most B2B businesses (see figure 40). Each building block will be a starting point for whittling down the potential options into a set that is appropriate for the category and for a specific B2B supplier in the category.

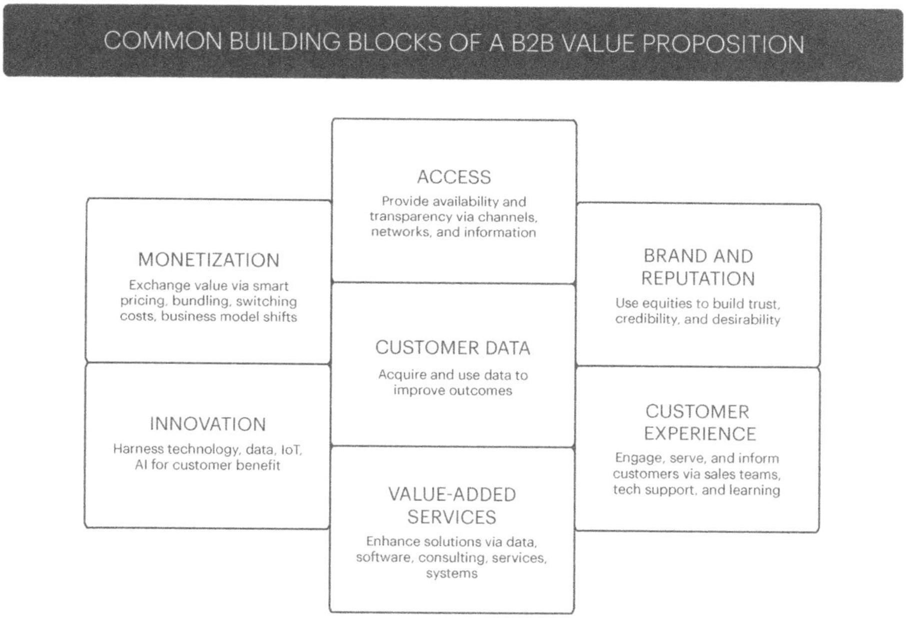

COMMON BUILDING BLOCKS OF A B2B VALUE PROPOSITION

ACCESS
Provide availability and transparency via channels, networks, and information

MONETIZATION
Exchange value via smart pricing, bundling, switching costs, business model shifts

CUSTOMER DATA
Acquire and use data to improve outcomes

BRAND AND REPUTATION
Use equities to build trust, credibility, and desirability

INNOVATION
Harness technology, data, IoT, AI for customer benefit

CUSTOMER EXPERIENCE
Engage, serve, and inform customers via sales teams, tech support, and learning

VALUE-ADDED SERVICES
Enhance solutions via data, software, consulting, services, systems

Figure 40. Common building blocks of B2B value proposition

The B2B value proposition building blocks represent an updated, digitized version of McCarthy's 4Ps: product, promotion, price, and place.[2] For a digital world, "product" translates into "innovation" and "value-added services" because the scope of product development broadens to include innovation in solutions and channel delivery, and digital provides opportunities to introduce value-added services as well as services bundled into the offering. "Promotion" becomes "brand and reputation" because brand and employee expertise are prized in the digital B2B world with so many competitors and a great deal of complexity. "Price" converts to "monetization" because the opportunities to obtain financial reward extend far beyond the price charged at the initial sale. And "place" translates to "access" because digital technologies provide options to change how channels are used to access information and procure solutions. Data and customer experience are new domains with no equivalents in the 4Ps.

IDENTIFY TERRITORY VALUE DRIVERS

Next, the company must narrow and redefine the common building blocks so that they are relevant to a specific demand territory. This step requires drawing on the emerging demand drivers (generated in the demand landscape mapping phase) as well as on the expertise of sales, marketing, and other customer-facing leaders. Each building block must reflect the specific dynamics of the demand territory and the benefits that customers seek.

- ▶ **Innovation.** How is the nature of innovation changing? Is there a certain aspect, type, or area of innovation that is most relevant to this demand territory?

- ▶ **Value-added services.** What might services look like in this territory? Could some form of advisory, troubleshooting, customization, data analysis, or technical support services be relevant to or sought after by customers?

- ▶ **Brand and reputation.** What types of expertise do buyers and users seek? Do they fit with the brand's reputation? How do the expertise and capabilities of the entire organization contribute to buyer trust, confidence, willingness to explore opportunities, and willingness to share data in this demand territory?

- ▶ **Customer experience.** What part of the customer experience matters most to customers? What aspects of the current experience will change as the territory matures?

- ▶ **Monetization.** How do customers determine value? How do they measure it? How do they determine the price they are willing to pay?

- ▶ **Access.** Is there a barrier or set of barriers to access that must be overcome to achieve success? Does the access relate to products? To information? Or to something else?

▶ **Data.** What types of data and specific data points are most important to the customer? What kind of data actually creates value for customers and enables them to enhance the services and offerings they provide or the operations they use to provide them?

Acme Proposition Building Blocks

Acme MD's chief strategy officer, Mats, enlisted Jannis, the company's marketing and sales leader, to adapt the common value proposition building blocks into the digital biosensing demand territory that he and Alison chose (see figure 41). Mats and Jannis focused on two customer targets: physicians (primary care providers and surgeons) and hospital management (including the C-suite and the purchasing department). They defined each building block in terms of the aspect most important to customers in the digital biosensing demand territory, using customer interviews and a customer survey Jannis had commissioned to explore customer interests over the next five years.

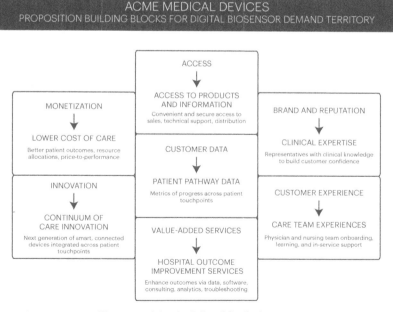

Figure 41. Category-specific proposition building-block pivots

- Innovation became Continuum of Care Innovation because of hospitals' shifting focus from individual care touchpoints to providing end-to-end care for the patient.

- Value-Added Services became Hospital Outcome Improvement Services because hospital decision makers were concentrating on boosting patient ratings and reducing the total cost of care and preventable errors.

- Brand and Reputation became Clinical Expertise because in this territory, brands are built on the distinct clinical expertise delivered to hospitals and physicians through the supplier's R&D team, technical support, learning facilitators, and sales team.

- Customer Experience became Care Provider Team Experiences because effective device-maker interactions with the care team through training and technical support are a key to successful patient treatment.

- Monetization became Lower Cost of Care because scarce resources are forcing hospital purchasing departments to move away from measuring unit costs to assessing total impact on patient outcomes.

- Access became Access to Products and Information because the customer survey spotted two key access barriers: on-time product delivery and hard-to-find technical specifications.

- Customer Data became Patient Pathway Data because physicians and hospital administrators want to better understand how patient outcomes can be improved across the continuum of care.

ADD THE ECOSYSTEM CONTEXT

It is important to surround the value proposition building blocks with context specific to the demand territory. Context helps those building the proposition see forces that must be addressed, understand important limitations that must be taken into account, and factor in constraints that could influence how the value proposition is designed or implemented.

The ecosystem context is best explored by examining regulatory, economic, social, and market-sector limitations and opportunities. For example:

▶ **Regulatory.** Financial service companies operating in Europe must take into account EU-mandated open banking standards (PSD2) and data protection standards (GDPR) when they consider data, monetization, access, innovation, and experience.[3]

▶ **Economic.** Macroeconomic shifts in cyclical industries such as construction can severely limit or expand customers' willingness to invest in new capital or solutions.

▶ **Societal.** Shifting norms about privacy and data ownership have increased the sensitivity and care with which temporary employment agencies must handle contractor data with their employers.

▶ **Market sector.** Software companies must take into account the impact of cloud computing and web services when they consider monetization, access, and value-added services.

Acme Ecosystem Context

Mats and Jannis asked their teams to submit a list of contextual considerations most relevant to operating in the digital biosensor demand territory (see figure 42).

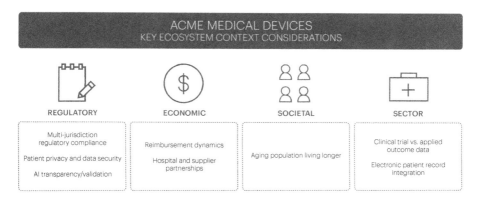

Figure 42. Ecosystem context considerations for proposition pivot

In the *regulatory* arena, multi-jurisdiction compliance and patient data security are ongoing concerns that must be addressed regardless of proposition. Regulatory demand for transparency and the validation of AI-derived care algorithms is an important development.

In the *economic* area, the expansion of supply chain partnerships has manifested itself in healthcare through hospital partnerships with life science companies. In the *societal* sphere, older adults living more active lives have altered conceptions of mobility, fitness, and health, with a profound impact on surgical viability and postoperative care. In the *sector* area, healthcare dynamics are changing so rapidly that it was hard for Mats and Jannis to decide what was most important.

Mats and Jannis settled on three issues: the growing replacement of controlled clinical studies with real-world, observed patient outcome data; the lack of integration between IoT device data, outside-the-hospital patient behavior data, and electronic medical records; and changing reimbursement dynamics that reward beneficial outcomes above all others.

ARTICULATE THE PROPOSITION

The proposition statement consists of a promise, differentiators, enablers, and foundational elements. Together they define the value a company will deliver to become the preferred supplier in a chosen demand territory.

To formulate the statement, leaders must first decide which of the proposition building blocks they will rely on to win in the demand territory; that is, which building blocks are most likely to drive competitive advantage. Competitive advantage comes from superior differentiation, focus, or cost competitiveness.[4] Differentiation is created by providing a unique and better offering, focus by fulfilling the needs of a specific niche or segment of the market, and cost competitiveness by providing a consistently lower cost for offers while still providing the essential benefits customers seek. Leaders must make a conscious choice about which building blocks they will use to drive competitive advantage and where they will pursue competitive parity. Choosing is crucial so that leaders avoid trying to be all things to all customers and can marshal the resources to invest where they can win.

The promise and the differentiators in the proposition statement reflect the choice of building blocks the company will seek to turn into competitive advantage. The promise describes the unique nature of the solution and its most important benefits for customers. The differentiators represent the unique aspects of the solution—what makes it different from and superior to competitive alternatives. It's important to limit the number of building blocks; otherwise, you'll diffuse the focus on becoming exceptional where it matters most to customers. After all, no company, despite its size, can be great at everything. For example, Electrolux Professional's cooking appliances differentiate through Electrolux's "chef-driven design" that relies on the company's expertise in customizing kitchens for the world's leading restaurant chefs. "Innovative design" is the category building block that is most important to professional-cooking-appliance buyers, and "chef-driven design" is Electrolux's key value driver and source of differentiation. Differentiators such as "chef-driven design" often require supporting information (storytelling) to make them fully understandable to broader audiences.

Next, the company must define the enablers that will support its pursuit of competitive advantage. The enablers describe how the company will bring the differentiators to life. They are the reasons customers believe that the promise and the differentiators will be delivered consistently and with high quality. Some enablers are things the company can deliver right away, and some are things the company will launch in the future. Enablers change and develop over time. Electrolux's key enablers are its relationships with professional chefs, the database it has built over time on how to meet the needs of chefs, and its dedication to advancing new methods of and practices in food preparation.

The foundational elements complete the proposition statement. Fulfilling these elements is essential for competing: for delivering on the proposition and for performing on a par with the competition. But foundational elements are not differentiating. With them, the company needn't strive for competitive superiority; it just needs to roughly match its competitors. Still, it is important that the foundational elements be explicitly stated in the proposition so that everyone in the organization stays mindful of their importance and customers are always aware of the company's fundamental capabilities. For Electrolux Professional, durability in tough kitchen environments, safety for the cooking and serving teams, precise temperature control, and reliable repair and service support are all foundational.[5] They are crucial to delivering the proposition, but they are also benefits that other leading competitors provide. If it slips in durability, Electrolux Professional loses customers. But choosing to win on durability is not a path to sustainable advantage because manufacturing advances are so easy to copy.

The proposition statement forces two types of decisions:

▶ **Competitive advantage.** What will we do to address the most important customer priorities in a unique and relevant way that will set our experience apart from the competitors? For example, if information about the status of their surgical implant is important to customers at different steps in the patient journey, how will Acme differentiate itself in this area—by providing this data on a real-time basis, in monthly updates, through the nursing staff, or directly online?

▶ **Hierarchy of benefits.** What is the relative importance of each proposition element? What will we promise and be known for? (This promise needs to be relevant and motivating to the customer.) What will differentiate us? (Here, we must win against the competition.) What are the key enablers? (We must identify how we will bring the differentiators to life.) What are the foundational elements? (In these, we needn't surpass the competition; we must just be strong enough to execute and allow no gaps that could sink our proposition or give competitors a window.)

Acme Value Proposition

Mats and Jannis advised Alison, the CEO, and the board that Acme needed to make a major pivot into a new customer value proposition. Part of the reason was the growing difficulty of competing in their core business—manufacturing surgical implant devices—and selling them globally to surgeons and hospitals. Data-driven commoditization had enabled low-cost, price-oriented competitors to gain a foothold and grow share at Acme's expense, while pressuring margins across the entire category. Continuing commoditization was likely over the next decade. The other reason was the potential of the biosensor demand territory. It was attractive and appealing because it offered manageable uncertainty and the opportunity to win in a large potential market with high margins. The prospect of winning and profitably growing in this demand territory was significant. The entire executive team and the board believed that Acme had the capabilities and the head start it needed to lead in this emerging territory.

Alison got the board's approval to launch a value proposition pivot that would transform Acme from a provider of advanced surgical implants to a solution provider of self-monitoring biosensing implant systems for better living. Self-monitoring implant systems report on the patients' ability to function and keep track of their own performance. They can request patient behavioral changes, such as alerting a patient to stretch or encouraging them to rest, and they can provide alerts on the device's status, such as needing to charge the battery or indicating a sensor needs to be recalibrated. Over time, the capabilities of the sensors will expand, from monitoring device performance to monitoring the performance of the organ in which the device has been inserted. The benefits of self-monitoring implant systems to cost of care and patient outcomes will grow as well, as the devices become increasingly capable.

The first system Acme Medical Devices will launch will place sensors in the body that relay implant performance metrics via IoT to patients and physicians. Over time, Acme's biosensor offering will expand from reporting on the performance of the device and the functionality of one part of the human body (such as the performance of a knee replacement) to also reporting on indicators of overall human health, such as blood chemistry and hormone levels.

Here is the summary of Acme's proposition statement Alison provided to the board (see figure 43).

The promise. It's forward looking and articulates the patient outcome and total cost-of-care benefits as the reasons to shift from standard implants to self-monitoring systems.

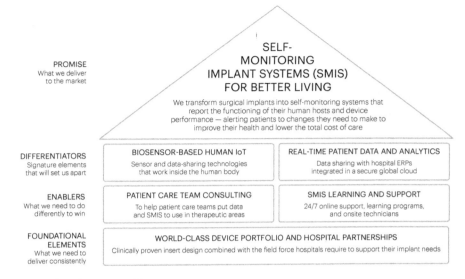

PROMISE
What we deliver
to the market

SELF-MONITORING IMPLANT SYSTEMS (SMIS) FOR BETTER LIVING

We transform surgical implants into self-monitoring systems that report the functioning of their human hosts and device performance — alerting patients to changes they need to make to improve their health and lower the total cost of care

DIFFERENTIATORS
Signature elements
that will set us apart

BIOSENSOR-BASED HUMAN IoT	REAL-TIME PATIENT DATA AND ANALYTICS
Sensor and data-sharing technologies that work inside the human body	Data sharing with hospital ERPs integrated in a secure global cloud

ENABLERS
What we need to do
differently to win

PATIENT CARE TEAM CONSULTING	SMIS LEARNING AND SUPPORT
To help patient care teams put data and SMIS to use in therapeutic areas	24/7 online support, learning programs, and onsite technicians

FOUNDATIONAL ELEMENTS
What we need to
deliver consistently

WORLD-CLASS DEVICE PORTFOLIO AND HOSPITAL PARTNERSHIPS
Clinically proven insert design combined with the field force hospitals require to support their implant needs

Figure 43. Value proposition statement

Differentiators. Acme R&D has already taken the lead in biosensor technologies. Real-time data and analytics are so crucial for delivering the total cost-of-care benefits that they are as important as the core technology and a key focus for Acme.

Enablers. Such a technologically advanced proposition requires services, learning, and technical support to pivot, by adding new consulting services and moving learning and tech support online.

The foundational elements. Acme's implant portfolio and hospital relationships are the foundation for success. But as the company's biosensors become able—as they must—to monitor competitors' implants, Acme's implant portfolio may shrink in importance over time.

Why does a proposition statement work so well? First and foremost, because it gives leaders a structured way to examine their options. It also organizes their choices and puts them in a hierarchy. Typically, we advise companies to have no more than three differentiators, three enablers, and three foundational elements. The proposition statement forces leaders to choose what they will do that will make a major impact on target customers. The proposition statement is a great litmus test. Alternative propositions can be constructed in a parallel form and tested among customers and other stakeholders before refining the final proposition.

ALIGN THE ORGANIZATION

The most important step in building a value proposition is enlisting the support of senior leaders by asking them to complete and endorse the proposition statement. Here's where growth leaders must lock in their decisions on how they plan to beat the competition in building block areas that are most important to their customers.

Leadership teams find it easy to talk about their need to focus. But—to put it plainly—they have a hard time putting their money where their mouths are. Even the most objective, team-oriented leader doesn't want to concede to peers that his or her area of the business may be better off just trying to stay even so that resources can be devoted to building differentiation in more significant areas. In organizations with a competitive culture, this often becomes a personal battle for resources. In addition, there is a widespread misperception among leadership teams that spreading resources across the organization is a form of risk management in the same way that a diversity strategy reduces risk for personal investors. Substantial evidence shows that the opposite is true. Differentiated and focused capital investment strategies, particularly for innovation, are more effective in gaining shareholder support and producing growth.

As the salient aspects of a winning proposition begin to emerge and leaders start finalizing the entire proposition, they must resist several common tendencies:

▶ **Product myopia.** Many leaders fail to change their orientation from a product to a solution mindset, a necessary shift in a data-driven world. This failure comes from having difficulty shifting from inside-out thinking to outside-in thinking. To do so, you must first ask, "What does the customer want to accomplish?" and then "What are we able to offer, given our capabilities?"

- **Including too much.** People tend to overload the proposition with too many elements. Often the additions are well intentioned, such as acknowledging every leadership team member's pet agenda item in order to build consensus. However, the more elements you add, the more the essentials get lost and the important choices get obfuscated.

- **Being too vague.** When a proposition isn't precisely worded, it's not actionable. Although you want to allow for flexibility, you don't want ambiguity, which leads to confusion and makes it hard for leaders and teams to take decisive action.

- **Being too wordy.** Propositions need to be concise enough to communicate clearly to customers and other stakeholders. The elevator test is helpful here; if you can explain your value proposition to a customer in the time it takes to get from the ground floor to the twentieth floor, you've nailed it.

DEFINE HOW TO IMPLEMENT

The proposition statement certainly helps leaders define the value proposition, but it needs more to define how the proposition will be implemented. For example, Acme Medical Devices' proposition calls for real-time data and analytics. But in delivering real-time data and analytics, the devil is in the details. Will the database be open so that hospitals using the company's tools can interrogate it? Or should it be closed, residing on Acme platforms and accessible to hospital customers only through Acme consultants and Acme analytic tools? Getting senior leaders, a typically opinionated group, to align on these crucial decisions can be a challenge. Robust and rational discussion based on the facts is critically important. Proposition pivots often involve adopting a new business model or solutions, and often, leaders struggle to recognize their options or lack the personal experience to evaluate them.

Our clients have had great success with a "support selector tool" that provides outside-the-category examples to illustrate and trigger discussion of important delivery decisions. Outside-the-category examples help leaders quickly and transparently come to grips with the implications of the delivery choices within their own category. They also help depoliticize the discussion of delivery options that so often clouds such decisions.

The support selector tool presents a set of choices for each important operating decision to be made. The options are illustrated with examples that make them accessible and easy for decision makers to understand and that stimulate dialogue, debate, and alignment. The selector tool helps leaders shed their preconceptions and biases by stepping outside their own frame of reference to conduct a fact-based examination of similar case examples. People with different perspectives can see the strategic implications of their choices more clearly by viewing them through the lens of other companies that faced similar choices but chose different paths.

Acme Proposition Delivery

In thinking through the options for monetizing Acme's self-monitoring implant system for maximum profitability, Xi, Acme's CFO, faced a difficult choice (see figure 44). Alison, the CEO, was at first inclined to stick with the current pricing model: an all-in product sale where revenue is captured through a single transaction at the time of shipment. Mats and Jannis favored a software-as-a-service model that called for collecting revenue on a monthly subscription basis. The analysis of Xi's finance team found no clear advantage for either revenue-capture option—or even for a hybrid option that involved collecting an up-front fee followed by monthly subscription revenues. The decision on the monetization model was therefore not financial but strategic, based on what would be best for the customer and for future initiatives.

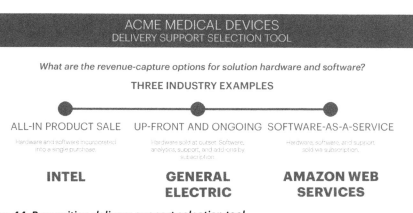

Figure 44. Proposition delivery support selection tool

Using the support selector tool reminded Alison, Mats, Jannis, and Xi that their monetization decision would have important implications for Acme's pivot and its operating model. The all-in product sale model was problematic because customers might be reluctant to pay for software upgrades or remote monitoring services, thinking these were already included in the all-in price. The software-as-a-service model would entail major conversion costs and cash flow challenges over a period of approximately one year as Acme moved from its current product-sale model to a subscription model. Acme could not afford such a level of business disruption. The up-front and ongoing model illuminated a path for charging for the sensors and implants up front and using a subscription model to earn monitoring revenues.

MAKE THE CASE FOR IMPACT

No new B2B proposition is complete without proof of impact: it's what buyers use in making their decision to purchase. The challenge is proving impact for something that doesn't yet exist. Here, you need to think of proof of impact as something that grows over time and helps set buyers' expectations. Early adopters don't expect every "i" to be dotted and every "t" crossed. They are looking for evidence from research, from the logic of your proposition, and from experts that their investment in time, people, resources, inventory, and the capital to buy your solution will be worthwhile. They are also looking for assistance in managing the risks of conversion to the new solution. Programs to help buyers pay for the cost of transitioning from their current suppliers to your new proposition, along with performance guarantees, can reduce their perceived risks and thus support the case for impact.

The first evidence of impact is that you actually have a case. We're not being glib; it's remarkable how many companies go to market in B2B environments with new offers and solutions that provide only a description of new features, leaving it to the salesperson to invent the benefits and the buyer to assess the potential impact. Merely having an impact case can be a point of differentiation.

Strong evidence of impact includes ascribing measurable value to the full range of benefits. In that sense, value isn't limited to immediate cost savings through unit price or better discounts. To envision the full scope of customer impact, create a benefit ladder. This visualization tool works as well for narrow point-solution propositions as it does for broad solutions from an entire business unit. Impact laddering entails taking what a solution does and converting it into a logic flow diagram that shows what it delivers for the customer and what outcomes it generates for the customer's business. The full range of outcomes includes intermediary as well as end-customer outcomes and can also include cost or risk avoidance, as well as incremental gains.

Acme Impact Ladder

Jannis and Mats undertook an impact-laddering exercise to help them assemble an impact case for the various decision makers among their target customer constituency: hospital administrators, purchasing professionals, surgeons, physicians, and insurance companies (see figure 45).

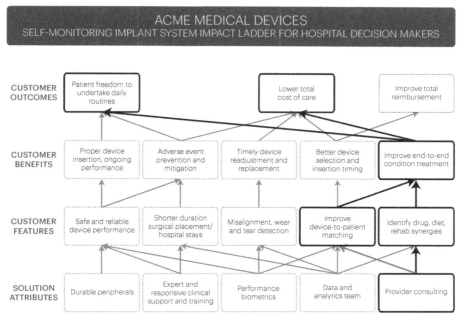

Figure 45. Proposition benefit impact ladder

Mats and Jannis started at the bottom of the ladder by breaking out the attributes of the solution, such as a consulting service for care providers, and then asking, "What specifically does this do for the customer?" In the case of provider consulting, it allowed physicians to more precisely match the right device to the patient and hospital care teams to identify drug, diet, and rehab programs that would work best with the device. Jannis and Mats then had to depict the customer benefits and the outcomes those benefits produced. For example, better device matching improved end-to-end patient treatment, which resulted in a lower total cost of care for the hospital and greater patient freedom in carrying out their daily routines. The impact ladder enabled Mats, Jannis, and Xi to quantify the total cost-of-care improvement for each hospital that adopted self-aware inserts. The ladder also revealed other outcomes. These outcomes include generating more reimbursement revenue for the hospital, improving patients' quality of life, recruiting new patients to the hospital, and hiring talented physicians who want to work in advanced areas such as implants.

Reducing the range of uncertainty is another kind of evidence of impact. As the adage goes, few company buyers are ever fired because they failed to save a few cents per unit, but shut down a line or harm employees because of a buying decision—that will get you fired. Guarantees, quality assurance programs, preinstallation verification, 24/7 support teams, on-demand call centers, and a host of other techniques can go a long way toward easing the fear of failure, no matter how unlikely the fear is. Having these assurances in place is, in fact, evidence that the company backs its own pivot and truly believes in it.

In making the case for impact, it is critically important to define the financial impact clearly and precisely. One common challenge suppliers face is getting buyers to switch from a simple per-unit cost savings metric (which is how most procurement models measure value) to looking at their organization's total cost to serve, the impact on the value of their customer, and the return on the investment in buying the solution. It is also important to incorporate metrics into the solution so that buyers can measure impact themselves. Total cost to serve and lifetime customer value metrics are not always easy for buyers to obtain for their organization or business unit. Suppliers may need to help buyers put these metrics in place and assist in conducting analysis to assess their progress and draw their own inferences.

As important as it is to project impact, you never want to let insufficient data stop you. Buyers recognize that no one can know the future with certainty. One has to make assumptions. It's OK to be a little wrong as long as the assumptions are reasonable, are transparent, and have a logical rationale. There are several ways to build assumption-based impact estimates. One is to use sensitivity analysis based on base, low, and high scenarios that help buyers account for data uncertainty. The other is to work in partnership with the buyer to build projections based on their own data and make estimates together when data gaps occur. Even though the buyer's estimates may be inaccurate, the buyer's participation adds a level of credibility that can go a long way toward making them feel confident about the impact.

3.4

What to Do in the Digital Proposition Pivot

Put the Proposition Pivot Strategy into Action via Growth Moves

As soon as the value proposition is tested among customers and agreed on by leaders, it's time for execution to begin. This point represents a critical juncture for leaders. They've raised expectations within the organization by completing the strategic work of How to Win, but they've not yet launched anything to bring the strategy to life and answer the question of What to Do. They must move quickly to deliver a series of growth moves to the market.

A growth move is an in-market initiative that delivers part of the new value proposition. In other words, a growth move brings a new value proposition to life. Michelin's introduction of the Michelin Tire Care solution for small fleets is an example of an individual growth move. Michelin's launch of a tire subscription service for large fleet owners is another.

Growth moves have both an internal and external impact. Internally, preparing for launch marshals the organization to shift its business model and build new capabilities. The urgency and immediacy of a launch deadline helps the organization accelerate its pace and sharpen accountability. Externally, the launch of growth moves produces an immediate impact on consideration, purchase, and loyalty. Customers' and other stakeholders' perceptions of the company change, and they are more prepared for and ready to adopt each subsequent growth move.

Companies that are most successful in making a Proposition Pivot launch a sequence of growth moves. Each growth move builds on the previous one, bringing more of the entire proposition to life. It's important to not view the digital proposition pivot as a one-and-done event. It is a transformation that must be brought to the market through a steady flow of innovative moves.

As we described in the introduction, "Digital Transformation and Uncommon Growth in B2B," Adobe is a great example of a B2B company that made a successful digital proposition pivot by transforming its core offering, the Adobe Creative Suite of prepackaged design software, to the Adobe Creative Cloud. This was just one of several growth moves that Adobe has made as part of their pivot into cloud-based subscription solutions.[1] Just one year before the Adobe Creative Cloud launch, the company premiered the Adobe Marketing Cloud of marketing and web analytics software. It integrated the software and technologies Adobe had acquired in Omniture into an integrated, cloud-based suite of eight major applications. Adobe followed the launch of the Adobe Marketing Cloud with a growth move that introduced mobile capabilities to its Marketing Cloud to enable analytics of smartphones and mobile devices. More growth moves are on the way as Adobe leverages its recent acquisitions—Magento, to add e-commerce applications, and Marketo, to enhance marketing automation applications—into what has become the Adobe Experience Cloud. Adobe's moves to expand its digital experience business illustrate the dual benefits of growth moves. On one hand, these moves bring innovation to the market, increasing revenue, and bolster competitive advantage. Beyond that, they build capabilities and shift the business model to one that's primed to deliver more innovation (with more valuable features) to the market faster.

Growth moves needn't be new solution launches. Adobe's shift to subscription pricing was a major growth move, as was its 2019 launch of Adobe Sensei, an AI-based marketing analytics enhancement.[2] A package of important usability and security enhancements Adobe made to the Experience Cloud is yet another growth move. What defines a growth move is simply that it realizes an important aspect of the value proposition in the market in a way that makes a significant impact on customers.

IDENTIFY GROWTH MOVES

Growth moves can be the launch of new solutions, new ancillary services, customer experience innovations, and new ways of monetizing customer benefits or other adjustments to the business model. Business leaders should also identify a few quick wins that can be taken to market rapidly and require relatively little investment while identifying growth moves. Quick wins can build momentum and signal to the rest of the organization that a proposition shift is formally underway.

Because growth moves are innovations that bring the proposition pivot to life, it makes sense that a company would identify them using the innovation best practice of searching for ideas from multiple sources, such as:

- **The pipeline.** Are there important innovations or acquisition plans for innovation already in development (or in the pipeline) that could be digitized, data-enabled, or repurposed to fit the proposition pivot? Can digital technologies and data enhance the value of innovation, lower their cost, or deliver data that will lead to further improvement or greater interoperability with other solution components?

- **Barriers.** Are there any major constraints or norms in the category that can be reshaped or rethought so the proposition can be fulfilled to customers' benefit?

- **Analogs.** Are there ideas from outside the category that can be imported and applied? Or are there any valuable innovations inside the category that can be obtained via corporate acquisition, licensing, or partnership?

► **Organic ideas.** Can existing organic innovation processes and concept development approaches be infused with data and digital thinking? Do innovation leaders and facilitators need retraining? Are there any tools and frameworks that would benefit from a redesign, or digital talent gaps that require filling?

Identifying potential growth moves is rarely a problem. Most companies already have a portfolio of good ideas just waiting to be resourced. For those without one, front-end innovation tools and methods such as crowdsourcing, brainstorming, design-thinking immersion sessions, and concept safaris are relatively easy to access or set up.

Acme Potential Growth Moves

Alison, Acme's CEO, was eager to get started plotting potential growth moves. She convened the senior leadership team, along with several of Acme's best salespeople and select go-to-market leaders from tech support, physician training, marketing, and supply chain. The group identified growth moves in four categories (see figure 46).

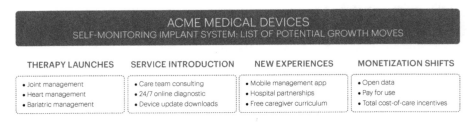

Figure 46. Potential growth moves for proposition pivot

Therapy launches. The launch of Acme self-aware devices into each therapeutic area was the most important growth move in terms of generating profitable revenue growth and seizing leadership in a niche of the biosensor demand territory. However, each launch would take significant capital and resources. The team prioritized three must-win therapeutic areas (by size and growth potential) where Acme already had considerable implant device expertise.

New services. These ideas sprang from thinking through how the devices could generate additional revenue streams and break the current product paradigm in surgical implants. The consulting service launch would be an important enabler of the introduction of Acme's solutions into each therapeutic area. Other services could follow, as their timing was not crucial to an early-stage win.

New experiences. These consisted of new ways that Acme and hospital decision makers and physicians could interact. Hospital partnerships were Acme's top priority in the first year of launch. Partnering with care teams was essential to codifying proper surgical implantation procedures and building best practices for the ongoing use of these self-aware devices.

Monetization shifts. These were important for ensuring that patients could afford Acme's solutions and that insurance companies would reimburse a large portion of the costs. A pay-as-you-go pricing scheme and total cost-of-care incentives were important for accomplishing these goals.

TURN GROWTH MOVES INTO ACTION

Turning growth moves into action is hard work. It is also the point where most growth moves get bogged down. Every growth move comes with its own set of requirements, contingencies, and constraints. Moves must be sequenced so that the enterprise can gain momentum with customers while building the capabilities and adjusting the business model to make the next growth move. A minimum viable product (MVP) mindset is extremely helpful for dealing with the size and complexity of launching growth moves. MVPs force development and launch teams to focus on the essentials—zeroing in on what matters most to the customer and what advances the company's success.[3]

Lean Canvas, a tool developed by Ash Maurya based on the thinking of Alexander Osterwalder, applies MVP and the spirit of the Lean Startup approach (Fast, Concise, and Effective) to building customer-centric growth moves and to guiding their rapid delivery to the market.[4] The Lean Canvas blueprint defines a growth move, describes its context, and specifies the resources needed to undertake it. The context clarifies when the move will happen, the goals and outcomes of the move, its target buyers and users, key customer insights, and desired brand and business impact. The Canvas also includes KPIs and questions for testing and learning, and specifies the key execution and resourcing considerations, costs, and investment needs.

Lean Canvas blueprints are living documents that follow each growth move from development all the way to launch. Like an engineer's blueprint, they are annotated and updated as the move progresses through each stage of development. Frequent updating ensures the Lean Canvas can keep the team centered on achieving the goal—delivering the move to the market in a way that brings the customer value proposition to life.

Acme Growth Move Lean Canvas

Mats realized that his sales team was ill equipped to be able to persuade key hospital decision makers to adopt self-monitoring solutions. A new care team consulting model of support for the patient care team of internists, nurses, primary care physicians, and surgeons was in order. The consulting team needed to partner with the care team to undertake tasks that were unfamiliar to the sales team, such as identifying appropriate candidates for a device, assisting with preoperative preparation, sharing best practices for surgical theater procedures, and delivering postoperative care and post-discharge patient support. These tasks are crucial to making sure the use of self-monitoring devices is efficacious and safe. Support in executing them is important for putting patient care teams' minds at ease so they will be willing to recommend the new solution to appropriate patient candidates.

As Mats worked through the Lean Canvas with Jannis, the two realized that this growth move would take more than just hiring people with consulting expertise (see figure 47). It required a concerted recruitment effort, extensive training and support for the new consultants, and piloting the consultant-patient care team engagement model. It also required optimizing ROI, measuring impact, engaging a wide array of partners inside the Acme organization, and making a multimillion investment that started modestly in the first year but became a double-digit investment by year two.

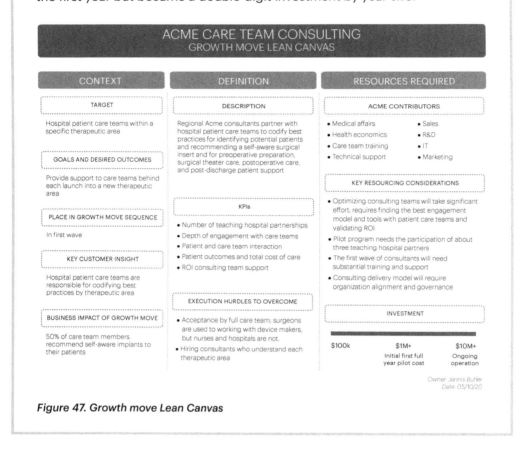

Figure 47. Growth move Lean Canvas

OVERCOME CONVERSION COSTS

Growth moves must include mechanisms to help customers cope with the cost, effort, and disruption of switching from their current supplier and ways of working to new inputs and processes. Too often the sales and tech support team are left holding the bag and asked to sort out issues, such as what to do with existing supplier inventories, without an increase in funding or resources. When conversion costs are not properly sorted, they become a barrier to purchasing or participating in the growth move.

A customer conversion plan helps buyers forecast the costs of transitioning to a new solution and helps them minimize or avoid these costs when the time comes. It also helps customers anticipate and overcome the inevitable hurdles they will encounter in transitioning to a new solution. To create a customer conversion plan, the supplier helps the buyer lay out the current portfolio of supplied products and services as well as the processes, training, inventory, systems, data, and people used to deploy them. The supplier then depicts how the portfolio will change and what the changes to processes, training, inventory, systems, data, people, and systems configurations will look like post-adoption. The differences between the current configuration and the new configuration can show up in a number of places in the customer's operation:

- Assets, such as inventory or equipment, that must be replaced
- People who must be retrained, hired, or reassigned
- Processes that must be redesigned or invented
- Systems that must be installed, retired, or integrated
- Data that must be gathered, reconfigured, made secure, and repurposed

In making the transition to a new value proposition, there will always be some ambiguity and uncertainty. But once the supplier and customer can identify most of the work to be done and where it happens, the supplier is ready to tackle the final step in the conversion plan: figuring out how to help the customer pay for the conversion, minimize disruption to their day-to-day operations, and obtain benefits from the new solution as quickly as possible. In some cases, particularly with early adopters, supplier-provided subsidies, loans, or co-investments are often appropriate. Conversion plans don't necessarily require incentives; their value comes from helping the customer see what's ahead, plan for it, and through planning, avoid waste and disruption during the transition.

Acme Customer Conversion Plan

Mats and the sales team targeted teaching hospitals for the first wave of Acme's Self-Monitoring Implant System launch into cardiac care. Teaching hospitals, they reasoned, are amenable to new products and services and are willing to invest their own resources in making them successful. Mats took the lead in conversion planning by developing a pilot plan with Aristotle

Medical Center, a leading teaching hospital that could help Acme develop a template for other teaching hospital customers (see figure 48). Although the plan's projected improvement in total cost of care for Aristotle was attractive, Aristotle's leaders felt they would need help with their conversion—in the form of forecasting, planning, and financial assistance.

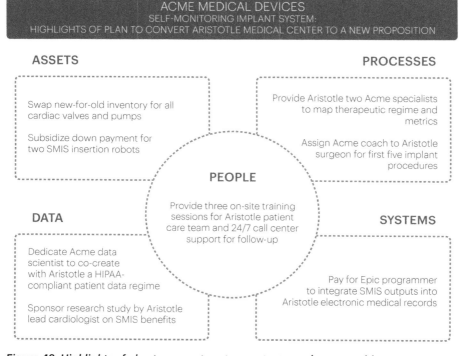

Figure 48. Highlights of plan to convert customers to new value proposition

The conversion plan called for swapping out old inventory and subsidizing a down payment on two insertion robots, as well as dedicating a variety of resources to Aristotle in the form of data science, programming, consulting, coaching, training, and tech support. Acme's investment would be offset by the revenues from the SMIS cardiac care system, the sale of the robots, and the support and training costs built into its cost assumptions on the SMIS P&L. Acme leaders were willing to invest in Aristotle's conversion because making the first few client adoptions a success is crucial to any growth move. It establishes a company's reputation in the market, while providing a platform for learning and optimization that can lower costs and boost impact later in the rollout.

CHART GROWTH ROAD MAP

Once a company develops and launches a growth move, it can now undertake a series of in-market initiatives that put competitors on the defensive as they struggle to keep up with each successive initiative. When sequenced well, each move builds on the previous one and enables the next. Pacing the moves requires executive judgment, and it demands that the entire organization understand how they can contribute; that's why a two- to three-year road map is a good idea. When Monsanto pivoted from being a seed and fertilizer manufacturer to providing a data, software, and input solution for crop-yield management, it made several growth moves in a well-thought-through sequence. The company deployed a field force of crop-yield advisors; launched Climate Basic and Climate Pro, applications that use satellite weather data and analytics to map farm microclimates; launched data and testing services through its new solution, Solum; and rolled out Climate FieldView, a cloud data and software platform for farmers that integrates their data and uses predictive modeling to improve crop yields.[5] All of these moves took place once Monsanto acquired Climate Corporation—an acquisition that profoundly changed the nature and pace of the company's pivot.[6]

Acme Growth Roadmap

With Jannis's assistance, Alison, Acme's CEO, guided the Acme senior leadership team and the board through the charting of a three-year growth road map (see figure 49). The road map sequenced Acme MD's growth moves so that each move built on the last one and established capabilities that were prerequisites to the next move.

The team designated three major SMIS launches for March of each year. They started with a cardiac care offering for two reasons. Acme's technology was the most advanced in this area. In addition, data readouts from implanted heart pumps had already conditioned surgeons and patient-care teams to the requirements for productive application and the changes in treatment regimens needed to ensure patient efficacy and safety. Each of the three launches is tied to an important enhancement.

SELF-MONITORING IMPLANT SYSTEMS FOR BETTER LIVING

BIOSENSOR-BASED HUMAN IoT	REAL-TIME PATIENT DATA AND ANALYTICS	PATIENT CARE TEAM CONSULTING	SMIS LEARNING AND SUPPORT

YEAR 1 | MARCH	YEAR 1 | SEPTEMBER	YEAR 2 | MARCH	YEAR 2 | SEPTEMBER	YEAR 3 | MARCH
Cardiac SMIS launch	Hospital partnerships	Bariatric SMIS launch	Mobile manager	Bone and joint SMIS launch
Care team consulting		Pay by use		Open data

Figure 49. Growth move roadmap

Care team consulting would accompany the cardiac SMIS launch because it is essential to adoption (in this and in every other therapeutic area). Pay by use would accompany the bariatric SMIS launch because follow-up monitoring is important to the success of bariatric corrective surgery but is usually not fully covered by insurers. The open data initiative is paired with the bone and joint SMIS because it is important for winning the support of the AO Foundation (Arbeitsgemeinschaft für Osteosynthesefragen), the board of leading surgeons that sets standards and best practices in the repair of bones and joints. In between the three major launches, Acme would introduce other offerings: a hospital partnership program and a mobile manager app. These would accelerate progress by enhancing the SMIS solution and extending access to more hospitals and patients.

3.5

Who Is Needed in the Digital Proposition Pivot

Enabling the Digital Proposition Pivot

igital Proposition Pivots depend on a cross-functional effort. For that reason, a transformation management office (TMO) is a necessity. Staffed by a cross-functional team to coordinate pilots, establish new governance routines, foster knowledge, develop talent, allocate resources, and undertake project management, the TMO is vital for accelerating the pivot and keeping it on track. At first, the TMO can be a one-person office, taking on more personnel as the nature and scope of the transformation expand.

ESTABLISH THE TMO

A TMO is far more than the typical project management office that tracks projects, coordinates resources, and facilitates planning. It plays five key roles (see figure 50).

Figure 50. *Transformation management office responsibilities*

▶ **Coordinating pilots and integrating capabilities.** The TMO serves as a coordinator for all pilots taking place throughout the organization. It helps develop methods and tools to ensure that pilots are indeed cross-functional efforts. The TMO taps the available capabilities and builds whatever ones are needed to fill gaps in pilot teams. It also ensures pilots have all the resources and support they need to succeed.

▶ **Instituting management routines.** The TMO establishes the key routines for leaders and teams—daily, weekly, monthly, quarterly, and annually. Whenever possible, it uses existing routines (such as weekly staff meetings or the annual planning process) as a starting point. The office helps develop measures, tools, and reporting procedures to ensure that leaders at all levels of the organization can monitor transformation progress and keep initiatives on track. New routines might need to be added; for example, when there is no system in place at the company for managing customer data and developing its future use.

▶ **Promoting knowledge sharing and development.** The TMO identifies useful methods and best practices from inside and outside the company. Working with the leaders of corporate learning and talent development, it holds forums to share knowledge and lessons learned.

- **Talent development.** For the TMO, this role is a delicate one. Talent development is most effective when handled by leaders in the business areas, with the help of HR professionals. In a transformation, however, the business and HR leaders may not be aware of the particular skills and capabilities that will be needed, because they won't necessarily understand the nuances of the new functions and roles. It's up to the TMO to anticipate the recruiting, learning programs, and organizational realignment that will be needed to supply the requisite talent for the transformation.

- **Project management.** Above all, the TMO keeps the entire effort on track by monitoring, planning, coordinating, and properly resourcing all of the activities of its team and by working with company divisions and functions to do the same.

Although these roles put the TMO in the center of the action, its team members do not carry out the actual work of the transformation. The TMO supports and advances the execution of the work associated with where to play, how to win, and what to do. If, however, TMO members begin to get involved, stepping in as resources themselves, the buy-in and commitment of the divisions and functions that need to own the work may wane as their responsibility and accountability is usurped by a central function.

MAKE THE TMO EFFECTIVE

Within the TMO's five roles, responsibilities can vary. The following best practices can be valuable in clearly delineating TMO roles and responsibilities.

- **Have the TMO report to a C-suite-level owner.** Unless the TMO reports to one senior executive who is accountable to the highest level of management in the organization, it will almost always fail. The C-suite-level owner is responsible for keeping other C-suite leaders informed and holding them accountable to hold regular transformation updates, receive input, and accelerate change in their areas of accountability. Division-wide transformations must do the same within their divisions but must also provide reports at the enterprise level so that leaders in other divisions and corporate function leaders are informed and can support the transformation wherever possible.

▶ **Include subject matter experts, not just project management experts.** Beware of overemphasizing project management expertise. As valuable as project management skills are, it is important to include in the office professionals with subject matter expertise in the particular type of pivot, as well as functional expertise in governance, metrics, change management, and talent development. A big mistake companies often make is assigning TMO project managers to dedicated roles while the other professionals split their time between their normal responsibilities and the TMO. A small, dedicated team of multifunctional professionals is far more effective in running a TMO than larger teams staffed with part-time members.

▶ **Use outside experts to help build internal capabilities.** Often it's necessary to bring in outside consultants to provide expertise for the TMO because there may not be enough employees in the organization with transformation experience. When relying on outside experts, be sure to team them with a handful of savvy, experienced employees whenever possible. In addition, make sure they focus on capability building—establishing people skills and creating the learning and development mechanisms that the transformation requires. Over and over we see the same sad story: external consultants that get the job at hand done but fail to help the organization build capability so it can carry on independently after the consultants are gone.

▶ **Drive cross-divisional and cross-regional coordination.** Appoint an advisory panel to charter and coordinate pilots and knowledge-sharing sessions across the organization. This is especially helpful for large global enterprises. This panel is not meant to substitute for senior-level oversight and participation; it's simply a way to speed the TMO's work and make sure that those who are involved in executing the proposition pivot remain committed and engaged.

▶ **Provide career-building rewards.** Participation on a TMO team can be a career stopper. In some cases, the TMO ends up being the repository of corporate staff who were unsuccessful at the division level. In other cases, we've seen companies put together a dream team of the best and brightest whose participation in the TMO advanced their careers—while the next wave of TMO members gets stuck in the role for extended periods. To avoid wasting talent or burning people out, be sure to reward excellent work in the TMO, be clear about the expected duration of the assignment, and maintain a recruitment effort for TMO roles.

► **Fund the TMO.** To be successful, the TMO needs an adequate budget. Avoid the scenario where the corporate center funds the TMO just enough to get started and perhaps to launch a pilot or two then runs out of funds needed to sustain progress. Don't let the business or functional areas shirk their investment in the actual work of the transformation; that will result in an underfunded TMO that is trying to make things happen at the margins instead of driving real change. The commitment to fund the TMO by the divisions, functions, and regions—the areas of the company that make things happen in the market—is a sine qua non for transformation. It ensures these leaders are themselves fully committed to the transformation and vested in making it happen.

WIND DOWN THE TMO

The roles of the TMO should never wind down. Proposition pivots don't end; either they continue and expand or the market changes and the company must make its next pivot. However, the TMO should transition over time into a more permanent resource for the company. This new incarnation can take one of two basic forms. It can be a central group led by a chief customer officer or the chief operating officer, or it can be divided up into smaller groups that report to division presidents, connected through a coordinating council. Whatever form it takes, it must, of course, continue to meet the company's needs by providing ongoing support: by developing, coordinating, and integrating pilots, routines, knowledge, talent, and project management to carry out the transformation.

3.6

Key Digital Proposition Pivot Takeaways

The Digital Proposition Pivot may well be the biggest and most challenging of the three transformations described in this book. By definition, it disrupts the organization, and when successful, it disrupts competitors in the market and drives lasting competitive advantage. Because value propositions can exist at different levels in a company, it is important to recognize and clarify the scope of the pivot. Does it apply across the entire business or to only a single business unit? Starting a pivot in a small unit of the business, then expanding it to an entire division and finally throughout the entire enterprise can be an effective way to manage the risks that disruption brings. But pivoting in waves works only if the company has time. The forces of digital and data innovation—the very forces that precipitate the need to pivot—don't wait while companies carefully manage their risks.

Leadership teams that see the need to pivot before their competitors do hold a great advantage. They can take the extra time to get the pivot right—to manage risks, to test out alternatives—because they are driving disruption, rather than being on the receiving end. They also have room to get it wrong and then pivot again, because they can start their pivot on a small scale before committing the entire enterprise. Even if they fail, they gain a valuable asset: knowledge and insights about their customers.

The principles of a successful proposition pivot remain the same, whether the pivot is at the unit, division, or enterprise level; whether it is small scale or large scale; or whether it's designed to disrupt or to respond to disruption.

▶ Choose where to play by identifying an attractive demand territory where uncertainties are manageable and the company has the best ability to win. Make this choice based on a demand landscape informed by an understanding of the segments and based on closely examining the emerging demand drivers that bring change to a market.

▶ Determine how to win by building a compelling value proposition that makes a central promise to your target customers and includes clear choices about what the company will do to gain advantage and to establish a foundation for success. Back up the value proposition with a business case for customers and guidance for the organization on how to execute key aspects of the proposition.

▶ Accelerate what to do by assembling a road map of growth moves that bring the proposition to life through in-market launches. Support these growth moves by helping customers manage their conversion to your new solution.

▶ Ensure you have who is needed to make the proposition pivot by empowering a transformation management office to drive the transformation. Fund it, resource it, and make sure division and region leaders have a stake in its success.

Once the digital proposition pivot is underway, B2B companies almost always undertake the digital experience makeover and often must undertake the digital selling shift as well. That's because a digital value proposition pivot to a solution will inevitably change the customer experience and will usually change how sales teams work—enough to warrant a shift to digital selling. There is no right time to start a value proposition pivot. As we've stated before, companies facing disruptive change don't get to choose the timing. Companies that have the opportunity to drive disruption should start as soon as possible so they can extract maximum value from disrupting others.

Part 4

ENABLE DIGITAL TRANSFORMATION

Unleash the power of customer data and empowered employees to drive transformation

► The challenges of enabling digital transformation

► Use customer data more effectively

► Mobilize for employee enablement

► Seize uncommon growth

4.1

The Challenges of Enabling Digital Transformation

C-suite leaders report that the three greatest barriers to successful digital engagement are the lack of customer focus, insufficient employee enablement (which would include structural and cultural impediments as well as the usual shortfalls in skills and capabilities), and ineffective use of customer data[1] (see figure 51). Up until this point, the primary focus of this book has been prioritizing customers in digital transformation strategy and execution. We now turn to enabling employees and making more effective use of customer data. Enabling employees is a major challenge that requires building a customer-centric culture, gaining management and leadership buy-in to customer-centric transformation, and empowering employees to be more autonomous in delivering and innovating around customer experiences. Using customer data more effectively is an equally complicated challenge that calls for measuring customer value and the ROI of customer experience investments, integrating systems and data across channels and products, and making data more accessible and visible to functional areas.

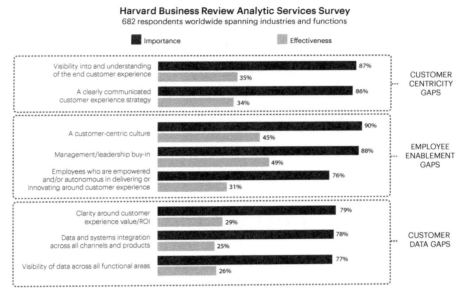

Figure 51. Key digital transformation enablers

It takes considerable attention on the part of senior leaders and middle managers to address these challenges because they are so multifaceted and extend so deeply within organizations. Large, game-changing investments, such as acquiring another company or investing in new technologies, are not the answer. Quite the opposite: they often exacerbate the challenges because people and data are so central to success. Fundamentally, leaders must help their organizations embrace change—change in the increasingly digital nature of work and change in how your employees see the customer and collect and use customer data.[2]

Embracing change, becoming more customer centric, and using big data are vast topics that are written about so extensively that it's beyond the scope of this book to deal with them in detail. Each involves a journey with many steps along the way, and no two journeys are alike.

In any digital transformation, the roles that data and employees play vary from business to business. The starting point for every company is different. But because data and employee enablement are so critical to success, we felt that addressing enablement would be useful to the reader, focusing on the aspects that are most germane to beginning a digital transformation. The next chapter focuses on data enablement and the importance of creating a customer data strategy to guide how the company collects, manages, and deploys data to support its digital transformation. In the subsequent chapter, we examine how organizational and cultural changes can prepare and support the workforce in executing a digital transformation.

4.2

Use Customer Data More Effectively

C ustomer data is the foundation for digital customer engagement. As such, it fuels the Digital Selling Shift, the Digital
Experience Makeover, and the Digital Proposition Pivot. But
using customer data effectively has proven challenging for
companies. There are so many types, sources, and uses of customer data
that companies become overwhelmed.

Constructing a complete 360-degree data view of customers' needs,
behaviors, and motivations is an ongoing process, not an end state that
can be achieved in a matter of months. Successful digital transformers
take a step-by-step approach to adding new data sources and putting
them to work. In doing so they build capabilities in data collection, storage, analysis, and deployment as the customer database grows larger,
richer, and more useful.

The most common misstep companies make is decoupling data collection from data use. They take pride in acquiring and assembling data and
building systems to store and manage it, without first thinking through
how it will be used to enhance the work their customers are trying to

perform. How the data will be applied should dictate how it is collected, and not the other way around. Discerning how richer data might improve or remake a customer experience and then finding ways to obtain that data is the key. Companies must connect market-facing functions (sales, customer service, call centers, and marketing) to those functions responsible for managing customer data (internal IT, data teams, and systems support) so that the two can collaborate.

Companies that have the foresight to look ahead to create and implement a customer data strategy are able to transform more quickly and more effectively. They are better able to uncover insights and turn them into action. In B2B, particularly in intermediated categories, a formal data strategy was rarely needed. The sales team or intermediaries would collect most customer data and use it for most customer interactions without sharing it broadly with the rest of the company. B2B companies would occasionally supplement the intelligence they received from their sales teams and intermediaries with field visits by headquarter staff and market research. In a world of data-driven solutions, this is no longer sufficient. Customers expect digital interaction with suppliers and are in fact wary of companies who do not provide digital access. Customers have been trained through all of their direct digital relationships with companies (in their work lives as well as their personal lives) to expect more online from their suppliers, even when dealing with them through intermediaries.

B2B companies seeking to utilize customer data more effectively (which ought to be nearly every B2B company) will benefit by implementing a data strategy. The benefit, moreover, will be immediate. You will develop capabilities and skills in data collection, management, analysis, and deployment—capabilities essential for future growth and competitiveness.

Building a data strategy is a step-by-step process that calls for the following:

- Taking inventory and connecting existing data

- Identifying customer data requirements

- Filling crucial customer data gaps

- Assembling the customer engagement stack

- Charting a data road map

TAKE INVENTORY AND CONNECT EXISTING DATA

A customer data strategy should start by identifying ways to make more effective use of the data already in the company's possession. Doing so will generate quick wins, which are the most persuasive way to make the case for a more significant investment in data use. It also gives leaders a preview of what it will take to build out the data strategy.

Most B2B company leaders are well aware that they already have a wealth of customer data buried within their business units and functional areas in formats that cannot readily be exported to the larger databases they rely on. (Indeed, some of the data isn't even in digital form.) To make better use of the data already on hand, companies must first inventory it, wherever possible connecting it and making it accessible to current users for their current applications (and even more quick wins).

A thorough inventory accounts for three data types: profiling data, behavioral data, and perceptual data.

▶ *Profiling data* describes the firmographics of the customer company and the characteristics of decision makers; it answers the "who are you" question. In a B2B company, profiling data is often kept by the sales force and functions such as shipping that interact directly with customers. It may also reside in financial functions that use it to qualify customers for pricing or incentives or to track sales tax treatment based on their profiles.

▶ *Behavioral data* describes what customers do. It includes everything from their transaction history to the channels they use and how they navigate the experience. Purchase records and financials are the most obvious source, but behavioral data also resides in customer relationship management (CRM) systems, customer service records, and sales and tech support systems, as well as in third-party databases that track online behavior.

▶ *Perceptual data* describes customers' goals, needs, and attitudes; it explains why they behave as they do. Perceptual data is often maintained by the market research, marketing, sales, or customer service teams, as they are the ones most likely to conduct customer surveys.

Together, these three types of data paint a 360-degree view of the customer (also called the "unified view" or the "single view" of the customer; see figure 52).

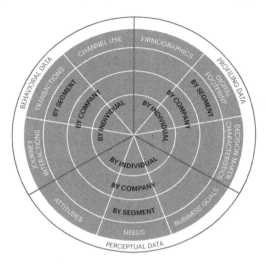

A 360-DEGREE VIEW OF THE B2B CUSTOMER

Figure 52. 360-degree view of B2B customer

Connecting the data relies on finding data "markers" that can tie different databases together. In B2B, the most common marker is company name. Many databases, such as revenue and cost databases and CRM databases, already include the company name. In other databases the company name can be inferred from the email address, phone number, or mailing address or the mention of the company name in a response to a question or in a social comment. The names of individual decision makers and influencers within a company can be obtained using the same approach. This can be very productive even if the data being linked is not as extensive. Just by knowing what company an individual is from can produce a quick win, by generating a lead or enabling a personal response to a request for information. Tying data for segments of customers uses this same inference approach. Here, tools to indicate or predict the segment can often be built that enable groupings by segment when only a few pieces of data are available.

IDENTIFY CUSTOMER DATA REQUIREMENTS

A customer data strategy should be customer driven.[1] It sounds self-evident, but it is often anything but. By this we mean the strategy relies on identifying the key interactions your company has with customers and is aimed at finding ways to use customer data to improve those interactions. Every type of customer interaction that can be improved is actually a use case for data; that is, for specifying customer data requirements, the use-case-based approach differs considerably from the data- and platform-led approaches that are common today. These approaches involve adding and combining different data types in systems and platforms to see how they enhance different business activities, including customer interactions. Because the combinations of new data and platforms are almost limitless, data- and platform-led approaches to setting data requirements must boil an ocean of possibilities. Customer-use-case based approaches are much quicker to develop and more actionable because they are centered on a narrower set of current and potential customer interactions.

Each of the three digital transformations described in this book reveal a set of potential use cases that can apply across different industries. We've assembled eighteen of the most frequently occurring ones. For example, in commercial insurance, medical devices, and software, customers and suppliers both can benefit from added data during the selling process or the service experience. The eighteen use cases (shown in figure 53) are not exhaustive, so it's worthwhile to seek out use cases that may be unique to a particular business. In commercial insurance, for example, the interaction of risk managers with customers about their future risk exposure is an important use case even though it is not described in the eighteen most common use cases.

COMMON CUSTOMER DATA STRATEGY USE CASES					
SALES		VALUE PROPOSITION		CUSTOMER EXPERIENCE	
CUSTOMER ACQUISITION	CUSTOMER LOYALTY	MARKET ENTRY	OFFER OF INNOVATION	CUSTOMER ENGAGEMENT	VALUE EXCHANGE
LEAD GENERATION AND SCORING	UPSELL, CROSS-SELL, UPGRADE	NEW GEOGRAPHIES	NEW PRODUCTS, SERVICES	CONTENT REDESIGN AND OPTIMIZATION	PRICING AND PROMOTION
TAILORED SELLING AND MARKETING	RETENTION AND FREQUENCY	NEW SEGMENTS OR INDUSTRIES	NEW DIGITAL SOLUTIONS	TOUCHPOINT OR SERVICE REDESIGN	VALUE-ADDED SERVICES
SALES TEAM ENABLEMENT	RECOMMENDATION AND PENETRATION	NEW CHANNELS OR E-COMMERCE	NEW BUSINESS MODELS	NEXT-BEST MOVE AND PERSONALIZATION	TOTAL COST TO SERVE/CARE

Figure 53. Common customer data strategy use cases

In defining their data requirements, companies need to take into account the ease and cost of data acquisition.

▶ *Profiling data* of B2B customers is usually easy to obtain. Databases containing firmographics and decision-maker characteristics are widely available and relatively inexpensive to build. Further intelligence, such as organization charts or the use of rival suppliers, can be obtained from sales teams or through tech support professionals who interact directly with customers. Data about a customer's digital footprint and its systems can be helpful to digital technology suppliers. But because it is not readily available for purchase, it may take some digging on the part of sales teams to unearth.

▶ *Behavioral data* of any kind can be challenging to obtain in the B2B world. Even with a straightforward transaction such as a purchase it can be difficult to know who made it, why, and for what purpose. Online B2B behavior data is similarly challenging. It's fairly easy to obtain the company name of an online user, but it is hard to know whether the behavior is that of a job seeker, a decision maker, or an influencer. The point is to connect individual behavior to company behavior. For example, recognizing a company's pattern for ordering corrugated boxes is relatively easy. But seeing a connection between a change in their ordering pattern and visits by the purchasing team to content on a website is harder to discern—but more valuable.

▶ *Perceptual data* is easy and inexpensive to collect from a sample of customers. You can discover what customers think, feel, need, and desire through surveys, interviews, and sales conversations, and by listening to their conversations online through social listening tools or offline via natural language processing apps that convert recorded conversations into data. Segmentation tools can group similar customers together and help you understand the perceptions of similar segment members to gauge their thoughts, needs, and feelings when it would be inappropriate to ask them directly.

FILL CRUCIAL CUSTOMER DATA GAPS

Data acquisition is all about building cost-effective and practical routes to filling in the most important data gaps. The gaps are relatively easy to identify: compare the inventory of data on hand with the data requirements generated from the customer data use cases. There are three ways to fill data gaps: by gathering data during customer interactions, by observing customers' online behavior, or by outright purchase.

With firmographic data, for instance, companies can collect data gleaned from sales interactions with customers. The sales force can be asked to use its knowledge to identify who decides what on customer management teams. Companies can always arrive at a similar result by buying data about senior executives from a source like D&B Hoovers, which can be filtered by job title.

Perhaps the most practical and cost-effective way to obtain data is to ask customers for it, within the course of a customer interaction. Here an important consideration comes into play: the value of a data exchange. Customers weigh the value of exchanging their data against the benefits they receive from providing it. Suppose a manager wants to download an industry report from a consulting company. If the manager is asked to provide minimal information and the report appears useful, the exchange is highly valuable and likely to occur. The consulting company could boost the value of this exchange by increasing the perceived benefits of downloading the report: revealing more of its contents in advance, adding extra features such as report updates, and providing testimonials from other report readers. The company could also lower the cost of the exchange to the visitor by making the questions easy to answer, promising to keep the visitor's data confidential, or committing to not follow-up with a sales pitch.

B2B companies can manage both sides of the data exchange with customers. On the cost side, they can be transparent to customers about the ways they plan to use the data, reassure them their data will not be abused or sold, make the data handover easy and quick, and focus on obtaining only the most crucial data. Companies can, and should, lower the cost to the customer of providing data by taking steps to ensure that customer privacy is respected and protected. They should see to it that there is sufficient security in place to protect data from hackers and unwarranted employee intrusion without making the data harder for the customer to access or use when interacting with them. On the benefit side, companies can offer rewards to customers who opt in by sharing their data. Rewards can take several forms. The most direct is to pay the customer for the data or to offer discounts on the supplier's offering to customers who share data. Another form of reward, and one of the easiest to implement, is to provide access to the supplier's data-derived insights in exchange for contributing data to inform them. Sharing customer trends or research is an example. Sharing other forms of helpful information or giving customers access to the supplier's resources can be a valuable reward to customers who share data. One of the best ways to reward data-sharing customers is to use their data to improve their experiences and interactions with you and to make sure the customer can see how their data contributed to the improvement. A simple way to accomplish this is by reducing the hassle to customers of repeatedly filling out the same personal information by using their stored data to prepopulate forms; another way is to recommend a service or product based on their profile.

The other main way to collect data is simply through observation. Observations can be made by an employee or online. A salesperson recording a sale, a conversation, or a service request is gathering observational data. An analyst could scan through customers' websites to learn (through requests for bids or proposals) what they buy, along with the rules for submitting bids. The explosion in customer data comes from observational data, which shows what customers do online by tracking what sites they visit, what engages them, and how they respond—and then linking it to actions they take later on.

A data acquisition plan for observational data needs to account for the platforms and tools that will be used to track all of this information and turn it into usable data. Should we acquire social listening software? Purchase a CRM program such as Salesforce, Marketo, or Eloqua? Add software to our website to track user time on the site? All of these questions must be answered, weighing the value of the data against the cost of the technology.

Beyond customer interaction and observation, the other main source of customer data is third-party providers. Companies can buy directly from one of the many B2B customer data providers, such as D&B Hoovers or TransUnion. Customer data is often bundled into an online purchase of a service or product. For example, when a B2B company places a paid search ad on an industry association's website, customer data might be rolled into the purchase. The company may also be asked (or required) to provide a link back to the association site or to share information with the association on their members' online behavior. The two-way nature of these exchanges highlights the importance of being mindful of the obligations implicit in the data exchange. Leaders must be careful to steer clear of conflicts of interest between the promises they make to customers to protect their data from third parties, and third-party vendors' desire to obtain user data for commercial gain.

As it turns out, most of the customer data that B2B companies acquire comes through direct requests from their customers and from observing them in one way or another. No matter what, the acquisition plan should evolve over time, as more tools for gathering observational data online become available—and as customers grow increasingly wary of sharing data without some sort of quid pro quo.

PUT IN PLACE PERSONAL DATA PROTECTION

One of the most sensitive data challenges that have emerged in recent years is the collection and use of customer data when the customer has an expectation of privacy. For example, customers who visit a supplier's facility expect that their data may be used when they sign in at the front desk, as long as the use is appropriate. They essentially give their permission for acceptable use in exchange for access. However, that same customer would not expect facial imaging software (whether in the lobby or elsewhere in the facility) to be used to classify them based on race, gender, or other observable traits—even though such use may be legal in itself, and even though tracking individuals in a facility via cameras is a legitimate security practice.

The challenge of respecting personal rights becomes even more complicated in cases when AI-based technologies generate new data such as predictions about future customer-buying behavior. The data sets used to construct the AI algorithms can be biased without the company realizing it. Suppose, for example, that predictions of future customer purchase were inadvertently based on the race of the purchaser. Preferential treatment, such as additional discounts or better credit terms, might be given based on race without the supplier being aware of the unfairness they were perpetuating. Susan Etlinger, an analyst at Altimeter who focuses on the business and ethical implications of AI, recommends approaching the use of big data and AI with a critical eye. The combination of data and intelligence, she says, is "a remarkable but blunt instrument." Though powerful, AI is prone to hidden bias. Because of the current limitations of machine learning technologies, it can also lead us to mistake correlation for causation. In assembling a customer data strategy, leaders should consider these issues and be sure to include human and digital monitoring in any application of AI.[2]

ASSEMBLE THE CUSTOMER ENGAGEMENT STACK

Building robust customer data is only half the data challenge executives say they face. The other half is putting that data to use assembling and integrating the systems and software platforms through what is known as the customer engagement stack. This is the array of systems that deliver content and experiences based on customer profiles and that collect customer data in the process. When a customer interacts with a B2B supplier's website or customer service mobile app, participates on a conference call with the supplier, talks to the supplier's call center, or receives a shipment from the supplier, that customer is interacting with the supplier's customer engagement stack.

The customer engagement stack consists of at least two layers of software that sit on top of a separate systems layer:

- ▶ **A user interface layer.** This is the software that the customer interacts with, enters data into, and receives a response from.

- ▶ **A foundational layer.** This is the software the customer never sees that performs the key functions of collecting data and inputs from the user interface layer. It links this data to achieve a 360-degree view of the customer, making decisions about the next best customer interaction (such as sending an automatic email) and delivering content and data to the user interface layer.

▶ **A systems layer.** This is the software that runs the computers, networks, servers, and underlying systems that make it all work. The transformation leader rarely has to worry about this layer, but the IT team does, so that the foundational and user interface layers have sufficient capacity to carry out their operations.

The stack does the work of interacting with prospects and customers. Building the stack requires thinking through how systems can work together to serve customers as efficiently and effectively as possible. As these platforms continue to move from company servers to cloud-based servers, many of the technical systems challenges companies once faced are being alleviated. The need to make big bets on inflexible long-term digital technology investments has also been reduced.

Figure 54 illustrates what a customer engagement technology stack looks like, using our fictional insurance company Acme Commercial Insurance.[3]

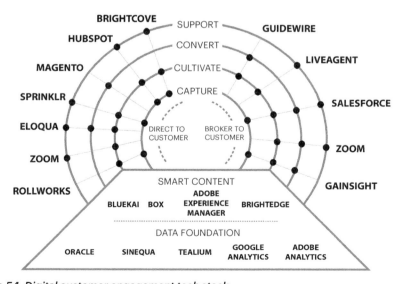

Figure 54. Digital customer engagement tech stack

As one might expect for an industry with so many different types of customers, Acme relies on numerous software applications to execute the many tasks required in customer engagement. Although visually complex, the stack is simple in structure: the circular part of the stack represents the *user interface layer*, which is organized around four rings, one for each of the major steps in a digital selling strategy: capture the customer's attention, cultivate their interest, convert their interest into buying and recommending to others, and support their needs after purchase. The user interface layer is further divided into the two main ways Acme interacts with customers: via commercial insurance distribution partners (broker to customer) and direct interaction (direct to customer). The *foundational layer* includes two main groupings: the Data Foundation for managing customer data and the Smart Content for managing content and delivering the right content to the right customer at the right moment in the experience.

A discussion of the specific platforms and tools for a given company to deploy is beyond the scope of this book; there are many potential vendors, and the features and benefits they provide evolve rapidly as their underlying technologies evolve. But it's worth underscoring the importance of three considerations that nontechnical leaders must be sure to address: functionality, data security and privacy protection, and metrics and dashboards.

▶ **Functionality.** What must the stack do at each key interaction with customers? That is, what types of content, tools, choices, prompts, and requests for input will the stack make at each interaction, and how will it respond to the customer? The "whats" of the customer interaction are the responsibility of business and functional leaders and their teams. The whats help determine the best software to acquire, systems configurations to establish, and underlying hardware to deploy. The transformation leader needn't manage the details of these choices; he or she must simply oversee the effort, focusing on what must change and improve for the sake of the customer and the business.

▶ **Data security.** This encompasses all of the considerations about how the data will be protected: how appropriate levels of privacy will be maintained and what rules must be established to avoid using the data in ways that don't align with customers' wishes, the brand's principles, or the company's values. Above all, these decisions should not be relegated to IT, legal, or other technical experts. Companies need the guidance of these experts, to be sure, but these areas require the involvement of leaders who are charged with building customer relationships and customer value. Clear governance and procedures, established from the top, are essential.

▸ **Metrics and dashboards.** These work in different ways depending on the needs of the leader or manager. Here, two best practices apply:

  ▸ *Differentiate outcomes from inputs.* When a problem arises, leaders and teams must understand its source: is it the strategy, or the execution of the strategy? If the inputs were correct and implemented as planned, but the outcomes did not achieve the objectives, then the strategy is to blame. All too often, however, the reason companies fall short of their objectives is poor execution. Companies need to systematically search for breakdowns in the flow from inputs to outcomes. That is the surest way to verify if execution was the problem, and where it went awry.

  ▸ *Distinguish between targeted impacts and secondary impacts.* Did targeted investments directly trigger behavior, perceptions, and outcomes, or was some other factor at work? Most companies judge the effectiveness of targeted investments based on overall sales gains in the period, without establishing a causal connection. It's important to segregate sustainable results, such as an improved loyalty score or an increase in the value of the customer base as opposed to immediate (and fleeting) spikes in sales. There is a big difference between a short-term incentive program that drives up the value of the customer base by adding new customers and a program that yields short-term gains through discounts to existing customers, which reduces the value of the customer base.

CHART A DATA ROAD MAP

The data road map sequences the initiatives required to fill the data gaps, securely provision data about customer interactions, build the customer engagement stack, enhance data analytics capabilities, and expand the application of data to new use cases over time. The road map is unique for each company because it must address the data use cases and because it depends on the company's starting point.

Developing the road map requires a robust assessment of the current state. The assessment must examine the breadth, completeness, accuracy, and usefulness of the data currently on hand, and how that data is being collected, deployed, analyzed, and secured. In effect, the assessment serves as a search for pockets of best practice and areas of weakness that must be addressed to ensure the digital transformation has the customer data needed to move ahead.

The data road map also requires corporate leaders to prioritize which use cases they will support today and in the near to distant future. The Where to Play chapters of the Digital Selling Shift, Experience Makeover, and Proposition Pivot transformations discussed the processes of identifying and prioritizing customer opportunities. These priorities determine which data use cases should be priorities—along with the practical consideration of how to sequence building the data enablement capabilities to support the use cases. Setting long-term data enablement priorities also requires envisioning how current and emerging technologies and tools will change the future data landscape. AI, virtual reality, and the IoT are examples of technologies that are becoming mainstream and influencing how data is put to use and what data should be collected in the near term, medium term, and long term. A strong data strategy looks ahead and anticipates what's next—including the implications for current investments, strategy, and execution.

The data road map represents the final step in building the customer data strategy. It combines data requirements with a current-state inventory and capability assessment to reveal gaps to fill as well as areas of strength to build upon. The most carefully conceived, well-wrought data requirements and the most robust customer engagement stack will expand and evolve continuously. As the organization gains capability and experience, it will be able to develop and implement new use cases for data faster and more effectively.

4.3

Mobilize for Employee Enablement

J ob one in mobilizing employee enablement is convincing transformation leaders to dedicate time and attention to this important task. Apart from pointing out what their peers in other companies might have learned about how important employee enablement is to a digital transformation, what can convince them that it is important enough to warrant their attention?[1]

At this stage of technological evolution, the most advanced technologies (AI included) may be able to observe and even predict certain types of customer behavior. But technology alone cannot explain why customers behave as they do. Employees who listen, watch, and pay attention to customers can. Employees who gain customer understanding can unlock plans and tactics for effective action that technologies cannot. In addition, B2B companies engage with their customers in so many different ways, at different times, and for different purposes, that only people can make sense of it all. Only people can design experiences, sales initiatives, or new propositions that synthesize different customer interactions into a comprehensible whole for serving the customer in the best way possible.

AI may be able to predict the future in limited circumstances, but it cannot envision new possibilities for the customer. Employees can. They can also fix customer issues in ways that technology has not yet learned to fix itself, and find workarounds that are beyond the scope of technology. Most important, employees remain, and will continue to remain for the foreseeable future, one of the most important touchpoints for customers in B2B. A digitally savvy employee ambassador can enhance customer value. An employee who is a digital laggard can damage customer value pretty quickly.

Employee enablement in the context of digital transformation is a broad and multidimensional subject, and one so open to interpretation that transformation leaders can easily get lost in the forest of possibilities. To help leaders focus on the digital transformation essentials, we've crystallized three primary employee enablement goals for leaders of a digital selling shift, an experience makeover, or a proposition pivot:

▶ To build employee ability to use the digital tools and data necessary for the given transformation. The extent of digital knowledge required will vary by function and role, but every transformation calls for some combination of training, hiring, rethinking job assignments, facilitating collaboration, and building team skills.

▶ To help employees learn how to listen to customers and address their needs. Data and digital technologies have expanded employees' ability to listen to an extent almost unimaginable in the predigital era—an ability that opens up a wide realm of possibilities for providing customer value, as long as employees can learn how to use these tools. Companies need to put in place the mechanisms that enable employees to observe how customers consume content online, to analyze their e-commerce buying behavior, to read their social media posts, and to conduct test-and-learn experiments.

▶ To cultivate a digital mindset, so employees think and act digitally in their work. The desired characteristics are those typically associated with digital start-up companies: moving quickly and with urgency, applying a test-and-learn approach to work, being entrepreneurial, always looking for ways to improve established processes and ways of working, being collaborative, and being vigilant in seeking opportunities to disrupt the status quo.

Enabling employees to develop their digital skills, listening abilities, and mindset is the responsibility of transformation leaders. But individual leaders cannot instill these improvements on their own. Employees must be open to change, and that is hard for most people—particularly those who worry that their contribution to the organization may no longer be valued or who simply see change as a threat to their position. Fostering employees' willingness to change and grow must be at the heart of any digital transformation.

It takes time and effort to enable employees. Senior transformation leaders must take several steps to mobilize the organization and build momentum that will boost enablement:

- ▶ Establish a common language for transformation.
- ▶ Assess employees' starting points.
- ▶ Build an employee value proposition.
- ▶ Chart an enablement road map.

ESTABLISH A COMMON LANGUAGE

Transformation leaders ought to clarify, for themselves as well as for employees, the aspects of the organization and culture that will (or could) change as part of the transformation. Doing so ensures that all the dimensions of organization and culture that are crucial to enabling the given digital transformation will be fully addressed. Clarifying the likely or possible changes also prevents miscommunication and mitigates the risk of alienating employees before the effort has even begun.

To provide clarity, leaders need a framework for thinking through all the different aspects of organization and culture that will enable the transformation. That framework should be simple and comprehensive enough that it can be used for all of the employees involved in the transformation. The framework can help leaders get beyond the obvious moves, such as recruiting or training, to tackle a full enablement agenda, which includes many less apparent changes in such areas as job assignments, performance, metrics, and incentives. Although changes in these areas are not always clear at the outset of a transformation, they are nonetheless extremely important to employees. Leaders' failure to be up front about the fact that changes are coming can arouse sensitivities later on, prompting surprise or even feelings of being deceived. Leaders must also beware of miscommunication. There are many ways to describe the same thing, whether it's a goal, an objective, an expectation, or a key performance indicator, but inconsistencies in language can inadvertently set off warning flags on all manner of employee-related issues, including how individuals will be measured and changes in performance reviews and their impact on bonuses and rewards. Employees get confused and suspicious when leaders don't speak a common language; it's a sign that leaders may not be on the same page.

So how do you forge an understanding with employees about the changes the company must make in a digital transformation and about what that means for them? How do you establish a common language that is straightforward but is also comprehensive? We think one useful way is through the Human-Centered Transformation model (see figure 55). Developed by Tyler Durham, Tony Fross, and Helen Rosethorn, the model uses a Body, Mind, Soul, and DNA analogy to highlight the different facets of organization and culture that must be tended to in a digital transformation. Human-Centered Transformation uses a common language and helps everyone involved see that employee enablement is a multifaceted effort.[2]

HUMAN-CENTERED ORGANIZATION TRANSFORMATION

Figure 55. Human-centered organization transformation model

Think of the Body as the structure, the operating model for how employee resources are deployed. The Soul represents the mindsets, values, and rituals that bind an organization together, and the Mind depicts the talent, capabilities, and skills by which the company achieves results. At the center, anchoring all three elements, is the DNA of the company—its vision and strategy, the essential driving forces of the transformation.

Link Transformation to Purpose (the DNA)

These days, one would have to be a total recluse to be unaware of digital transformation and the impact it is having on society, business, and individuals. But it is not a terribly motivating topic to employees. In established B2B companies, digital transformation for its own sake seems to come with more baggage than benefit in the eyes of many employees. Those uncomfortable with technology fear the changes it might bring about in their jobs; those who are comfortable wonder why it's taking so long to get underway.

Leaders must put digital transformation into context. When companies link digital transformation to higher goals by demonstrating its importance to the strategy, when they show that it is crucial to achieving the company's purpose, they can reposition digital transformation from a force to be feared to a cause worth enlisting in. In the case of companies with a clear strategy and purpose (or mission, or combination of the two), making the link usually requires putting forward a thoughtful case. Tell people why the transformation is essential to achieving the strategy and purpose. The tighter the link, the more convincing the case, the more inspiring the cause will be.[3]

Most B2B company leaders have routines in place to articulate their strategy to employees, shareholders, customers, and other stakeholders. When articulating the strategy, they often treat digital challenges and opportunities as a separate topic or strategy. Transformation leaders need to avoid this trap and show how the digital transformation is a tool that will support and accelerate the execution of other key strategies. They must show that digital transformation is crucial to success in adding more customers, growing revenue, becoming more efficient, and building a brighter future. Transformation leaders must also add an explicit employee enablement strategy or set of initiatives to the larger strategic framework so that employees can see that they are part of the plan and avoid the fear that the digital strategy will make them obsolete.

Because some leadership teams are not always as diligent about articulating enterprise purpose as they are about articulating their business strategy, the task of linking the digital transformation to purpose is often more complicated than linking it to the strategy. However, it is no less important because aligning transformation with purpose, the contribution the company makes to customers and society and the values on which this contribution is based, is one of the best ways to enlist and motivate employees.

A simple test of purpose clarity is if leaders and employees can fill in the blanks in the following two statements: "We believe that _____" and "We exist to _____." Johnson & Johnson's current website offers an example of a clearly articulated purpose: "At Johnson & Johnson, we believe good health is the foundation of vibrant lives, thriving communities, and forward progress. . . . We strive to improve access and affordability, create healthier communities, and put a healthy mind, body, and environment within reach of everyone, everywhere."[4]

When the purpose is not clear, transformation leaders can instigate a process to bring it to the forefront of leadership concerns and, in so doing, create a powerful tool to support the transformation. This sounds easier to execute than it may be, however. When companies don't have a clear purpose, there is often an underlying reason (a major shareholder who doesn't believe in it, a lack of leadership alignment) that may be hard to overcome. In these cases, the customer benefits and the customer-centric nature of the transformations can be a viable, although not ideal, substitute for a higher transformation. Most employees want to do right by the customers they serve. Focusing on that simple fact can make a difference in enlisting employees to support a digital transformation.

In cases where the purpose is clear, the task for transformation leaders is quite different. In most companies there are a few "keepers of the purpose flame"—individuals whom employees look to for inspiration and clarity when it comes to purpose. This may be the CEO, a set of prominent senior leaders, a founder, or a mix of all of these. The task of the transformation leader is to enlist these keepers of the flame and help them promote the transformation and make the link between executing the transformation and coming closer to achieving the company purpose.

Renovate the Operating Model (the Body)

Organizational silos and hierarchical decision-making are the enemies of agile teamwork and iterative development—two ways of working that are essential for a digital selling shift, an experience makeover, or a proposition pivot. Leaders of customer-centric digital transformations must renovate their operating model—the Body—in three main ways:

- ► By *redesigning business processes* so they are more customer driven and less encumbered by internal bureaucratic constraints

- ► By *forming agile teams* with clearly defined roles and structure

- ► By *shaping metrics and management forums* to make it easier and more rewarding for employees to be customer centric and digitally oriented

In the course of this book we've tackled the first two: customer-focused processes and agile teaming. Metrics and management forums (the activities related to monitoring progress, allocating resources, and making decisions about transformation issues) require discussion because they are so vital to overcoming the biggest Body barriers to transformation: fear and ambition.

What gets measured gets managed—and done.[5] This oft-repeated adage from the legendary business thinker Peter Drucker is particularly applicable to digital transformation. However, with the explosion of digital data and tools, it's tempting for B2B leaders to add metric upon metric to their scorecards, dashboards, and trackers, and to pile on new management forums and coordinating bodies instead of discontinuing old measures and repurposing existing meetings. As a result, the transformation gets bogged down. The metrics that matter for the transformation—those that will provide the needed incentives and spur the right kind of decision-making—get lost in the shuffle.

The status quo suits those whose success came from playing by its rules. Change threatens their chances for promotion, power, and greater compensation. Change threatens those who fear losing control, information access, status, and influence.

In most B2B companies, ambition and fear are most salient among middle managers, but they are not confined to their ranks. Research on organizational transformation and innovation indicates middle managers are the greatest barrier to change.[6] Metrics, along with governance, is an important lever for countering their ability to undermine the transformation effort. But metrics and governance can work only if senior leaders do the following:

- ▶ Replace the old business performance metrics with new ones relevant to the transformation. In that way, the new metrics will be embedded in decision-making, progress monitoring, resource allocation, incentives, rewards, and performance reviews.

- ▶ Reconfigure the agendas of key monthly meetings, the annual planning process, strategic planning activities, talent planning, and board meetings so that they incorporate the topics most important to the transformation even when this requires delegating old business topics to lower-ranking managers or dropping them altogether.

In vetting the existing metrics and management practices, leaders should focus on those that are most compatible with so called "blue line management."[7] Blue line management advocates that leaders base their decisions on the factors that reflect value creation: customer satisfaction, the time it takes to go from patent to production, employee productivity, and so forth. These are the kind of factors that will increase the value of the enterprise and its share price over the long term. Indicators that promote maximizing the short-term share price—for example, by smoothing quarterly income gains or hoarding cash to embellish the balance sheet (red line management)—should be scrapped.

Mobilize the Talent (the Mind)

When undertaking a digital selling shift, an experience makeover, or a proposition pivot, the company will almost always realize that there's a mismatch between the new work to be done and existing skills and capabilities. That means filling gaps (through learning and development) and filling voids (through recruiting and outsourcing). In some cases, the company will need to ask people to find a job at another company or retire. The challenge for senior leaders is to know when to train or recruit and when to show employees the door. It's also in determining whether company leaders, themselves included, have what it takes to make talent decisions. Consider these practical rules of thumb:

▶ Skills and capabilities based on deploying processes, such as running a scrum agile team or using collaboration tools, can generally be learned quite readily. It will take initial training and ongoing support from experts (often outside contractors or consultants), who transfer knowledge and tools to a cadre of insiders who then teach and coach teams in the organization. This approach generates waves of learning and deployment; this is how Six Sigma methods have been disseminated throughout many B2B companies.

▶ Highly technical skills and capabilities associated with advanced disciplines (such as data science or AI programming) or the complex interplay of systems, science, and technologies require recruiting and outsourcing. No one—not even talented internal candidates—can acquire these sorts of skills quickly on the job.

▶ Skills and capabilities that are based on expertise and the accumulation of knowledge and understanding through practical experience can be learned, but with conditions. The learners must already have foundational skills (for example, a marketer specializing in organic and paid search must have strong data analysis skills). They must be working side by side with other team members and a team leader with that expertise who can share it. Forming a customer data analytics team is a good example: despite the complexity, it's feasible to teach employees with strong quantitative backgrounds— but only when leaders (and ideally other team members) have the expertise and managerial skills. One of the biggest mistakes companies make is putting talented junior leaders in charge of teams where they must help others build expertise in areas where they have none. This might work in highly stable environments (where the junior leader has time to learn best practices and approaches from more experienced people), but in a transformation, where the tasks are evolving and new tasks are constantly being added, such an arrangement quickly becomes a case of the blind leading the blind. It can easily end up damaging the careers of high-potential leaders and eroding team members' faith in the transformation.

How to best build skills and capabilities is a tough call for senior management. They must determine whether they or their leadership teams have what it takes to guide a transformation when they themselves may not have sufficient expertise to judge what's required. In these cases, it can make sense to bring a new senior leader into the mix, one with the desired expertise who can guide other senior leaders in evaluating the skills and capabilities required to execute—including helping them identify their own gaps and voids.

Shift the Culture (the Soul)

For each transformation we've described the importance of working with agility and speed and of following a test-and-learn approach. We emphasize how critical it is to listen to the customer and adapt to their needs. These requirements amount to culture change—they force the organization to accept new ways of doing things, to be resilient in the face of the failures that will inevitability result, and to be ready to forge ahead to the next horizon. The key to success with these types of changes is to foster an innovation mindset (or "digital mindset") among employees.[8] Fostering an innovation mindset, like any culture change goal, takes the guidance and support of senior management and team leaders. It also requires innovation tools and incentives and rewards that align with an innovation mindset. At the same time, senior leaders must actively work to engage and win over those middle managers who are willing to change, while blocking those who are intent on stifling an innovation mindset because it may threaten their control or influence.

Some employees can feel that the very soul of a company is being challenged by a major digital transformation because the routines, values, and stories that are bellwethers of culture evolve. Few companies, primarily in high tech, have cultures that openly embrace change, because change has traditionally been viewed as the enemy of the efficiency, consistency, and reliability that are so prized in large enterprises. Most companies have a mix of characteristics that support and inhibit digital transformation. A commercial insurer may have a predilection for data-driven decision-making, which would facilitate a transformation based on customer data, but that same company may also be extremely consensus driven in its decision-making, relying on time-consuming processes for alignment that inhibit agile ways of working and block transformation progress.

The Soul, like the Body and Mind, brings the company's DNA—its purpose and strategy—to life. Unlike changes to the Body and Mind, changes to the Soul mean encouraging behaviors that are much harder for leaders to control—rewarding and incentivizing the desired behaviors and discouraging undesired behaviors, in ways that won't be misunderstood. The carrots and sticks that organizations have at their disposal rely greatly on the perceptions and attitudes of most employees. In striving to shift an organization's culture, leaders must recognize that culture is the result of collective inputs, not something that can be changed directly. Because of this, efforts to change the Soul of a company to make it more conducive to a digital mindset and digital transformation can easily veer off track. As daunting as the challenge may be, it cannot be overlooked. Culture is vital to success.

Leaders have multiple levers at their disposal for driving culture change that supports digital transformation. In our experience, leaders migrate to overarching levers such as new mindsets, strategies, and values because they are easier to link to the transformation. By articulating these goals and ideals, leaders hope they can win hearts and minds and thus foster the culture change that will support the transformation. These levers also tend to be less controversial, because they are broader and more conceptual and thus open to individual interpretation. Leaders tend to avoid addressing the more mechanical levers, such as changes to governance, decision rights, incentives, and talent gaps, because the results create winners and losers in the organization and have the potential for arousing conflict and intense debate.

While it's important to communicate the more conceptual levers, it takes concrete levers that spur the desired behaviors to get people on board. And addressing the concrete levers more aggressively enhances the overarching levers. A move to reconfigure incentives supported by decision-rights improvements drives new behaviors when the right talent has been recruited and training has been undertaken. When employees feel incentivized, empowered, and skilled, they have a fresh mindset about what's possible. They will express values differently and execute the strategy with new vigor.

Leaders who work on both the overarching and concrete levers can enhance their chances of success if they execute a few fairly obvious but often overlooked best practices of culture building.

▶ **Cultivate an honest dialogue around the need for cultural change.** Acknowledge any missteps or failures as they occur. Employees will tolerate mistakes and contribute to the dialogue when the intent is transparent, the rationale is well founded (they don't have to agree), and the overall approach celebrates what works and should continue to be valued in the current culture. Make sure the concrete levers are included in the dialogue even though they are more sensitive and likely to generate conflict.

▶ **Revamp routines, establish new ones, and eliminate old ones.** Focus on routines that are effective in advancing culture change. Routines such as looking over a dashboard at the beginning of every management review, rewarding leading salespeople at annual leadership gatherings, and including the discussion of profitability KPIs at every quarterly business review are the main ways that employees see leaders in action in their daily work. By instigating routines, leaders shift the emphasis to what's important. It's essential that leaders, especially senior leaders, be consistent when altering routines; otherwise they can undermine the changes they are trying to embed.

▶ **Solicit active and consequential employee participation.** At every level in a hierarchy there are leaders of all sorts and kinds: opinion leaders, spirit leaders, thought leaders, leading problem solvers. Positive culture change occurs when these individuals lead by example: fostering productive routines and discouraging nonproductive behavior. Those at the top must listen to these leaders, confer decision rights on them, and assign them roles to encourage their participation.

ASSESS THE CURRENT STATE

An organization-wide assessment of the current state of Body, Mind, and Soul lays the foundation for the employee enablement necessary for a successful digital transformation. Effective assessments for each area have several features in common:

- **They combine extensive listening and employee engagement.** Surveys and interviews are important tools in this work. They work best when employees are given the opportunity to participate in helping to interpret the results and to influence the implications for action. Participation uncovers deeper insight and helps build the understanding and alignment that will be crucial to embed lasting change.

- **They look at best practices from outside the company and benchmark against them.** An external view is important to help leaders and employees see opportunities and reexamine norms that are outside their experience or ability to envision.

- **They are based on reasonable goals that serve the strategy and purpose.** Aspiring to be the greatest in every dimension compared to external best practices is not the point. Best practices are useful when they are relevant and the topic is important to accomplishing concrete goals.

- **They look for strengths as well as weaknesses.** Building on your strengths may seem like an obvious move, but it's remarkable how many organizations think assessments are only about pointing out weaknesses. That's simply not pragmatic. Moreover, it's much more encouraging to employees when the challenges they confront are a mix of positive (building on strengths) and negative (addressing shortcomings and gaps).

- **They are shared broadly across all levels of the organization.** Sharing the results of an assessment is a powerful tool for generating buy-in on the need to change. That never works if results are shared only with senior leaders or a small transformation team. Leaders must adapt the message and the forums for sharing depending on the audience, but transformation requires a common understanding of what must be improved.

Body, Mind, and Soul assessments each call for a different approach:

- **The Body assessment.** For this assessment, you must first define how digital transformation will change the work that must be done by the various groups and teams throughout the organization. Then, analyze how well suited existing organization structures, management routines, processes, systems, and metrics are to doing it. To what extent will existing structures, routines, processes, systems, and metrics accelerate (or delay) progress according to the relevant transformation leaders? How do these areas of the company Body compare to those of companies that have transformed successfully? Assessments of this type are best carried out by external consultants with experience in the field and should be based as much as possible on best practices of companies within and outside the industry who are at a more advanced state of digital maturity. The use of stories about best practices is particularly effective in making the assessment actionable.

▶ **The Mind assessment.** Assessing talent, skills, and capabilities (the Mind) always follows a Body assessment because the Body assessment defines the requirements for the work that the organization must undertake. Assessors must have deep knowledge of the three areas of mastery (processes, technical skills, and expertise) relating to the particular type of transformation (digital selling shift, experience makeover, or proposition pivot). Mind assessments are different from most types of talent assessment because they must be undertaken at three levels (individual, team, and leadership) so that they address not only the skills required to do the work but also the skills and capabilities to work together and the skills to motivate and guide teams. This type of assessment often requires contribution from experts outside the company who have seen firsthand what it takes to carry out a specific transformation in different situations. Often a partnership between HR and business unit leaders makes the best sponsors because of the wide variety of skills that must be assessed.

▶ **The Soul assessment.** To evaluate the organization's Soul, you must probe how employees think and feel about the culture and about the changes they anticipate will occur. Often one-on-one interviews with employees, employee focus groups, and employee surveys are all useful for a Soul assessment. Benchmarking versus other companies must be used sparingly, if at all, and only by those with extensive and deep understanding of both the company and the comparison set. Culture is unique to each company, and the nuances in employee research results can be difficult to interpret. A senior HR sponsor working with the endorsement of a CEO or COO is usually the best way to oversee this work and avoid the bias that individual business unit leaders may bring to it.

REVAMP THE EMPLOYEE VALUE PROPOSITION

Being engaged and invested in a goal and taking action on it are highly motivating to employees. Most are motivated by enhancing value for customers and being part of an endeavor that is helping the company fulfill its purpose. But the excitement and enthusiasm may not be enough to sustain motivation over time or to retain or recruit the specific talent you need for your transformation. Employees and potential recruits need to know what's in it for them. How will the transformation provide them with work that interests them, enrich their careers, allow them to work with people they enjoy, and help them achieve their financial goals? Every current employee has a baseline proposition that forms the reason they come to work and try to do their best. Because transformations demand more of employees, employees want more from the value proposition they receive. Transformation leaders must think through what has to change in order to deliver value to employees—what will attract new talent, retain top talent, and motivate employees to embrace change and take on new roles?

What is the employee value proposition? Like the customer value proposition, it articulates how the organization will deliver value to employees in ways that enhance the value of the company. But instead of the value exchange being based on a purchase, it's based on the rewards that the company gives the employee in return for the work the employee does, which contributes to the company's operations, strategy, and purpose. Employees derive value from many sources, based on their personal priorities and values: intrinsic rewards, such as recognition and a sense of achievement, as well as extrinsic (tangible) rewards, such as compensation, opportunities for promotion, and working conditions. An employee value proposition has seven key characteristics (see figure 56).

- ▶ **It is purposeful.** It answers the question, Are our employees able to make an important contribution to something that matters?

- ▶ **It's stimulating.** Do we offer work that is interesting and appropriately challenging?

- ▶ **It's career building.** Can our people advance their careers and future job prospects?

- ▶ **It's developmental.** Do we provide employees a place to learn, build their skills, and enrich their capabilities?

- ▶ **It promotes work/life balance.** Does our work environment give our people the ability to balance their work life and home life?

- ▶ **It offers a cultural fit.** Can employees find enjoyable colleagues and customers whose interests and values they share?

- ▶ **It's rewarding.** Do we reward and recognize our people for their contribution to the company?

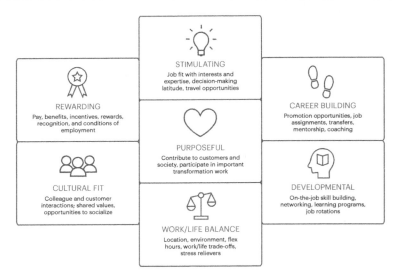

Figure 56. Elements of employee value proposition

The challenge for digital transformation leaders is to figure out what changes they need to make to the baseline employee proposition (the one already in place, if only implicitly) to attract new talent and motivate current employees who are important for the transformation. In doing so, they must consider a few sometimes competing factors.

► Of the seven elements, some will require more investment, while others might be best kept as is. It's neither realistic nor sustainable to change everything, and certainly not overnight. Transformations must be ambitious but also authentic. Just as with a customer value proposition, leaders need to make choices, focusing on a few critical areas in which to stand out and excel.

► Balancing resource constraints with the need to stay competitive in the talent market. Some aspects of a proposition (such as remuneration) cannot vary too much from the market standard, so fulfilling this requirement may require rejiggering some transformation investments or else securing funds elsewhere from the company budget.

► How to equitably distribute benefit enhancements between people contributing directly to the transformation and those in comparable positions who help maintain the company's day-to-day operations. For example, it's fine to give bigger bonuses to those who have taken on more risks or achieved higher targets. However, increases will be perceived as being unfair if they are not based on taking greater risks or greater responsibility. Perceptions of unfairness can, in turn, trigger resentment that undermines transformation progress.

Being part of a digital transformation, whether as a leader or an employee, can be a dream job when it visibly involves making a real contribution—advancing the company's purpose or strategic vision—and when the value proposition of the transformation has meaning for the employee. As long as remuneration is at market levels, it is rarely the deciding factor in taking a position. What attracts and motivates people is the potential for fulfillment, which means different things to different people: career opportunity and impact on company growth for some, social interactions and a supportive culture for others. Transformation leaders must be mindful of these factors, not only in seeking to shift the employee value proposition, but in ensuring they live up to it as they design roles and determine responsibilities.

CHART AN ENABLEMENT ROAD MAP

Now leaders have assessed the Body, Mind, and Soul of the company—the strengths to bolster and the skill gaps and voids to address. And they have identified how the employee value proposition must be modified in order to retain, motivate, and recruit those needed to carry out the transformation.

The next step is to draw an employee enablement road map. This lays out the initiatives the company must undertake to help employees execute the transformation. We've found that organizing the road map in waves and grouping initiatives by Body, Mind, and Soul makes it easier to think through the necessary initiatives and their sequencing (see figure 57).

KEY CONSIDERATIONS FOR EMPLOYEE ENABLEMENT ROADMAP

REQUIREMENTS	WAVE 1 | INITIATE	WAVE 2 | SUSTAIN	WAVE 3 | EXPAND
Governance, tools, roles, process, organization, systems	What are initial team structures? Who will lead/sponsor key teams? What forums and metrics?	How will teams sync together? What changes to annual plans? What routines stop, start, continue?	Change organization structure? New business model required? Raise goals and KPIs?
Talent, capabilities, skills, training, rewards	What is basic learning curriculum? Where will recruiting start? Are senior recruits needed?	What is advanced learning? How must rewards be revamped? What's next for recruiting?	Change performance management? Is it time for layoffs or hiring surge? Right time for center of excellence?
Values, behaviors, stories, symbols, rituals	How will leaders show commitment? How to foster innovation mindset? What are new success stories?	What changes to values? How are agile teams supported? What project is symbol of success?	Who are new culture champions? Next culture barrier to tackle? What's next for team performance?
Purpose, strategy, brand	How to show link to strategy, purpose? Who will oversee overall effort? How will CEO and board support?	What changes in the strategy? How does role of brand change? Where to reinforce what we do best?	Has purpose evolved? Is it time to enter new business? Is it time to pivot business?

Figure 57. Key considerations for employee enablement roadmap

The road map is a high-level depiction of the major initiatives for employee enablement. By plotting the road map, leaders can get a better idea of the issues they need to tackle and why they must avoid cramming too much into the first wave of the effort.

Each initiative will require an owner, a project charter, and a work plan. Coordinating all of this activity often falls to the HR head, which, given their background and expertise, makes sense, provided certain conditions are met. First and foremost, HR leaders should receive special coaching and learning support to ensure they understand the fundamental aspects of the transformation. This coaching and learning step, often overlooked, can severely hamper the effectiveness of the transformation. HR leaders also need to interact frequently with other senior leaders to make sure the enablement initiatives (and their outcomes) are linked to the transformation work goals. Finally, they should be given project management support to coordinate all of the enablement activities.

To be useful and actionable, every enablement road map should feature the following:

- **A system for measuring progress, built into every initiative and wave.** Apart from having metrics that tie to the transformation, the system should also include mechanisms for capturing employee feedback and for tracking their progress against goals and initiatives. For example, a training initiative on scrum agile methods should be measured not only in terms of participation and engagement but also by extent of its deployment by participants post-training. Companies should also take participants' feedback into account, including suggestions for improvement.

- **Explicit links to desired transformation outcomes.** Too often, employee enablement programs are separated from the specific transformation initiatives on the assumption they will be mutually reinforcing. Employee enablement initiatives such as a new approach to incentives, changes in learning programs, or a new way to organize a team should be embedded, tested, and improved within go-to-market transformation initiatives before they are rolled out to the broader organization. This ensures the programs are effective and that employees know they have been battle tested and are therefore to be taken seriously.

Road maps must also be monitored on a regular basis by leaders. It may take only one person to track and coordinate progress against the road map, but the entire senior leadership team bears responsibility for supporting implementation. Leaders can dispatch their responsibility only by routinely reviewing road map metrics and contributing their ideas for adapting and improving the enablement program.

Employee enablement can be a significant barrier to digital transformation, but with the right strategy, planning, and preparation, it can also be overcome. It is a complex challenge, and one that requires a deep well of knowledge to effect change. Here, we have merely touched on its importance and on how to approach it.

We encourage readers to explore the extensive body of thought leadership on leadership, teaming, organization design, and culture. Consider the principles and best practices as they apply not only to sectors facing digital disruption but also to employees whose attitudes and perceptions of their employers are changing in a modern, more digital world.

4.4

Seize Uncommon Growth

S ustainable, profitable growth in the age of digital disruption and changing customer behavior is uncommon. Only thirty-seven of the five hundred largest publicly traded US companies with substantial B2B sales grew their revenues and profits for three consecutive years for the period 2016 to 2019.[1] Companies that have been able to grow consistently demonstrate that the tried-and-true growth strategies of geographic, category, offer, and channel expansion are necessary but insufficient to face a rapidly evolving present and a disruptive digital future. Digital transformation is clearly the path forward for companies with the will to sustain success. Leaders must navigate the organization through the steps of Where to Play, How to Win, What to Do, and Who Is Needed for a Digital Selling Shift, an Experience Makeover, a Proposition Pivot, or some combination of the three. The need for sustained growth also reinforces that notion that digital transformation has no end point. It is an ongoing evolution that brings customers closer to the company and improves business results, as long as leaders commit to sustaining, supporting, and continuously improving it.

The central premise of this book is that customer centricity is the key to success in navigating a B2B company through digital transformation. Customer centricity drives uncommon growth. This premise is built on research cited in the introduction, "Digital Transformation and Uncommon Growth in B2B," which points out the failure of transformations that put technology and systems before the needs of the customer. It is also based on the examples of successful transformations at Air Liquide, Maersk, and Michelin that put the customer at the center of their transformations. In every one of their transformations, uncommon growth did not come from transitory gains in customer happiness or temporary gains from discounting. Uncommon growth was generated by instilling changes in customer behavior that resulted in increased customer adoption and loyalty to the supplier's solutions. Sustainable growth is built on a virtuous cycle of investment in selling, experience, and proposition innovation, which in turn yields repeated improvements in customers' purchasing behavior, which in turn drives profitable revenue and thus generates further investment. As we pointed out in the preceding two chapters, the investment that fuels the virtuous growth cycle must include building customer data and employee capabilities. Together they are a major stumbling block to successful transformations.

Transformations take hold through a combination of declaration and implementation. Declaring the transformation vision and strategy and the case for change is essential to mobilizing the organization and inspiring employee, investor, and customer confidence in the company's future. But declarations are meaningless unless they are backed up with concrete implementation plans about where to play, how to win, what to do, and who is needed—and supported by the people, processes, tools, metrics, and organization structures to turn plans into action. Insufficient declaration leads to a lack of strategic clarity that spawns disjointed initiatives and investments. These moves may appear rational and worthwhile at the outset but later stall because they do not work together toward a common strategic vision and strategy. Declaration without sufficient implementation raises customer, employee, and investor hopes that later are dashed and can turn stakeholders against the transformation before it has a chance to gain momentum. Blending both declaration and implementation together is crucial to helping the transformation locomotive gain momentum as it leaves the station of the current state. Stretching our locomotive analogy a bit further, the customers and workers on board the transformation train must have enough confidence that they will arrive at their destination and feel comfortable with the pace of implementation that they don't bail out at any stops along the way.

We urge leaders to think about the transformation in phases.

- ▶ In the initial transformation phases, leaders outline the vision and strategy in aspirational terms and put the greatest emphasis on the need for change. This leaves room for the vision and strategy to evolve but makes it clear that clinging to the status quo is not viable. Implementation efforts in the first phase should focus on "doing the doable, then push it."[2] They should aim to tackle customer opportunities that can be solved relatively quickly and have the potential for future improvement, through the customer-driven, iterative innovation we've described in this book. This approach builds momentum and quickly helps build proof points around the case for change.

- ▶ In successive phases of the transformation, leaders should make the vision and strategy more specific as employees and customers become more engaged in the company's new direction. Leaders should push implementation further by tackling bigger and more audacious innovation initiatives on behalf of the customer and by making larger investments in capabilities and systems that are informed by previous efforts.

The key choice facing business leaders is not whether to undertake digital transformation but which of the transformations—the digital selling shift, digital experience makeover, or digital proposition pivot—to undertake first.

Companies should start by asking whether a digital proposition pivot is what they most need. That's because, of the three transformations, it is the most disruptive, and typically most expensive, and has the most uncertain outcome. If the company's current value proposition has a bright future—if the proposition is a force for disruption rather than a likely casualty of it—then it is best to start with either the digital selling shift or the digital experience makeover to attract more customers and build loyalty to the proposition. If the proposition is vulnerable to disruption, then a selling shift or experience makeover will be a wasted effort until a proposition pivot is underway. (Why optimize the fax machine if people want email?) For many companies, a proposition pivot would entail substantial transformation in the customer experience or in selling, so undertaking one could actually require tackling more than one transformation simultaneously. Many propositions are in that middle ground between "bright future" and vulnerable: robust enough to compete successfully but at risk from conditions in the industry that are evolving in unpredictable ways. Proactive leaders in such businesses often empower small teams to test future proposition pivots while the bulk of the organization focuses on transforming selling and the experience.

The next question is whether to use the digital selling shift or the digital experience makeover to fortify a viable value proposition. Because it is generally more efficient and effective to encourage existing customers to buy more, more often, and for more money, a digital experience makeover is a smart starting point for mature businesses with a large customer base. Companies or business units with low market penetration can often benefit by starting with the digital selling shift because it has the greatest potential to accelerate new customer acquisition, cross-sell, and upsell. As selling, marketing, and experience are so intertwined, most companies implement transformations that involve both a digital selling shift and a digital experience makeover. Since experience makeovers can be tackled in modular fashion, one touchpoint or one moment in the journey at a time, they are ideal for combining with a digital selling shift or multiple experience makeovers.

Once the choice of transformation has been made, get going as soon as possible so there is little gap between establishing expectations among employees, investors, and customers and taking action. Do the doable and push it further by following the steps we've described in this guide.

- ▶ **Start with a customer-driven opportunity.** Find a place to help customers or customers' customers and determine where to play.

- ▶ **Craft a strategy to build customer preference.** Determine how to win in this opportunity in the face of competition and a changing environment.

- ▶ **Implement effectively and continue to improve.** Drive the organization to action by supporting teams that uncover what to do and how to do it better as they learn from the impact their initiatives have on the customer.

- ▶ **Build the expertise necessary to do the work.** Identify who to win with and rally the team to move iteratively and rapidly. Enlist teams that are truly motivated to make it happen. Focus on getting the right people to do the most important tasks.

- ▶ **Show results.** The best way to get a company, a business unit, or a team to shift is to demonstrate that the shift is worth it. Prioritize one or two quick wins to demonstrate proof of concept. Don't make the great be the enemy of the good.

In undertaking these steps, use the frameworks and templates in this handbook. You can obtain them at *www.B2BDigitalTransformation.com* or ask for help by reaching out to Fred or Joerg through our LinkedIn accounts.

ACKNOWLEDGMENTS

We have been privileged to collaborate with some of the world's most renowned thinkers and business leaders on the topic of business growth and digital transformation in a changing world.

Our first thanks go to the business executives and students we've interacted with through the Prophet consulting projects and INSEAD educational programs we've undertaken over the past several years. Their insights and experiences are the foundation for this book.

INSEAD and Prophet have been the greenhouse for our thinking for more than a decade. Our colleagues are an inspiration and have contributed in innumerable ways to the thinking, frameworks, and methods we recommend. A few deserve special thanks for their particular contributions to this book.

From Prophet, Fred would like to thank in particular Abram Sirignano and Peter Dixon for their input on customer experience; Nicolle D'Onofrio for her guidance on scrum agile; Tony Fross and Helen Rosethorn for their contributions to employee enablement and the DERPA model; Gibran Lalani and Mike Welch for their assistance with the transformation management office; Mat Zucker, Peter Stubbs, Ted Moser, and John Ellett for their digital marketing thinking; Darrell Ross for insight into customer data strategy; and Chan Suh and Samantha Papadakis for opening Fred's eyes up to the potential of digital transformation.

Joerg would like to thank Wolfgang Ulaga and David Dubois from INSEAD for the input they provided on several case studies used throughout the book; Pierre Chandon for being a great champion and for supporting Joerg in his teaching at INSEAD from the beginning; and Mohammed

El-Desouky for helping us tremendously in screening and identifying relevant research for the three transformational shifts.

This book would not be complete without the many business cases and examples that we have included. We especially thank Sonny Wilkens Dahl and Vincent Clerc for their valuable input on the Maersk case and Olivier Blachier for guiding us through Air Liquide's digital transformation. This exciting journey would not have been possible without the help of their teams and many other executives from the B2B organizations cited in this book.

Putting a book together takes many contributors. Thanks to Maureen Forys at Happenstance for our elegant book design; Susan Berge for a final copyedit; Kelly Redling for our glorious book cover; Harold Cheng for the insightful graphics; Nick Geyer for our website, *B2BDigitalTransformation.com*; Amanda Nizzere, Nichola Seeley, Julian Boudier, Chris Howells, and Ben Kessler for marketing support; and Charlene Li and David Aaker for their invaluable advice on the entire process of bringing a book to life.

Jan Koch deserves special recognition. She has been an amazing editor, sharpening each turn of phrase and ensuring every idea will be clear to readers. Her remarkable attention to detail and business insight exceeded our expectations.

We are particularly grateful to our families' support throughout this project. Fred's wife, Alison, gave up countless weekends and evenings and a good bit of vacation time with enthusiastic encouragement and love. Joerg would like to thank his wife, Hilke. He could not have done this project without her love and support. And thanks go to his sons, Mats and Jannis, who inspired his creativity and continue to make every day special. They all kept us going.

The work of helping digital transformation in B2B succeed continues—with clients, students, and executives applying many of the frameworks we talk about in this book. If you would like to join the community and receive ongoing updates and examples, sign up at *www.B2BDigitalTransformation.com*.

Many thanks to all of you.

NOTES

PREFACE

1   George Westerman et al., *The Digital Advantage: How Digital Leaders Outperform Their Peers in Every Industry*, CapGemini Consulting and MIT Center for Digital Business, MIT Sloan School of Management, November 2012, *https://www.capgemini.com/wp-content/uploads/2017/07/The_Digital_Advantage__How_Digital_Leaders_Outperform_their_Peers_in_Every_Industry.pdf*.

2   David Abood et al., *Rethink, Reinvent, Realize: How to Successfully Scale Innovation to Drive Growth*, Accenture Research, 2019, *https://www.accenture.com/_acnmedia/thought-leadership-assets/pdf/accenture-ixo-hannovermesse-report.pdf*.

3   Steven ZoBell, "Why Digital Transformations Fail: Closing the $900 Billion Hole in Enterprise Strategy," Forbes Technology Council, *Forbes Blog*, March 13, 2018, *https://www.forbes.com/sites/forbestechcouncil/2018/03/13/why-digital-transformations-fail-closing-the-900-billion-hole-in-enterprise-strategy/#793c1da67b8b*.

4   Saul Berman, Josh Goff, and Carolyn Heller Baird, *The Experience Revolution: Digital Disappointment—Why Some Customers Aren't Fans*, IBM Institute for Business Value, IBM Digital Strategy and iX, 2017, *https://www.ibm.com/downloads/cas/Q1K5AKNQ*.

5   Kestutis Reklaitis and Lina Pileliene, "Principle Differences between B2B and B2C Marketing Communication Processes," *Management of Organizations: Systematic Research* 81, no. 1 (October 30, 2019): 73–86; Severina Iankova et al., "A Comparison of Social Media Marketing between B2B, B2C and Mixed Business Models," *Industrial Marketing Management* 81 (August 2019): 169–179.

6   Thomas Abrell et al., "The Role of Users and Customers in Digital Innovation: Insights from B2B Manufacturing Firms," *Information & Management* 53, no. 3 (April 2016): 324–335; Michael Brown, "How Boosting People Skills Helps in Digital Transformation: A Case Study," *Strategic HR Review* 18, no. 6 (November 11, 2019): 254–257.

7   Joerg Niessing, "Successful Digital Transformation Starts with the Customer," *The European Business Review*, September 23, 2016, *https://www.europeanbusinessreview.com/successful-digital-transformation-starts-with-the-customer/*.

INTRODUCTION

1   Fran Brosan, "Democratisation of Digital in B2B: The Marketing Challenge," *Market Leader* (Quarter 4, 2015): 12–13.

2   Blake Morgan, "B2B Digital Transformation 2020," *Forbes*, CMO Network Blog, June 14, 2019, *https://www.forbes.com/sites/blakemorgan/2019/06/14/b2b-digital -transformation-2020/#1a6d80b21a5f*.

3   Eric Almquist, "How Digital Natives Are Changing B2B Purchasing," hbr.org, March 14, 2018, *https://hbr.org/2018/03/how-digital-natives-are-changing-b2b -purchasing*; Sam Del Rowe, "Buyer Enablement Is the Key to B2B Sales: Much of the Sales Process Happens Before Sales Reps Get Involved," *CRM Magazine* 22, no. 8 (October 2018).

4   Stephen Kudyba and Thomas Davenport, "Machine Learning Can Help B2B Firms Learn More about Their Customers," hbr.org, January 19, 2018, *https:// hbr.org/2018/01/machine-learning-can-help-b2b-firms-learn-more-about-their -customers*; Rob Markey, "Run B2B Sales on Data, Not Hunches," hbr.org, September 12, 2016, *https://hbr.org/2016/09/run-b2b-sales-on-data-not-hunches*.

5   Anuj Kopadia et al., *Medical Devices 2030—Making a Power Play to Avoid the Commodity Trap*, KPMG Thriving on Disruption Series, KPMG, 2018, *https:// assets.kpmg/content/dam/kpmg/cn/pdf/en/2018/04/medical-devices-2030.pdf*.

6   Joerg Niessing, Wolfgang Ulaga, and Andrew Carrick, *Engie: Transforming an Incumbent—Creating Competitive Advantage in B2B and B2T Through Smart Data, AI and Digital Technologies*, INSEAD case library, March 6, 2020.

7   Jasmine Pennic, "Change Healthcare Acquires National Decision Support Company," *HIT Consultant* blog, January 18, 2018, *https://hitconsultant.net/2018/01/18 /change-healthcare-acquires-national-decision-support-company/#.XmKEqZP7RQI*.

8   *The Digital Savvy HCP Survey: Top Trends 2019*, Indegene, PharmaFuture, January 2020, *https://www.indegene.com/digitalSavvyHcp/pdf/hcp-survey-2019.pdf*.

9   Frederick Geyer, notes from presentations at 2019 Eyeforpharma Conference, Philadelphia, October 2, 2019.

10 Thomas Abrell et al., "The Role of Users and Customers in Digital Innovation: Insights from B2B Manufacturing Firms," *Information & Management* 53, no. 3 (April 2016): 324–335.

11 Joerg Niessing, "Why Companies Shouldn't Rush Their Digital Transformation," *South China Morning Post*, December 29, 2017, *https://www.scmp.com/business /article/2126070/why-companies-shouldnt-rush-their-digital-transformation*.

12 Mahmoud Dasser, "Marketing, the Change Catalyst for Digital Business Transformation: Lessons Learned from the Modernisation of a B2B Marketing Organisation," *Journal of Brand Strategy* 8, no. 1 (2019): 20–41.

13 Claire Fletcher, "Schneider Electric Helps Electricians with Innovative Quotation App," *Electrical Contracting News*, July 14, 2017, *https://electricalcontractingnews .com/news/schneider-electric-quotation-app/*.

14 "Thyssenkrupp Lays the Foundation for Intelligent Buildings with Digital Twin Technology," *Microsoft Customer Stories*, September 24, 2018, *https://customers .microsoft.com/en-us/story/thyssenkrupp-manufacturing-azure-iot*.

15 Anasia D'mello, "Siemens Aims to Make It Faster and Easier to Develop Industrial IoT Apps," *IoT NOW*, April 16, 2019, *https://www.iot-now.com/2019/04/16 /95026-siemens-aims-make-faster-easier-develop-industrial-iot-apps/*; Kumba Sennaar, "AI in Pharma and Biomedicine—Analysis of the Top 5 Global Drug Companies," *Emerj Weekly*, February 3, 2020, *https://emerj.com/ai-sector -overviews/ai-in-pharma-and-biomedicine/*; *Chipless RFID Market Insights 2019, Global and Chinese Analysis and Forecast to 2024*, HTF Market Intelligence, Report HTF2162377, September 13, 2019.

16 Stefan Michel, "Hilti Fleet Management: Strategically Moving from Products to B2B Solutions," *IMD*, Case library reference no. IMD-3-2354, 2013.

17 Maria Minsker, "Adobe Reaches for the Peak," *CRM Magazine* 18, no. 6 (June 1, 2014): 16; "How Adobe Initiated a Digital Reinvention and Is Getting a Makeover," *FRPT—Software Snapshot*, 2015: 23.

CHAPTER 1.1

1 John Rounseville, "A Brief History of Salesforce: from Telegraph Hill to the Tower," *J2 Interactive*, April 15, 2019, *https://www.j2interactive.com/blog/brief -history-salesforce/*.

2 N. Buratti, F. Parola, and G. Satta, "Insights on the Adoption of Social Media Marketing in B2B Services," *TQM Journal* 30, no. 5 (2018): 490–529.

3 Fred Geyer and Mat Zucker, "Four Digital Marketing Trends Poised to Disrupt in 2020," *Prophet Thinking*, December 12, 2019, *https://www.prophet.com/2019/12 /four-digital-marketing-trends-poised-to-disrupt-in-2020/*; Järvinen et al., "Digital and Social Media Marketing Usage in B2B Industrial Sector," *Marketing Management Journal* 22, no. 2 (2012):102–117.

4 "The World's Largest Sales Forces," *SBI Magazine*, Spring 2016: 34–37.

5 *Digital Intelligence Briefing: 2017 Digital Trends in B2B*, Econsultancy, April 2017, *https://econsultancy.com/reports/ digital-intelligence-briefing-2017-digital-trends-in-b2b/*.

6 Mark Brohan, "Why GE Healthcare Is Shaping Up Its B2B Ecommerce Site," *Digital Commerce 360*, Vertical Web Media, June 21, 2019, *https://www .digitalcommerce360.com/2019/06/21/why-ge-healthcare-is-shaping-up-its -ecommerce-site/*.

7 Rob Petersen, "33 Inspiring B2B Digital Marketing Case Studies," *{grow}* (Mark Schaefer blog), May 21, 2015, *https://businessesgrow.com/2015/05/21 /b2b-digital-marketing-case-studies/*.

8 "Why B2B Sales Still Has a Crucial Digital Gap: and How to Fix It," *Crankwheel*, March 1, 2018, *https://crankwheel.com/why-b2b-sales-still-has-a-crucial-digital -gap-and-how-to-fix-it/*.

9 Amy Gesenhues, "Oracle Eloqua Adds Automated ABM Capabilities with Meta-data Integration," *Martech Today*, October 8, 2019, *https://martechtoday.com /oracle-eloqua-adds-automated-abm-capabilities-with-metadata-integration -236076*; Juan Martinez, "Salesforce Einstein ABM Could Be a B2B Marketing Game-Changer," *PC Magazine*, June 8, 2017, *https://www.pcmag.com /news/salesforce-einstein-abm-could-be-a-b2b-marketing-game-changer*; "Adobe Introduce ABM Essentials Solution for Marketo Engage," *B2B Marketing News*, ABM, June 19, 2019, *https://www.b2bmarketing.net/en/resources/news /adobe-introduce-abm-essentials-solution-marketo-engage*.

10 William Larcom, "Exploring RollWorks for ABM and B2B Marketing," *PPC Hero*, January 14, 2019, *https://www.ppchero.com/exploring-rollworks-for-abm-and-b2 b-marketing/*; Jon Brody, "What to Know about Demandbase as a Growth Tool," Ladder Blog, November 18, 2019, *https://blog.ladder.io/demandbase/*.

11 Leonardo Calisse, "6 Artificial Intelligence Use Cases in B2B Sales," *Momentum Data*, December 11, 2019, *https://momentumdata.com/6-artificial-intelligence -use-cases-in-b2b-sales/*.

12 Matthew Cook, "Why Artificial Intelligence Will Eliminate Millions of Sales Jobs," *Forbes*, Forbes Agency Council blog, January 2, 2018, *https://www.forbes .com/sites/forbesagencycouncil/2018/01/02/why-artificial-intelligence-will -eliminate-millions-of-sales-jobs/#7d1828d3d3b8*.

13 Shep Hyken, "57 Percent of Sales Reps Missed Their Quotas Last Year," *Forbes*, Leadership Strategy (blog), September 2, 2018, *https://www.forbes.com/sites /shephyken/2018/09/02/77-of-sales-reps-missed-their-quotas-last-year /#50199d6e52e4*.

14 David Dubois and Jean-Michel Moslonka, "Digitally-Powered Customer-Centric-ity in the Industrial Gas Sector: The Air Liquide-Airgas Merger," *INSEAD*, Case library reference no. 6446, March 25, 2019.

15 David Dubois, "Driving B2B Digital Transformation through Customer-Centric-ity," *INSEAD Knowledge*, May 20, 2019, *https://knowledge.insead.edu/marketing /driving-b2b-digital-transformation-through-customer-centricity-11581*.

CHAPTER 1.2

1 Sergio Zyman, *The End of Marketing as We Know It* (New York: Harper Collins, 1999).

2 David Dubois and Gilles Haumont, "Leading Effective Insights & Brand Strategy in a Digital World: The 4S Data Framework," *European Business Review*, July 4,

2018, *https://www.europeanbusinessreview.com/leading-effective-insights-brand
-strategy-in-a-digital-world-the-4s-data-framework/?*.

3 Yanna Dharmasthira, Julian Poulter, and Neha Gupta, *Market Share Analysis: Customer Experience and Relationship Management Software*, Gartner Research, ID: G00351975, July 31, 2018.

4 Jim Dickie, "Salespeople Face an Uphill Battle, and AI Is Ready to Help: Sales Enablement Divisions Are Gaining Valuable Technology Partners," *CRM Magazine* 21, no. 9 (September 2017): 6; Leonard Klie, "Death of a (B2B) Salesman?" *CRM Magazine* 19, no. 7 (July 2015): 15.

5 R. Premo et al., "The One Ratio Every Subscription Business Needs to Know," *BCG Henderson Institute*, February 19, 2017, *https://www.bcg.com/publications /2017/corporate-development-one-ratio-subscription-business-needs-to-know .aspx*.

6 Frank Cespedes and León Poblete, "How B2B Companies Can Win Back Customers They Have Lost," hbr.org, June 3, 2019, *https://hbr.org/2019/06/how-b2b -companies-can-win-back-customers-theyve-lost*; Paul Harney, "Make Customers Your Best Salespeople: The Advocacy of a Satisfied Customer Can Make All the Difference in B2B Sales," *CRM Magazine* 23, no. 3 (April 2019): 5.

CHAPTER 1.3

1 George Westerman et al., *The Digital Advantage: How Digital Leaders Outperform Their Peers in Every Industry*, CapGemini Consulting and MIT Center for Digital Business, MIT Sloan School of Management, November 2012, *https:// www.capgemini.com/wp-content/uploads/2017/07/The_Digital_Advantage __How_Digital_Leaders_Outperform_their_Peers_in_Every_Industry.pdf*.

2 Amy Kotsenas et al., "The Social Media DNA of Mayo Clinic and Health Care," *Journal of the American College of Radiology* 15, no. 1, part B (January 2018): 162–166.

3 Justin Grossman, "Going Omnichannel? There's a Method for That," *DTC in Focus, DTC Perspectives*, October 21, 2019, *http://www.dtcperspectives.com /going-omnichannel-theres-method/*.

4 Sheena Iyengar and Mark Lepper, "When Choice Is Demotivating: Can One Desire Too Much of a Good Thing?," *Journal of Personality and Social Psychology* 79, no. 6 (December 2000): 995–1006.

5 Elly Yates-Roberts, "Microsoft and Dell Technologies Expand Partnership," *The Record*, Tudor Rose, May 2, 2019, *https://www.technologyrecord.com/Article /microsoft-and-dell-technologies-expand-partnership-80709*.

6 Sam Holzman, "The Beginners Guide to Lead Scoring," *Zoominfo* (blog), August 2019, *https://blog.zoominfo.com/lead-scoring/*.

7   Mark Hollmer, "Nationwide Expands Small Business Insurance Direct Platform," *Insurance Journal*, April 3, 2019, *https://www.insurancejournal.com/news /national/2019/04/03/522661.htm*.

CHAPTER 1.4

1   Hirotaka Takeuchi and Ikujuro Nonaka, "The New New Product Development Game," *Harvard Business Review*, January–February 1986.
2   Ronald Moen, "Foundation and History of the PDSA Cycle," paper presented to Asian Network for Quality Conference, Tokyo, September 17, 2009.
3   "Six Sigma Case Study: Ford Motors," *6Sigma.us*, Articles, May 19, 2017, *https:// www.6sigma.us/uncategorized/six-sigma-case-study-ford-motors/*.

CHAPTER 2.1

1   Joerg Niessing, "The Value of Focusing on Customer Centricity," *IBM Think Blog*, February 28, 2018, *https://www.ibm.com/blogs/think/2018/02/training-reten-tion/*; *State of Marketing, Insights and Trends from 3500 Global Marketing Lead-ers*, Salesforce Research, 2017, *https://www.salesforce.com/content/dam/web /en_us/www/assets/pdf/datasheets/salesforce-research-fourth-annual-state-of -marketing.pdf*.
2   Alessandro Di Fiore and Simon Schneider, "Stop Treating B2B Customers like Digital Novices," hbr.org, May 10, 2016, *https://hbr.org/2016/05/stop-treating -b2b-customers-like-digital-novices*.
3   Heiner Evanschitzky et al., "The Relative Strength of Affective Commitment in Securing Loyalty in Service Relationships," *Journal of Business Research* 59, no. 12 (2006): 1207–1213.
4   Gerald Kane et al., "Strategy, not Technology, Drives Digital Transformation: Becoming a Digitally Mature Enterprise," *MIT Sloan Management Review*, July 14, 2015, *http://sloanreview.mit.edu/projects/strategy-drives-digital-trans-formation/*; Thomas Jensen, Jonas Hedman, and Stefan Henningsson, "How TradeLens Delivers Business Value with Blockchain Technology," *MIS Quarterly Executive* 18, no. 4 (December 2019): 221–243; Kirstine Helvig Kromberg, "How to Achieve Digital Mastery at Maersk Line: The Journey Towards Sustainable Digi-tal Innovation," Copenhagen Business School, 2016, *https://research.cbs.dk/en /studentProjects/b6b8a78c-62d5-4002-b827-695ea2710eb3*.

CHAPTER 2.2

1   "Incumbents Strike Back: Insights from the Global C-suite Study," *IBM Institute for Business Value*, Global C-suite Study, 19th ed. (February 2018), *https://www .ibm.com/downloads/cas/Y9JBRJ8A*.

2 Lou Carbone, in a presentation to healthcare marketing class at Questrom School of Business, Boston University, November 5, 2019; based on his book *Clued in: How to Keep Customers Coming Back Again and Again* (New York: Prentice-Hall, 2004).

3 Jane Sarasohn-Kahn, "The Mobile Health App Glut," *Healthcare IT News*, October 21, 2016, *https://www.healthcareitnews.com/blog/mobile-health-app-glut*.

4 "Zurich Launches New Brand Campaign," *Insurance Journal*, September 22, 2008, *https://www.insurancejournal.com/news/international/2008/09/22/93898.htm*.

5 Jason Little, "How Salesforce Accelerates Onboarding Using Journey Builder," *Salesforce Blog*, August 23, 2019, *https://www.salesforce.com/blog/2019/08/journey-builder-for-customer-onboarding.html*.

6 Heiner Evanschitzky et al., "The Relative Strength of Affective Commitment in Securing Loyalty in Service Relationships," *Journal of Business Research* 59, no. 12 (2006): 1207–1213.

7 Ping-Lung Huang, Bruce Lee, and Ching-Chin Chen, "The Influence of Service Quality on Customer Satisfaction and Loyalty in B2B Technology Service Industry," *Total Quality Management & Business Excellence* 30, no.13 (September 2017): 1449–1465.

8 Lori Molinari, Russell Abratt, and Paul Dion, "Satisfaction, Quality and Value and Effects on Repurchase and Positive Word-of-Mouth Behavioral Intentions in a B2B Services Context," *Journal of Services Marketing* 22, no. 5 (2008): 363–373; Ivan Russo et al., "The Combined Effect of Product Returns Experience and Switching Costs on B2B Customer Re-purchase Intent," *Journal of Business & Industrial Marketing* 32, no. 5 (April 2017): 664–676.

9 Maxi Bergel, Phillip Frank, and Christian Brock, "The Role of Customer Engagement Facets on the Formation of Attitude, Loyalty and Price Perception," *Journal of Services Marketing* 33, no. 7 (2019): 890–903; Jana Lay-Hwa Bowden, "The Process of Customer Engagement: A Conceptual Framework," *Journal of Marketing Theory & Practice* 17, no. 1 (2009): 63–74.

10 Hans Bracke et al., *Standing Out in Business-to-Business Customer Engagement*, IBM Research Insights, IBM Institute for Business Value (April 2019), *https://www.ibm.com/downloads/cas/ZK0E7O23*.

CHAPTER 2.3

1 The "Run, Build, Explore" model and the approach to touchpoint, service, product, and end-to-end experience design described in this book were developed under the leadership of Abram Sirignano, a partner at Prophet, for use by Prophet clients.

2 William Toh, "American Airlines & SABRE," *ISORG Case Studies*, University of London, September 28, 2011, *https://sites.google.com/site/uolext/home/isorg/isorg-case-studies/untitledpost*.

3   IBM Cloud Education, "Cloud Migration," *IBM Cloud Learn Hub*, April 3, 2019. *https://www.ibm.com/cloud/learn/cloud-migration*.

4   Adam Muspratt, "How to Be a CX Leader: Lessons from FedEx," *CX Network*, May 29, 2019, *https://www.cxnetwork.com/cx-experience/articles/how-to-be-a-cx-leader-lessons-from-fedex*; Blake Morgan, "Leading the Future of Customer Experience with FedEx Express," *Forbes Blog*, November 9, 2016, *https://www.forbes.com/sites/blakemorgan/2016/11/09/leading-the-future-of-customer-experience-with-fedex-express/#426e7a7f468b*.

5   "Johnson & Johnson Business Case Study, Competitive Advantage and CSR," *RWC Business Case Series*, National Safety Council, 2008, *https://www.coursehero.com/file/p1hp2csh/When-Professor-Lee-Mitchell-invited-students-to-submit-questions-to-Mr-Weldon/*.

6   Charles Arthur, *Digital Wars: Apple, Google, Microsoft and the Battle for the Internet*, 2nd ed. (New York: Kogan Page, December 2014).

CHAPTER 2.4

1   Peter Neufeld, "The Minimum Viable Experience: Creating Services with Both Real Human Benefit and Sustainable Business Impact," Medium, May 21, 2017, *https://medium.com/@PeterNeufeld/the-minimum-viable-experience-creating-services-with-both-real-human-benefit-and-sustainable-e243dfd1acf4*.

2   Tanawat Hirunyawipada, Audhesh Paswan, and Charles Blankson, "Toward the Development of New Product Ideas: Asymmetric Effects of Team Cohesion on New Product Ideation," *Journal of Business & Industrial Marketing* 30, no. 7 (August 2015): 855–866; Min Kay, Devon Proudfoot, and Rick Larrick, "There's No Team in I: How Observers Perceive Individual Creativity in a Team Setting," *Journal of Applied Psychology* 103, no. 4 (April 2018): 432–442; Roger Schwarz, "What the Research Tells Us about Team Creativity and Innovation," hbr.org, December 15, 2015, *https://hbr.org/2015/12/what-the-research-tells-us-about-team-creativity-and-innovation*.

3   Thomas Malone and Michael Bernstein, eds., *Handbook of Collective Intelligence* (Cambridge: MIT Press, October 2015).

4   "Sermo Launches Redesigned Global Physician Platform with Enhanced Product Features," *Business Wire*, September 18, 2019, *https://www.businesswire.com/news/home/20190918005221/en/Sermo-Launches-Redesigned-Global-Physician-Platform-Enhanced*.

5   "Jamf Kicks Off 2019 Jamf Nation User Conference," *Intrado Globenewswire*, November 12, 2019, *https://www.globenewswire.com/news-release/2019/11/12/1945675/0/en/Jamf-Kicks-Off-2019-Jamf-Nation-User-Conference-Showcasing-Powerful-New-Product-Line.html*.

CHAPTER 2.5

1   Tony Fross, "Creating Smarter, Faster Product Teams for the Digital Age," *Medium*, November 4, 2018, *https://medium.com/@tfross/creating-smarter-faster -product-teams-for-the-digital-age-cace327ce1b9*.

CHAPTER 2.6

1   Joerg Niessing, "Digitisation for the Short, Medium and Long-Term for Better Customer Experiences," *The European Business Review*, March 13, 2018, *https:// www.europeanbusinessreview.com/digitisation-for-the-short-medium-and-long -term-for-better-customer-experiences/*.

CHAPTER 3.1

1   Clayton Christensen, Michael Raynor, and Rory McDonald, "What Is Disruptive Innovation?," *Harvard Business Review*, December 2015: 44–53; Elisa Konya-Baumbach et al., "Making a First Impression as a Start-Up: Strategies to Overcome Low Initial Trust Perceptions in Digital Innovation Adoption," *International Journal of Research in Marketing* 36, no. 3 (February 2019): 385–399.
2   Theodore Levitt, "Marketing Myopia," *Harvard Business Review*, July–August 1960: 3–13.
3   Wolfgang Ulaga, Frédéric Dalsace, and Chloé Renault, "Business Model Innovation: Michelin Fleet Solutions - From Selling Tires to Selling Kilometers," *IMD Case*, no. IMD-5-0793, June 2013.
4   "Google Ventures Seeks to Make Name as Farsighted Health Investor," *The Business Times*, February 12, 2016, *https://www.businesstimes.com.sg/technology /google-ventures-seeks-to-make-name-as-farsighted-health-investor*.

CHAPTER 3.2

1   Charlene Li, *The Disruption Mindset: Why Some Organizations Transform While Others Fail* (Oakton, VA: Ideapress Publishing, 2019), 17.
2   Caroline Robertson, "Nine More Questions for 3M Industrial Business Marketing Leader Penny Wise," *Forrester Featured Insights*, Forrester, November 21, 2018, *https://go.forrester.com/blogs/nine-more-questions-for-3m-industrial-group -marketing-leader-penny-wise/*.
3   Joerg Niessing, "What Brands Need to Survive in a Digital World," *The Business Times*, May 31, 2016, *https://www.businesstimes.com.sg/sme/what-brands-need -to-survive-in-a-digital-world*.

4 Alexa Tietjen, "How Ouai Uses Dash Hudson and Instagram for Crowdsourcing," *WWD*, February 26, 2019, *https://wwd.com/beauty-industry-news/beauty-features/how-ouai-uses-dash-hudson-and-instagram-for-crowdsourcing-1203052918/*.

5 *Open Banking Standards, PSD2*, European Commission, Directive 2015/2366/EU (January 2018).

6 Katy Stalcup, "AWS vs. Azure vs. Google Cloud Market Share 2020: What the Latest Data Shows," *ParkMyCloud blog*, February 5, 2020, *https://www.parkmycloud.com/blog/aws-vs-azure-vs-google-cloud-market-share/*.

CHAPTER 3.3

1 Chris Hare, "An Overview of AWS Rekognition," Medium, September 30, 2019, *https://medium.com/@labrlearning/a-five-minute-overview-of-aws-rekognition-562b34a885fc*.

2 Jerome McCarthy, *Basic Marketing. A Global Managerial Approach* (Homewood, IL: Irwin, 1964).

3 Mark Phillips, "International Data-Sharing Norms: From the OECD to the General Data Protection Regulation (GDPR)," *Human Genetics* 137, no. 8 (2018): 575–582.

4 Michael Porter, *Competitive Advantage* (New York: The Free Press, 1985).

5 Cristina Cristalli, *Electrolux Professional Case Study*, GOoD MAN project, 2019, *http://goodman-project.eu/category/technical-activities/electrolux-case-study/*.

CHAPTER 3.4

1 "How Adobe Became a Successful $95 Billion SaaS Company," *Product Habits Blog*, 2018, *https://producthabits.com/adobe-95-billion-saas-company/*.

2 "Adobe Unveils AI-Powered Technology Previews in Adobe Experience Cloud to Accelerate Customer Experience Management (CXM)," *Adobe Blog*, June 14, 2019, *https://news.adobe.com/press-release/experience-cloud/adobe-unveils-ai-powered-technology-previews-adobe-experience-cloud*.

3 Steve Blank, "Why the Lean Start-Up Changes Everything," *Harvard Business Review*, May 2013.

4 Alexander Osterwalder and Yves Pigneur, *Business Model Generation: A Handbook for Visionaries, Game Changers, and Challengers* (Hoboken: John Wiley & Sons, 2010).

5 Chris Kanoracus, "Monsanto Bets Big on Data Science," *CIO* 27, no. 3 (2013): 11; David Bennett, "Climate Corporation Wants to Push Precision Agriculture to New Heights, Focus on R&D," *Delta Farm Press* 74, no. 3 (January 2017): 20; Brett Ryder, "Digital Disruption on the Farm," *Economist* 411, no. 8888 (May 24, 2014): 64.

6 Betsy Atkins, "Making the Best Deal in 2017," *Directors & Boards* 41, no. 2 (March 2017): 43–46.

CHAPTER 4.1

1   *Closing the Customer Experience Gap*, Harvard Business Review Analytic Service (August 28, 2017), *https://hbr.org/sponsored/2017/08/closing-the-customer-experience-gap*.

2   Joerg Niessing and James Walker, "The Demand Analytics Premium," INSEAD Faculty & Research Working Paper (October 2014), *https://www.consultancy.uk/news/878/strategy-demand-analytics-boosts-commercial-performance*.

CHAPTER 4.2

1   Theos Evgeniou, Vibha Gaba, and Joerg Niessing, "Does Bigger Data Lead to Better Decisions?," *Harvard Business Review*, Digital Article, October 21, 2013, *https://hbr.org/2013/10/does-bigger-data-lead-to-better-decisions*.

2   "Women in AI Ethics, Names Susan Etlinger One of 100 Brilliant Women in AI Ethics," *Lighthouse3*, December 17, 2019. A selection of Susan Etlinger's writings on the topic of AI and ethics can be found at *www.linkedin.com/in/susanetlinger/*.

3   Figure 54 was inspired by Cisco's customer engagement stack as described by Shantha Kumar, "Cisco's Amazing Marketing Technology Stack," *Blueoshan*, October 29, 2018, *https://blog.blueoshan.com/ciscos-amazing-marketing-technology-stack*.

CHAPTER 4.3

1   Sam Del Rowe, "An Empowered Workforce Needs a Culture of Engagement: Employee Engagement, Employee Experience, and Employee Enablement Have to Come Together," *CRM Magazine* 22, no. 8 (October 2018): 12–13; "Employee Engagement Impacts Bottom Line," *Management Report for Nonunion Organizations* 35, no. 10 (2012): 7–8.

2   Tyler Durham, Tony Fross, and Helen Rosethorn, *Catalysts, the Cultural Levers of Growth in the Digital Age, a Global Research Report*, Prophet, Prophet Thinking (May 2019): 13, *https://www.prophet.com/download/catalysts-the-cultural-levers-of-growth-in-the-digital-age/*.

3   Joerg Niessing, "Don't Be Paralysed by Digitisation Revolution," *The National*, October 5, 2017, *https://www.thenational.ae/business/technology/don-t-be-paralysed-by-digitisation-revolution-1.664463*.

4   "About Johnson & Johnson," Johnson & Johnson (website), accessed April 7, 2020, *https://www.jnj.com/about-jnj*.

5   Peter Drucker, *The Practice of Management* (New York: Harper and Row, 1954).

6   Julia Balogun, "From Blaming the Middle to Harnessing Its Potential: Creating Change Intermediaries," *British Journal of Management* 14, no. 1 (2003): 69–83; Eric Dent and Susan Goldberg, "Challenging "Resistance to Change," *The Journal of Applied Behavioral Science* 35, no.1 (1999): 25–41; Giovanni Radaelli and

Lucy Sitton-Kent, "Middle Managers and the Translation of New Ideas in Organizations: A Review of Micro-Practices and Contingencies," *International Journal of Management Reviews* 18, no. 3 (2016): 311–332.

7   Kevin Kaiser and David Young, "Blue Line Management: What Value Creation Really Means," INSEAD, Faculty & Research Working Paper, 2009.

8   Rafael Berges and Fabian Kon, "'We Want Change,' but Who's We? How to Transition Cultural Change in the Digital Era as a Team," *Strategic HR Review* 18, no. 5 (September 2019): 210–214; Thomas Abrell et al., "The Role of Users and Customers in Digital Innovation: Insights from B2B Manufacturing Firms," *Information & Management* 53, no. 3 (April 2016): 324–335.

CHAPTER 4.4

1   Analysis of *Fortune* 1,000 companies, using data sets for 2017, 2018, and 2019; research conducted by Prophet Analytics, February 2020.

2   Leigh Buchanan, "How Great Entrepreneurs Think," *Inc. Magazine*, February 1, 2011, *https://www.inc.com/magazine/20110201/how-great-entrepreneurs-think.html*.

INDEX

functional leaders, service design, 127
functionality, customer engagement
    stack, 256
future-state maps, 105–106

G

GE
    Life Sciences, 16
    service design, 127
growth moves. *See also* uncommon
    growth
    explained, 217–218
    identifying, 219–221
    overcoming conversion costs, 223–224
    pacing, 226
    roadmap, 227
    turning into action, 221–223
growth opportunities, identifying and
    prioritizing, 179
growth road map, charting, 226–227
growth territory, choosing, 191–195

H

Hartz, Peter, 92
Hilti, 9
Human-Centered Transformation
    model, 262
hybrid segmentations, building, 181
hypothesis draft, journey mapping, 110

I

IBM
    differentiating value, 123
    reliance on sales forces, 16
    research on journey mapping, 100
impact, making case for, 212–215
implementation
    defining, 210–212
    and improvement, 283
industry ecosystem, emerging demand
    drivers, 185, 187
influencers, paying attention to, 182
information access, 2
innovation
    from competitors, 144
    data driven, 3
    digital experience makeover, 6–8
    territory value drivers, 200, 202
    within companies, 185, 187
innovation-igniting tools, 146–147
INSEAD, research on journey mapping, 100
insight draft, journey mapping, 110

inspiration, accessing sources of, 143–144.
    See also concept creation
insurance. *See* ACI (Acme Commercial
    Insurance)
interest, cultivating, 44–45, 53–58
intermediaries
    bypassing, 2–3, 62
    gauging use of, 182
    relationships, 138
IoT (Internet of Things)
    and Air Liquide, 21
    data control, 137
    devices, 173
    digital proposition pivot, 8
    impact of, 1
    Maersk case study, 96
    and Microsoft technology, 7
iteration, feedback, and speed, 142

J

J&J Medical Devices, 132
Johnson & Johnson, 2, 9
journey mapping. *See also* customer
    experience; map type; road maps
    building foundation, 101
    designing, 103–106, 125
    drafts, 110
    end-to-end, 104
    importance of, 100
    interviewing employees, 106–107
    process, 106–110
    using, 99

K

knowledge sharing and development,
    promoting, 230

L

last move, data acquisition, 135
leadership improvement, promoting, 67
lead-scoring process, 54
lead-to-conversion rates, 16
Lean Canvas, 221–222
Lean Startup approach, 221–222
Levitt, Theodore, 173
Li, Charlene, 179
Lillie, Jason, 112
LinkedIn, 17
listening
    creating culture of, 6–8
    and employee engagement, 271
LTV (lifetime value) of customers, 35

M

Maersk case study, 91–96
management forums and metrics, shaping, 265
management routines, instituting, 230
map type, choosing, 103–106. *See also* journey mapping
mapping demand landscape, 188–189
market sector ecosystem context, 203
market-fit phase, DERPA maturity model, 161
marketing
    account based, 50–51
    and selling objectives, 4, 25–26
mature phase, DERPA maturity model, 162–163
Maurya, Ash, 221–222
MAX system, 7–8
Mayo Clinic, thought leadership, 49–50
McCarthy's 4Ps, 199
medical devices industry, 173–174, 177–178
Medtronic, 2
metrics
    and dashboards, 257
    and management forums, 265
Michelin Solutions case study, 174–177
Microsoft
    Azure technology, 7
    and Dell, 53
    Willow Twin, 8
Mind
    assessment, 272
    mobilizing talent, 266–268
mobile app, electrical contractors, 7
module prototype, creating, 152
Møller, A.P. – Maersk, 91–96
monetization
    emerging demand drivers, 186, 188
    territory value drivers, 200, 202
Monsanto, 226
MVE (minimum viable experience)
    building, 142
    module prototype, 152
MVP (minimum viable product), 221

N

"next best move," 54

O

objectives and outputs, clarifying, 66
observational analysis, 46
Ohio State University, 3
omnichannel campaigning, 50, 60

online customer data, 17. *See also* customer experience
operating model, renovating, 265–266
opportunities
    filtering for importance, 114–118
    and strategies, 77
    uncovering, 111–114
opt-in, data acquisition, 135
Optum US health services, 16
Oracle, 17
organic ideas, growth moves, 220
organizations
    aligning, 209–210
    assessing readiness, 36–39
Osterwalder, Alexander, 221–222
outsourcing routine tasks, 31, 33

P

pain point resolution, 6–7, 107, 109
perceptual data, 247–248, 250
personal data protection, putting in place, 253–254
pharma marketing, 5–6
physicians and pharma marketing, 5–6
piloting experiences, 142
pilots
    coordinating, 230
    launching, 153–155
pipeline, growth moves, 219
pivot. *See* digital proposition pivot
planning-executing-measuring-analyzing-executing differently, 76
post-purchase experience, journey map, 108
predictive modeling, 7–8
"price adjustments," 62
product, promotion, price, and place, 199
product design, 128, 131
product proposition, outdated, 173
profiling data, 247–248, 250. *See also* customer data; data
project management, 231
proposition
    articulating, 204–209
    building blocks, 199–200
    thinking in terms of, 171
prototyping rapidly, 142, 150–153
purchases
    barriers, 28–29
    behavior, 28
    data acquisition, 135
    decision-making funnel, 47
purpose, linking transformation to, 263–265

talent
    development, 231
    mobilizing, 266–268
talent plan, establishing, 83
target, clarifying, 44
target decision maker, clarifying, 45–48
tasks, outsourcing, 31
teams, configuring by experience maturity,
    159–163
technology orientation, considering, 182
technology trends, emerging demand
    drivers, 186, 188
technology-first transformation
    paradigm, 12
templates and frameworks,
    downloading, 283
territory value drivers, identifying, 200–202
test-and-learn lead, 80
testing versus prototyping pilots, 153–154
thought leadership, 49–50
Thyssenkrupp's Elevator unit, 7–8, 89
TMO (transformation management office)
    establishing, 230–231
    making effective, 231–233
    winding down, 233
touchpoint design, 126, 130, 143–144, 148
touchpoint engagement, journey
    mapping, 109
touchpoint maps, 105
Toyota Motors, 77
tracking mechanisms, 17
TradeLens open digital platform, 94–95
transformations
    considering in phases, 281
    digital experience makeover, 6–8
    digital proposition pivot, 8–11
    digital selling shift, 4–6
    linking to purposes, 263–265
    occurrences of, 280
TransUnion, 253
travel agents, providing distinctive value
    to, 122
trends, sources of inspiration, 144
troubleshooting video, providing, 100

U

uncertainty
    reducing range of, 214
    thinking about, 192–193
uncommon growth, 11–12, 279–283. *See also*
    growth moves
understanding, lack of, 27
United Airlines, Apollo system, 122, 137
upselling, 26–27, 29, 54. *See also* cross-sell/
    upsell
urgency, creating sense of, 66
use cases
    evaluating attractiveness, 33–36
    identifying, 29–33
    prioritizing, 39–42
user interface layer, customer engagement
    stack, 254, 256
users, emerging demand drivers, 185, 187

V

validation phase, DERPA maturity model,
    161–162
value proposition. *See also* digital
    proposition pivot; employee value
    proposition
    boosting, 30
    defining for customers, 25–26, 29
    differentiating, 122
    digitizing, 9–10
    fortifying, 282
    making transition to, 224
    use cases, 34–35
value-added services, territory value
    drivers, 200, 202
visualization tools, using, 80

W

weaknesses versus strengths, considering,
    271
website traffic, 16
Willow Twin, Microsoft, 8

Z

Zyman, Sergio, 25–26

ABOUT THE AUTHORS

Fred Geyer is a senior partner at Prophet, one of the world's leading digital transformation consultancies. He has helped B2B clients in the financial services, healthcare, and technology industries—including Zurich Financial, AXA, Johnson & Johnson Medical Devices, Medtronic, and Avery Dennison—undertake customer-first transformations and address the challenges of digital disruption. Fred's prior experience as president of Crayola Canada and chief marketing officer, North America, of Electrolux Floor Care, enables him to bring a practitioner's perspective to making digital transformation work in the real world.

Joerg Niessing, a member of the faculty at INSEAD, is a globally recognized expert and strategic advisor on digital transformation, digital strategy, customer centricity, and data analytics. He is the program director of INSEAD's flagship programs, "B2B Marketing Strategies" and "Leading Digital Marketing Strategy." Over the past five years, Joerg has engaged with more than three thousand executives from a wide range of companies in Europe, the Americas, the Middle East, and Asia, including Google, KONE, Roche, Maersk, Michelin, IBM, Thales, PwC, and KION. Joerg's prior experience as head of Prophet's Insight and Analytics practice, along with his previous work as a marketing data scientist, informs his insights on ensuring that digital transformations are data driven, are customer centric, and drive sustainable growth.

.